TRINITY FORUM STUDY SERIES

THE TRINITY FORUM

DOING WELL AND DOING GOOD

Money, Giving, and Caring in a Free Society

OS GUINNESS

Edited by Ginger Koloszyc
Reader's Guide by Karen Lee-Thorp

NAVPRESS

Bringing Truth to Life
P.O. Box 35001, Colorado Springs, Colorado 80935

OUR GUARANTEE TO YOU

Copyright © 2001 by The Trinity Forum
All rights reserved. No part of this publication may be reproduced in any form without written permission from NavPress, P.O. Box 35001, Colorado Springs, CO 80935.
www.navpress.com

Library of Congress Catalog Card Number: 00-049544
ISBN 1-57683-161-2

Cover design by Dan Jamison
Cover photo of money by Zephyr Images / Tim Mantoani
Cover photo of hands and bread by Stock Connection / Mimi Forsyth
Creative Team: Karen Lee-Thorp, Darla Hightower, Pat Miller

Unless otherwise identified, all Scripture quotations in this publication are taken from the *HOLY BIBLE: NEW INTER-NATIONAL VERSION®* (NIV®). Copyright © 1973, 1978, 1984 by International Bible Society. Used by permission of Zondervan Publishing House. All rights reserved.

All quotations from *We Gave Away a Fortune* are used by permission of More Than Money, 2244 Alder St., Eugene, OR 97405, (541-343-3420), www.MoreThanMoney.org.

Guinness, Os.
    Doing well and doing good : money, giving, and caring in a free society / by Os Guinness ; edited by Ginger Koloszyc ; reader's guide by Karen Lee-Thorp.
        p. cm.
    Includes bibliographical references.
    ISBN 1-57683-161-2
        1. Charity. 2. Postmodernism. I. Koloszyc, Ginger. III. Title.

BV4639.G86 2001
241'.682—dc21   00-049544

Printed in the United States of America
1 2 3 4 5 6 7 8 9 10 / 05 04 03 02 01 00

FOR A FREE CATALOG OF
NAVPRESS BOOKS & BIBLE STUDIES,
CALL 1-800-366-7788 (USA)
OR 1-416-499-4615 (CANADA)

THE TRINITY FORUM and design are a registered service mark of The Trinity Forum, Inc.

THE TRINITY FORUM

Contents

THE TRINITY FORUM

"Contributing to the transformation and renewal of society through the transformation and renewal of leaders."

The Trinity Forum would like to recognize the following people for their work on this project:

Project Director: Os Guinness

Selections and Introductions: Os Guinness and Mark Filiatreau

Academic Consultants: Gary Ferngren, Michael Novak, Marvin Olasky, Robert Payton, Daniel Russ, and Robert Wuthnow

Researchers: Mark Filiatreau and David Legg

Research Assistants: Dustin Salter and Peter Edman

Editor: Ginger Koloszyc

Copyeditors: Amy Boucher and Peter Edman

NOT SO MUCH A BOOK
AS A WAY OF THINKING

The 'Why' and 'How' of the Trinity Forum Study Series

Thinkers from the time of Socrates to our own day have believed that the unexamined life is not worth living. Today's unique challenge is to lead an examined life in an unexamining age. The sheer pace and pressure of our modern lives can easily crowd out time for reflection. To make matters worse, we live in a war zone against independent thinking. Television jingles, advertising hype, political soundbites, and "dumbed down" discourse of all kinds assault an individual's ability to think for himself or herself. Carefully considered conclusions about life and the best way to live it are too often the casualties.

Into this challenging landscape The Trinity Forum launches its *Study Series,* inviting individuals to think through today's issues carefully and deliberately— in the context of faith—to reach deeper and more firmly established convictions.

About The Trinity Forum

The Trinity Forum was founded in 1991. Its aim: to contribute to the transformation and renewal of society through the transformation and renewal of leaders. Christian in commitment, but open to all who are interested in its vision, it has organized dozens of forums for leaders of all sectors of modern life—from business to education, from fashion to government and the media.

Hundreds of leaders from many faiths across the United States, Canada, and Europe have taken part in these forums.

A distinctive feature of The Trinity Forum is its format. There are no lectures, addresses, or talks of any kind. A curriculum of readings on a given topic is sent out in advance and then explored at the forum in a Socratic-style open discussion led by moderators. This give-and-take challenges the participants to wrestle with the issues themselves and—importantly—to reach their own thought-out conclusions.

By popular demand, The Trinity Forum now offers these curricula to a wider audience, enhanced as the *Trinity Forum Study Series* and designed for individual readers or study groups in homes, churches, and colleges. Each *Study* is intended to help thoughtful people examine the foundational issues through which faith acts upon the public good of modern society. A reader's guide at the back of each book will aid those who want to discuss the material with a group. Those reading the book on their own may also find that the reader's guide will help them focus on the *Study's* big ideas. The reader's guide contains basic principles of small group leadership, an overview of the *Study's* main ideas, and suggested selections for groups that don't have time to discuss every reading in the *Study*.

Adult in seriousness and tone, yet popular rather than scholarly in style, the *Trinity Forum Study Series* probes each topic through the milestone writings that have shaped its development. This approach will be fresh and exciting to many and, we trust, stimulating to all. It is worth laying out some of the assumptions and convictions that guide this approach, for what is presented here is not so much a book as it is a way of thinking.

Defining Features of the Trinity Forum Study Series

First, the Trinity Forum Study Series *explores the issues of our day in the context of faith.* As stated earlier, The Trinity Forum is Christ-centered in its commitment, but opens its programs to all who share its aims—whether believers, seekers, or skeptics. The same committed but open spirit marks this series of books.

For people of faith, it should be natural to take into account the place of faith when discussing the issues of life, both historically and presently. But it should also be natural for all citizens of Western society, of whatever faith. For no one can understand Western civilization without understanding the Christian faith which, for better or worse, has been its primary shaping force. Yet a striking feature of many of today's thought-leaders and opinion-shapers is their "tone deafness" toward faith of any kind—which means that, unwittingly or otherwise, they do not hear the music by which most people orchestrate their lives.

For example, a national media executive recently admitted his and his colleagues' befuddlement about Americans' deep reliance upon faith. Citing the outpouring of public prayer in response to a tragic school shooting in Kentucky, he confessed, "We simply don't get it." These readings aim to remedy that neglected dimension of understanding, and thereby reintroduce to the modern discussion the perspective of faith that is vital both for making sense of the past and dealing with the present.

Second, the Trinity Forum Study Series *presents the perspective of faith in the context of the sweep of Western civilization, recognizing the vital place of the past in the lives of nations as well as individuals.* A distinctive feature of the modern world is its passion for the present and fascination with the future at the expense of the past. Progress, choice, change, novelty, and the myth of newer-the-truer and latest-is-greatest reign unchallenged, while ideas and convictions from earlier times are boxed up in the cobwebbed attic of nostalgia and irrelevance. By contrast, Winston Churchill said, "The further backward you can look, the farther forward you can see." For him, as well as the American framers in the eighteenth century and the writers of the Bible before them, remembering is not foremost a matter of nostalgia or historical reverie, and it is far more than mental recall. For all of them, it is a vital key to identity, faith, wisdom, renewal, and the dynamism of a living tradition, for both nations and individuals.

By reintroducing important writings from the past, the *Trinity Forum Study Series* invites readers to a living conversation of ideas and imagination with the great minds of our heritage. Only when we know where we have come from do we know who we are and where we are going.

Third, the Trinity Forum Study Series *presents the perspective of faith in the context of the challenge of other faiths.* If the first feature of this series is likely to offend some unthinking secularists, this one may do the same to unthinking believers. But the truth is, some believers don't appear to know their own faith because they know *only* their own faith. Familiarity breeds inattention. It is true, as essayist Ronald Knox quipped, that comparative religion can make us "comparatively religious." But it is also true that contrast is the mother of clarity.

One important benefit of understanding one's own faith in distinction to others is the ability to communicate ideas and positions persuasively in the public square. Believers properly hold their beliefs on the basis of divine authority. Such beliefs, however, must be conveyed compellingly in a society that does not accept the same authority. An important part of meeting that challenge effectively is the ability to grasp and highlight the differences between faiths.

This series of books, therefore, sets out the perspectives of the Christian faith in the context of the challenge of other faiths. If "all truth is God's truth," and if differences truly make a difference, then such contrasts between one faith and another are not only challenging, but illuminating and important for both individuals and society.

Fourth, the Trinity Forum Study Series *is unashamed about the necessity for tough-minded thinking.* Much has been made recently of Christian anti-intellectualism and the scandal of the lack of a Christian mind. As Bertrand Russell put it, "Most Christians would rather die than think — in fact, they do." But failure to think is not confined to any one community or group. Former Secretary of State Henry Kissinger is quoted as saying, "In Washington D.C. there is so little time to think that most people live forever off the intellectual capital from the day they arrive."

In contrast, Abraham Lincoln's greatness was fired in times of thoughtful reflection during the Civil War. Today's profound crises call for similar thoughtful reflection and courage by men and women prepared to break rank with a largely unthinking and conformist age. Just as an earlier generation broke with accepted practices of little exercise and bad eating, restoring a vogue for fitness, so our generation must shake off the lethargy of "dumbed down" discourse and recover the capacity to think tough-mindedly as the issues and our times require.

Fifth, the Trinity Forum Study Series *recognizes that many of the urgent public issues of our day are cultural rather than political.* Much recent discussion of public affairs oscillates uneasily between heavily moral issues (such as abortion) and more strongly political issues (such as campaign finance reform). Yet increasingly, many of the urgent concerns of our day lie in-between. They are neither purely moral nor purely political, but integrate elements of both. In other words, many key issues are morally grounded "pre-political" issues, such as the role of "trust" in capitalism, "character" in leadership, "truth" in public discourse, "stewardship" in philanthropy and environmentalism, and "voluntarism" in civil society.

To be sure, it is a symptom of our present crisis that such foundational issues have to be debated at all. But the *Trinity Forum Study Series* addresses these often neglected issues, always presenting them in the context of faith and always addressing them in a nonpartisan manner that befits such cultural discussion.

Finally, the Trinity Forum Study Series *assumes the special need for, and the possibility of, a social and cultural renaissance in our time.* As we consider our present crises with clear-eyed realism, one of the great challenges is to be hopeful with a real basis for hope while always being critical of what is wrong without collapsing into alarmism or despair. To be sure, no freedom, prosperity, or success lasts forever in this life, in either spiritual or secular affairs. But, equally, the grand cycle of birth, growth, and decline is never deterministic, and no source of renewal is more sure and powerful than spiritual revival. The *Study Series* is born of this conviction.

Giving up hope in the worthwhileness of the worthwhile—in God, the good, the true, the just, and the beautiful—is another name for the deadly sin of sloth. Venturing out, under God, to be entrepreneurs of life is another name for faith. Thus, while always uncertain of the outcome of our times, always modest about our own contribution, and always confident in God rather than ourselves, those who present the *Trinity Forum Study Series* desire to encourage people to move out into society with constructive answers and a sense of a confidence born of faith and seasoned by history. In so doing we seek to sow the seeds for a much-needed renaissance in our own time.

INTRODUCTION—
DOING WELL AND DOING GOOD

EVER SINCE THE FIRST COIN WAS MINTED IN THE SEVENTH CENTURY B.C., MONEY HAS been central to human society. Along with sex, power, and glory, money is one of the elemental forces driving the affairs of individuals and nations. But the last two decades of the twentieth century were particularly significant for the place of money in the modern world.

First, in the downfall of the Soviet Union in 1989 and the broader collapse of communism worldwide, democratic capitalism gained a stunning victory over its rival economic systems, such as socialism and state-run economies. Second, led by Wall Street in the 1980s and Silicon Valley's high-tech revolution in the 1990s, free-market capitalism made possible the greatest legal creation of wealth in history. Third, these two decades saw the beginning of the largest transition of wealth from one generation to another in history.

All in all, the second millennium closed with two decades that stood Karl Marx on his head, handed the victor's crown to Adam Smith, and ushered in what Jim Clark, founder of Netscape, called the era of "the wealth of the masses."

These momentous events, however, were offset by a simple but equally profound fact: For all the preoccupation with the *making* of money, little attention has been paid to the *meaning* of money. Likewise overlooked is the companion question of the culture of giving and caring that automatically accompanies any dominant view of money.

For all the preoccupation with the making of *money, little attention has been paid to the* meaning *of money.*

Doing Well and Doing Good has been written to address this blind spot. What is the meaning of money? What are the deepest motives to give? Why should we care for those outside our own groups, especially for the poor and needy outside any group? Answers to questions such as these are decisive for the character of any society, but especially for the citizens of free societies that would remain free. It is not too much to say that as a society creates wealth, gives, and cares, so it is.

15

ATTENDING TO BLIND SPOTS

The gap between the preoccupation with making money and the inattention to the meaning of money is only the first of a series of blind spots bedeviling the subject of money, giving, and caring. A second blind spot is the abysmal ignorance of the topic.

Paraphrasing a famous line of Winston Churchill's, it might be said that never in the entire field of human need has so much been asked so often of so few. There is, in short, much giving and caring to be done, including the important part played by institutional philanthropy. But at a time when more and more is being asked of the willing volunteer and the generous giver, most of the talk is of the "nuts and bolts" of philanthropy—taxes, law, foundations, and politics—with too little discussion of the wellsprings of the great ideals of giving and caring.

But at a time when more and more is being asked of the willing volunteer and the generous giver, most of the talk is of the "nuts and bolts" of philanthropy—taxes, law, foundations, and politics—with too little discussion of the wellsprings of the great ideals of giving and caring.

A third blind spot concerns the fact that giving, caring, and volunteering are insufficiently appreciated even in countries with a strong philanthropic tradition. The United States, for example, has the most developed culture of giving and caring in history. But do Americans realize how the influence of philanthropy has gone far beyond "charity" to be a vital factor in education, in reform movements, and in democracy itself? (Philanthropy's proud credits as "the moral goad to politics" include the abolition of slavery, creation of the public schools and libraries, women's suffrage, and child labor laws.) How many realize that there are more people employed full-time in philanthropic work in the United States than are employed full-time by the federal and state governments combined?

"Quick! Is there a philanthropist in the audience?"

Reprinted from The Chronicle of Philanthropy by permission of the artist, Bob Schochet.

"We have long thought of ourselves immodestly as a nation of philanthropists," writes American historian Daniel Boorstin. Yet a Carnegie Corporation study of more than fifty American textbooks used in history, social studies, and civics classes revealed not a single reference to philanthropy and volunteering. Young Americans could go through a supposedly thorough education without ever learning of the distinctive and decisive role of the voluntary sector in their nation. To be sure, scholarly material on philanthropy is always mounting, but the gap between the academic and the understanding of ordinary people is troubling. When Professor Robert Payton was president of the Exxon Education Foundation, he commented, "The new Brittanica overlooks philanthropy, as far as I can tell, although its predecessors dealt with it quite adequately. That's the way it goes: One day you take it for granted, and the next it's gone."

A fourth blind spot is the neglect of individual giving because of the preoccupation with organized giving. In North America, again, most discussions of giving focus on foundations and associations of foundations, corporate giving programs, regional associations of grant makers, and so on. This preoccupation is understandable because the philanthropic foundation is one of America's two distinctive contributions to philanthropy. (The other, as we shall see later, is the voluntary association.) The neglect of individual giving, however, is unfortunate because the largest potential for philanthropic growth in the next few decades will likely come from individuals and families. Contrary to public perception, individuals already account for 90 percent of all giving; even such large foundations as Lilly and Ford or such giant corporations as Exxon only contribute to the other 10 percent.

The neglect of individual giving, however, is unfortunate because the largest potential for philanthropic growth in the next few decades will likely come from individuals and families.

A fifth blind spot is the most surprising of all. The contemporary discussion of giving—and contemporary leaders in institutional philanthropy—has a characteristically secular cast that generally ignores the beliefs and attitudes that gave rise to a culture of giving and caring in the first place. But it is exactly these ideals that are now required to sustain it. Robert Payton of Indiana University's Center for Philanthropic Studies speaks bluntly of a "rejection of religion and religious values by the educated elites and the wealthy of our society." Such people, he says, often see in their good education and comfortable lives a way of life superior to those less fortunate. Thus, "the educated dismiss the faith of the uneducated as ignorance, and the wealthy dismiss the appeals of the poor as envy."

One 1986 study of nearly a thousand American research projects on philanthropy found that fewer than 5 percent dealt with religion—when the centrality to philanthropy of faith and faith-based institutions is indisputable. On the one hand, religious organizations are the largest recipients of giving; on the other hand, religious motivation is one of the strongest impulses toward giving. To ignore faith and religion in philanthropy is as absurd as describing Egypt without mentioning the Nile. Unless treated, this disregard for religion may become a cancer in Western philanthropy that no sentimental trust in "the universal charitable impulse" can cloak and for which no amount of tough-talking professionalism can compensate.

Doing Well and Doing Good addresses these missing dimensions of today's discussion by exploring the big ideas that shaped the rise of the Western tradition of giving and caring. Recognizing that true giving and caring involve more than the transfer of money from one person to another, these readings go beyond the "whats and hows" to the "whys and wherefores" that make giving entrepreneurial and effective as well as generous. Sometimes controversial, often challenging, always illuminating, the issues of money, giving, and caring are fascinating and vital themes that stand at the crossroads of many issues in contemporary society. They are topics that no responsible citizen or leader can afford to ignore.

MUCH GIVEN, MUCH REQUIRED

There are several straightforward reasons why money, giving, and caring are so important today. First, the recent explosion of wealth—the so-called "wealth of the masses"—puts increased responsibility on wealthy families and individuals. Much has been made recently of the stupendous movement of wealth from the World War II generation to its heirs. Nobody really knows how much this generation has amassed in pensions, savings, stocks, insurance policies, and real estate—estimates vary between seven and ten trillion U.S. dollars. But certainly this will be the greatest transfer of wealth in history. Thus the post–World War II generation of Americans, the baby boomers, will inherit more in the next two decades than any other generation in the history of the world. And the richest one percent will inherit one-third of the total (study by Cornell University's Department of Economics and Housing).

Yet this transfer is only one of many indications of the quantum leap in the wealth created and the fortunes left in recent decades. In 1984, U.S. President Reagan was quoted in *Money* magazine as saying, "What I want to see above all is that this remains a country where someone can always get rich." Clearly he was successful. Between 1980 and 1992 the increase in wealth in the United States was staggering. The number of millionaires grew from 574,000 to 2,320,000; the number of "centi-millionaires" (note the new term) from 400 to 2,560; and the number of billionaires from 13 to 73. Conversely, however, and quite strikingly, individual giving has dropped significantly during this boom in individual wealth. Those with annual earnings of more than $500,000 reduced their average donations from $47,432 in 1980 to $16,062 in 1988. When Sam Walton's net worth reached $4.5 billion (one-sixth of his family's fortune) it was estimated that his lifetime giving was one-thousandth of his net worth.

Today the multibillion-dollar fortunes of Bill Gates, Warren Buffett, Sam Walton, and Larry Ellison have eclipsed the legendary wealth of Andrew Carnegie and John D. Rockefeller. And such eclipses now occur faster and faster. Thus financier and philanthropist George Soros, head of the aptly named Quantum Fund, made $958 million in a single day's trading (in September 1992) and earned $1.1 billion on Wall Street in one year (1993). Hailed as "The World's Greatest Investor," "the man who broke the Bank of England," and "the man who moves markets," Soros is a twentieth-century Carnegie who puts his own wealth behind his own ideas. In light of his Eastern European philanthropies, he has been described by *Newsweek* as being on a similar scale as a "One-Man Marshall Plan."

AS RICH AS SOROS

"If Soros were a corporation, he would have ranked 37th in profitability, between BancOne and McDonald's. His compensation exceeded the gross domestic product of at least 42 member nations of the U.N. and was roughly equal to that of Chad, Guadeloupe, and Burundi. Put another way, he could buy 5,790 Rolls Royces at $190,000 a pop. Or pay the annual tuition for every student attending Harvard, Yale, Princeton, and Columbia combined for more than three years."

—*Financial World,* putting Soros's 1993 earnings into perspective

Not surprisingly, responses to this explosion of wealth have been widely divergent—especially because it has highlighted the widening gap between rich and poor, as illustrated by the disparity between corporate downsizing and CEO remuneration. Positive responses to the new wealth include euphoria about capitalism and an astute marketing of prosperity books and seminars. Deepak Chopra's *The Seven Spiritual Laws of Success,* for instance, offers the specious promise of a system that "will give you the ability to create unlimited wealth with effortless ease." Such predictable negative reactions as anxiety, resentment, guilt, and cynicism are also common. But at the heart of the host of ethical, political, and social issues raised is the inescapable question of individual responsibility.

As Aesop said two and a half thousand years ago, "Wealth unused might

"Wealth unused might as well not exist."
—Aesop

as well not exist." In the same sense, Andrew Carnegie calls philanthropists "administrators of surplus wealth" and Warren Buffett refers to wealth, such as his own, as "claim checks" that should benefit society. Put differently, it might be said that if the vast enterprises of medieval philanthropy depended on a vow of poverty, the equally vast enterprises of modern philanthropy depend on what is essentially a vow of wealth. At the very least, the problems of poverty and the other great issues facing wealthy nations can only be addressed with a deep understanding of wealth and the active participation of the wealthy themselves.

BEWARE THE GAP

"I believe that the poor hate the rich and that the rich are afraid of the poor. It will be ever thus. It is as futile to preach love to the one as to the other. The most urgent thing is to educate the rich, who after all are the stronger."

—Gustav Flaubert

"The inherent vice of capitalism is the unequal sharing of blessings; the inherent virtue of socialism is the equal sharing of miseries."

—Winston Churchill, House of Commons, October 22, 1945

"When individual wealth gets above 'a certain rather indefinite average,' a mood develops that works toward a 'leveling policy.'"

—Thorstein Veblen, *The Theory of the Leisure Class*

"If a free society cannot help the many who are poor, it cannot save the few who are rich."

—John F. Kennedy, Inaugural Address, 1960

JERUSALEM AND ATHENS

For a start, the voluntary sector confronts a mathematical and moral crunch as it is asked to pick up the slack created by the rolling back of government.

Second, money, giving, and caring require special attention because they go to the heart of the challenges facing institutional philanthropy. For a start, the voluntary sector confronts a mathematical and moral crunch as it is asked to pick up the slack created by the rolling back of government. Can charities make up for budget reductions? Some even say that cutbacks in government programs will spur a nonprofit revival. Far from it, others reply. For charities to bridge the gap is not only unlikely but impossible.

There are many reasons why the evidence leans toward the less sanguine. Participation in voluntary activities is down. Private giving has never risen in the past as fast as it would be required to do so now. Private donations to nonprofits are already outstripped by other sources of income, such as membership fees. In many cases, nonprofits themselves are heavily dependent on government grants, so they too must come off the dole before they can help wean others of government welfare. Besides, today's public-private partnership is in

"Faster than rising inflation, able to cut through government red tape in a single bound . . . Philanthropyman!"

Reprinted from The Chronicle of Philanthropy *by permission of the artist,* Joseph Brown.

part a reaction to the failure of voluntarism in earlier ages. Above all is the fact that voluntary giving sets its own priorities and may not change them radically even if government cuts back its responsibilities and leaves certain groups unprotected.

But this practical challenge is only the beginning of a series of challenges taxing the leaders in the independent sector. Another is dissatisfaction with the name. To call the sector "nonprofit" or "non-governmental" is to define it in purely negative terms, whereas to call it the "third sector" suggests only a third-rate importance. Yet to call it the "voluntary sector" suggests an amateurishness that obscures its high degree of professionalism and significant commercial component.

A far more serious challenge is the emerging division over how philanthropy should be defined and run. On the one hand are those—sometimes called "the soup-kitcheners"—who see philanthropy as *acts of mercy* to relieve *suffering,* commonly called "charity" in domestic situations and "relief" in foreign aid. On the other are those—sometimes called "the symphonyites"—who see it as *acts of community* to enhance *the quality of life* and ensure a better future, commonly called "philanthropy" in domestic situations and "development" in foreign aid.

Various distinctions are made to support the split. Supporters of "charity" see their work as directed toward the poor and the present situation; they, however, are criticized for "short-term solutions" and for dealing only with "the symptoms" of a problem. Supporters of "philanthropy," in contrast, see their work as directed toward society and the future, and pride themselves in "long-term solutions" and in dealing with the underlying "causes" of problems. The Rockefeller Foundation, for example, states its purpose grandly: "To promote the well-being of mankind throughout the world."

Supporters of "charity" see their work as directed toward the poor and the present situation; they, however, are criticized for "short-term solutions" and for dealing only with "the symptoms" of a problem. Supporters of "philanthropy," in contrast, see their work as directed toward society and the future, and pride themselves in "long-term solutions" and in dealing with the underlying "causes" of problems.

In fact, the ultimate difference between the two camps lies in their roots. Supporters of "charity" keep alive the imperatives of Jerusalem, the example of Jesus, and the distinctive Christian concept of love as *agape*. Supporters of "philanthropy" are realigning their work with the far more limited imperatives of Athens, the example of Prometheus (first philanthropist and "champion of the human race"), and the distinctive Greek concepts of love as *eros* and *philanthropia*.

Still another challenge is the fact that some of the recent, dominant trends in the philanthropic sector run counter to its character. The managerial drive toward "efficiency," for example, often undermines the voluntary spirit. The drive toward "professionalization" can create a new institutional class of bureaucracy and experts who could lead a nonprofit in a direction counter to the aims of its founders. The trend toward "secularization" characteristic of foundation leaders—as of most educated elites—can lead foundations away from the faith and commitment that has been their major originating power. Or yet again the imperatives of the market, such as cost-benefit analysis, and the crippling fear of litigiousness have a tendency to block the sources of true charity.

PHILANTHROPIC SCLEROSIS

"Philanthropic organizations are increasingly constrained in their work by legal and even legalistic interpretations of the law. It occurred to me to think of the Good Samaritan walking down from Jerusalem to Jericho accompanied by his friend, a lawyer. At the Good Samaritan's first movement to help the victim, his friend the lawyer would grab at his sleeve and say, 'Don't you *dare* get involved with that!'"

—Dr. Robert L. Payton,
first professor of philanthropic studies in the United States

In sum, the present situation in philanthropy raises very basic questions: Who gives and who gets? Is the private-public relationship to be one of competition or collaboration? And so on. The issues, however, run to the heart of effective philanthropy and its vital contribution to a free and just society. In his book *Self Renewal*, John Gardner writes, "Unless we attend to the requirements of renewal, aging institutions and organizations will eventually bring our civilization to moldering ruin." In other words, free societies are not machines. Keeping alive traditional ideas and ideals is not a matter of nostalgia or ancestral piety, but of practical urgency.

In today's world with capitalism in the ascendancy, we have no shortage of enthusiasts for Adam Smith's celebrated "invisible hand" of the market forces. But what we need now is a renewal of what has been called "the other invisible hand"—the invisible hand of generosity, help, and moral commitment that not only balances the forces of the market but expresses and sustains a sense of human caring, community, and mutual responsibility.

DEVOLUTION CHIC

Third, money, giving, and caring require attention because they are vital to the health of "civil society." Whereas the recent explosion of wealth has been restricted to a few countries, a seismic shift in the relationship between government and citizens (or public-private partnerships) is a global phenomenon. In countries of the Eastern Bloc this shift takes the form of the gigantic effort to replace centralized governments and command economies with democracy and market capitalism. In Western countries the shift has created an open season for government bashing and talk of decentralization and devolution. The air is abuzz with notions of "reinventing government," "dismantling bureaucracy," "downsizing the Nanny State," "rolling back the Great Society," "leveling hierarchies," and so forth.

Money, giving, and caring are central to this transition and the surrounding debates because they are essential to a "civil society" and the creation of the "social capital" needed to sustain it. As used now, these terms refer to the myriad tissues of trust, association, cooperation, community engagement, and entrepreneurial energy that are vital to a healthy, free society. In short, they signify the famous voluntary associations that so impressed Alexis de Tocqueville on his visit to the young American democracy in the 1830s.

"Social capital" deserves special underscoring. Using the analogy of physical capital and human capital (the tools and training that enhance productivity), proponents of social capital use the term to refer to features of community life that foster cooperation among individuals for the mutual benefit of the community as a whole. Such binding features include shared vision, shared trust, shared virtues, and shared associations. For many reasons life is better and easier in a nation or neighborhood with a rich stock of social capital.

We should be cautious about the rage for devolution, because the decentralizing trend is not as simple as it looks. Another countervailing trend is taking place simultaneously. The effect of modernization (through market capitalism and industrialized technology) is to centralize and decentralize the world *simultaneously*. Unification and fragmentation are *both* going on apace. Our

But what we need now is a renewal of what has been called "the other invisible hand"—the invisible hand of generosity, help, and moral commitment that not only balances the forces of the market but expresses and sustains a sense of human caring, community, and mutual responsibility.

world is being globalized and localized *at the same time.* Depending on our jobs, class, and income, some of us are closer to being "one worlders" and others to being "little worlders."

A political example of the countervailing trends is the fact that centripetal forces are pulling Europe toward the European Community at the same time as centrifugal forces are pulling toward national separatism (Scottish independence from Britain, Basque independence from Spain, and so on). The parallel trends in the world media are simultaneously toward larger and larger info-entertainment conglomerates (such as Viacom) and also toward more and more niche-sensitive narrow-casting through cable channels, interactive shopping, and entertainment.

Overall, the "little world" trends may be carried by technology and a desire for a human scale of life. But these are balanced by such "one world" trends as capital, information, popular entertainment, and labor, all of which are making national boundaries artificial and unenforceable. Thus, although devolution is supposedly in vogue because governments have become bloated and overbearing, another reason applies too: governments and nation-states are weaker today because power has shifted in a borderless world now dominated by international communications and the global market.

Where social capital in a local community is strong—including giving, caring, and volunteering—devolution will be wise and successful; where social capital in a local community is weak, devolution will be foolish and a failure.

The implications for the devolution trend are obvious: *Where social capital in a local community is strong—including giving, caring, and volunteering—devolution will be wise and successful; where social capital in a local community is weak, devolution will be foolish and a failure.* It is not enough to be vehement about the purported evils of centralization, authoritarianism, collectivism, and bureaucracy if there is nothing to support society on the local or regional level. Too much talk of decentralization does not do justice to the requirements of a healthy civil society. So although fashionable, this trend is likely to prove simplistic, shortsighted, and impractical.

It is true, for example, that many older corporations have been hierarchical in their structures and paternalistic in their attitudes. But for all their inadequacies, they were also usually solidly anchored in their local communities. The newer style of company may be more modern, efficient, and competitive, but it also is absentee-owned, quarterly performance-driven, and globally footloose. Thus these modern corporations often show no more loyalty to a local community than to a flag of convenience—and in their blind indifference to local considerations they can become prime destroyers of a community's social capital.

Even Americans, with their rich heritage of social capital, cannot afford to be complacent. As we shall see in later readings, there is evidence of serious erosion in the United States too. Indeed, many argue that market excesses will do just as much damage to "social capital" and "civil societies" as government excesses. But, again, the point is critical. Money, giving, and caring may not appear as influential as more obvious political and economic factors, such as the interest rates and the unemployment figures. But these pre-political issues are just as vital for creating and sustaining free, just societies.

INTERNATIONAL CULTURE WARS?

Fourth, money, giving, and caring require special attention because they go to the heart of differences between civilizations. An economics professor from the University of Singapore stated his view of this conflict succinctly: "What we in Singapore want," he said, "is the modern world, not the West. We want the Asian way, not the American way. We want to follow Confucius, not Christ." Having given rise to the modern world, he explained, the Jewish and Christian faiths now have been reduced to ruins by the modern world. The result has been "the social squalor and a moral slum" of the West, which Asian countries should avoid by pursuing modernity within the setting of their own beliefs and cultures.

And what did the professor believe were some of the key problems with which each civilization and its own distinctive worldview must grapple and supply practical answers? The state of the family would be on most lists, he said. But because of the central importance of capitalism to modernity, all lists must also include the meaning of money and its proper enjoyment and use in a good society.

In short, we can no longer afford the lazymindedness of recent thinking that religious and ethical beliefs don't matter or that all beliefs are basically the same. In the bracing climate of current international competition, differences can be seen to make a difference. *Why* we do what we do is becoming as important as *what* we do. And nowhere is this point plainer than in the story of the origins and rise of the distinctive Western tradition of giving and caring, with its implications for the challenge of meeting global human need today.

Most people are unaware of the differences and tensions between civilizations. Others shrug off the differences as being abstract and impractical. But two things should make us take them seriously. One is the global dimension of human need in a world of instant communication. (We will look later at the "CNNing" of compassion.) The other is the fact that Western capitalism already shows signs of its capacity to undermine the very Western values it requires to thrive.

THE GLOBAL VILLAGE

"If there were a representative global village of 1,000 people, its principal make-up would be as follows:

"584 would be Asians, 124 Africans, 84 Europeans, 84 Latin Americans, 55 former Soviets, 52 North Americans, and 6 Australians and New Zealanders.

"Of the main linguistic groups, 165 would speak Mandarin, 86 English, 83 Hindi, 64 Spanish, 58 Russian, and 37 Arabic.

"329 would be Christians, 178 Muslims, 167 secularists, 132 Hindus, 60 Buddhists, 45 atheists, 3 Jews, and 86 claiming other affiliations.

"Out of the group of 1,000, 60 would receive half of the total income, 500 would be hungry, 600 would live in shantytowns, and only 330 would have access to clean drinking water."

—**Donna Meadows, systems analyst and writer**

Daniel Bell of Harvard University called attention to the "cultural contradictions" of capitalism. In the past, he argued, the menace of unrestrained economic impulse was held in check by the Protestant ethic—people worked in response to their calling. But now, with the Protestant ethic dissolved, including its moral attitudes toward hard work and saving, there is only the ethic of hedonism. "The greatest single engine in the destruction of the Protestant ethic," he wrote, "was the invention of the installment plan, or instant credit. Previously one had to save in order to buy. But with credit cards one could indulge in instant gratification."

Others have put the point differently. Robert N. Bellah of the University of California at Berkeley says that the menace of Soviet totalitarianism has been replaced by that of "market totalitarianism"—as more and more of life is reduced to its market value as a commodity. The late Christopher Lasch warned that the higher life of a society could be judged by its capacity to preserve things that were valued for their own sake and could not be reduced to "pecuniary values." Peter L. Berger of Boston University says that capitalism, having defeated all challenges such as socialism, now faces its greatest challenge—itself, because of its self-devouring nature. *The Wall Street Journal* says simply that "God has a new co-pilot: Midas" (April 5, 1996). Despite the variations, one thrust is the same. For most observers today, the triumph of democratic capitalism is unarguable on *market* grounds but is far less assured on *moral* and social grounds.

If ever an institution required the guiding hand of decisive beliefs, it is the revolutionary force of capitalism.

If ever an institution required the guiding hand of decisive beliefs, it is the revolutionary force of capitalism. Is it conceivable that the runaway engine can be restrained and redirected? That money can be kept simply as a medium of exchange and not allowed to grow into an idol? There are no easy answers here, but one thing is certain. Only those who grapple profoundly with the long human story of the meaning of money and the meaning of giving and caring know the questions that must be faced.

A WISE AND HUMBLING ART

For all the advances of a sophisticated, scientific understanding of philanthropy, giving remains an art—a wise art that must be learned and practiced accordingly after being won in the teeth of all its difficulties, disappointments, and failures. As Seneca wrote in his essay, "On the Happy Life": "Whoever believes that giving is an easy matter, makes a mistake; it is a matter of very great difficulty, provided that gifts are made with wisdom, and are not scattered haphazard and by caprice." The wise giver, he continued, is one who has "his pocket accessible, but it will have no hole in it—a pocket from which much can appear and nothing can drop."

Jesus said famously, "The poor you will have with you always." Many have commenced their war on poverty seeing this statement as a fatalism to be overcome—only to come full circle and realize that its realism is actually reassuring because it is an antidote to utopianism. There have been great and effective givers. There have been examples of giving that have changed societies, affected history, and brought hope into the darkness of human misery. But there is no golden age of giving. There is no philanthropic panacea with guaranteed consequences. There is no business best seller with the sure-fire secrets of the successful giver. Hope is essential in philanthropy, but the utopian are advised to work elsewhere. Giving can be a slippery business. Many of the best intentions and most skillful initiatives have had unforeseen consequences and contradictory outcomes. No success in giving and caring is forever.

POVERTY IS NOT ABOLISHABLE

"There are blessings and benefactions that one would willingly forego—among them the poor. Quack remedies for poverty amuse; a real specific would kindle a noble enthusiasm. Yet the world would lose much by it; human nature would suffer a change for the worse. Happily and unhappily, poverty is not abolishable: 'The poor ye have always with you' is a sentence that can never become unintelligible. Effect of a thousand permanent causes, poverty is invincible, eternal. And since we must have it let us thank God for it and avail ourselves of all its advantages to mind and character."

—Ambrose Bierce, "Charity"

So as we set out on this exploration and wrestle with the issues that trace the road to the present, it is helpful to remember why this art is so humbling and why effective giving sometimes seems so baffling and elusive.

First, giving and caring are humbling because money carries with it three distinct challenges, not just one—making money, enjoying money, and giving it away. Those with singular success in one area may be less accomplished in the others. It is one thing to make money intelligently and another to be wise in giving it away. Money is the end of business but the beginning of giving and caring, and many are greatly disappointed when, after accumulating wealth, they don't know how to use it wisely. As one millionaire complained, "One really needs two lives. One to get to the top. The other to enjoy it all."

MORE TO MONEY THAN MAKING IT

"The rich man who was not generous would be but a miserly beggar. What brings happiness to the possessor of wealth is not the having but the spending of it, and by that I mean spending it well and not simply to gratify his own whims."

—Miguel Cervantes, *Don Quixote*

"It is well to remember that it requires the exercise of not less ability than that which acquires it, to use wealth so as to be really beneficial to the community."

—Andrew Carnegie

"The type of man most likely to grow very, very rich is the type of man least likely to enjoy it."

—Max Gunther

Second, giving and caring are humbling because they contain three distinct components, not just one—giving money, giving time, and giving of ourselves. Those rich in one sort of giving, usually the first (hence the term "checkbook charity"), actually may be poor in the other two and thus ineffective in their overall giving.

Third, giving and caring are humbling because they carry recurring temptations to conceit. Three are prevalent today. One kind of conceit is that of the rich, who are easily flattered by their resources into forgetting that proportionately, poorer people give much more than they do. Jesus' commendation of "the widow's mite" has ample corroboration today. For example, in 1989, American households with incomes under $10,000 gave 5.5 percent of their income to charities, whereas those earning over $100,000 gave 2.9 percent (*Los Angeles Times*, October 25, 1990).

Another kind of conceit is the conceit of Americans, who are easily flattered by their past into seeing themselves as the world's great philanthropists forever and ever. The record is indeed striking. Economist Walter Williams claims that 80 percent of privately contributed gifts in all of human history have been donated by U.S. citizens, and the impact of public largesse, such as the Marshall Plan, is legendary. But Americans are now being left behind in certain important areas by people of other nations. For example, Organization for Economic Cooperation and Development figures for 1996 show that when foreign aid is taken as a percentage of gross national product, the United States ranks twenty-first and last among major industrialized countries—down from ranking first in the years after World War II.

Yet another kind of conceit is that of Christians, who are easily flattered by their role in the origins and record of giving into forgetting that correct beliefs do not make up for lack of deeds. In the parable of "The Good Samaritan," after all, Jesus castigated the smugly orthodox and commended the despised outsider who truly saw the need and responded in practice to his "neighbor"—the "neighbor" simply being the person next to us in need.

Fourth, as we shall explore, giving and caring are humbling because their history gives repeated lessons on their sometimes-baffling character. One recurring theme is that, however well-intentioned a donor may be, the consequences of a gift for the recipient are often ironic, unforeseen, and unintended.

Another recurring lesson is that, however farsighted a donor may be in anticipating problems in the recipients, there are even more problems on the side of the donors. It is currently fashionable to highlight the damage unwise giving causes to recipients—centering mainly on problems such as humiliation, dependency, entitlement, and the reinforcement of beggars (or "pauperizing"). But this is a scanty list compared with history's lengthy catalogue of the crimes and follies surrounding donor abuse. Examples abound of giving as a form of self-interest, as a pursuit of recognition, as a sop to conscience, as a type of snobbery, as a desire to deceive and dominate, as a mask of hypocrisy, as a way of folly or fanaticism, as a means of social control (or "riot insurance," as nineteenth-century philanthropy was described). The story of the Trojan horse and Virgil's advice, "Beware Greeks bearing gifts," is a reminder worthy of wider application. All donors should be humble and self-critical.

Yet another recurring lesson is that, however successful giving may be in individual projects, it is always limited in the face of the limitlessness of human need. Jesus' statement "The poor you will have with you always" is echoed by John D. Rockefeller Sr.'s 1909 statement after conferring $530 million on benevolent causes: "We must always remember that there is not enough money for the work of human uplift and that there never can be." The first and last attitude of the entrepreneurial giver must always be humility.

NO SMALL PRINT HERE

The great Jewish storyteller Sholem Aleichem once told of a poor Jew from Kasrilenke who went to Paris to see the great financier Baron Rothschild. When they met, he tried to persuade the baron to come back to his humble village—and promised him eternal life if he would do so.

"How is that possible?" Baron Rothschild asked.

"Because," the poor Jew answered, "we've never seen a rich man die in Kasrilenke."

The fields of philanthropy and fundraising are replete with misrepresentations far less innocent and humorous than this one. So it is important to state clearly what *Doing Well and Doing Good* offers, and what it doesn't.

First, this book contains no fundraising agenda of any sort, and is not directed toward any charity or cause. Neither is it partisan or ideological. Nor does it contain any appeal to guilt.

PASTOR TOMMERDAHL'S ANNUAL SERMON: "THE TRUE MEANING OF CHRISTMAS"

"If you went to the church with visions of sugarplums dancing in your head, he stopped the music. Santa Claus was not prominent in his theology. He had the gift of making you feel you'd better go home and give all the presents to the poor and spend Christmas with a bowl of soup, and not too many noodles in it either. He preached the straight gospel, and as he said, the gospel is meant to comfort the afflicted and afflict the comfortable. He certainly afflicted the Lutherans."

—Garrison Keillor, *Lake Wobegon Days*

From the perspective here, guilt-motivated giving is neither right nor successful in the long run. Instead, for reasons that we shall examine, sustained and effective giving stems from a joy in generosity.

Second, this book is neither an encyclopedia of good works nor a history of philanthropy. Both are beyond our scope here. For example, simply because we are modern people there is little included on the medieval era with its defining "vow of poverty"; instead there is much more on the modern period, with its "vow of wealth." The readings have been chosen with two things in mind: the big *ideas* that have animated giving and are in need of *renewal* today; and the big *issues* that have shaped and challenged giving and are in need of *resolution* today.

"Well, this is crazy. Every time we talk about likely donors for the project, it sounds like me."

©1994 Mark Litzler, The Chronicle of Philanthropy.

Third, this book has been written for citizens in all walks and levels of life. In an important sense, all citizens of Western democracies already benefit from various acts of generosity and philanthropy. We have only to be cared for in a hospital, refreshed in a park, attended to in a library, delighted in a symphony concert, or welcomed in a church or synagogue to begin to trace the myriad ways in which the generosities of others have enriched our lives. Our own responsibility to "pass on generosity" is therefore strong. But it is also worth considering whether some have further levels of responsibility. For example:

- Individuals and families with wealth who are reflecting on their responsibilities in society
- Senior business leaders and executives who are weighing their corporate responsibilities to wider society
- Political and community leaders and public policy specialists who are contending with the public issues involved in giving and caring
- Leaders in the philanthropic and foundation world who are wrestling with the fundamental institutional issues raised today

ROADMAP TO THE READINGS

What will be our approach in this book? In part 1 we will examine the meaning of money from a classical perspective. First we will weigh different responses to basic questions that underlie the rise of philanthropy—in particular, Whose is it? and What are the problems with money? Then we will look at different explanations for the generally agreed problems, such as the "insatiability" of desire for money.

In part 2 we will focus on the meaning of giving and caring, also from a classical perspective. Largely trivialized today because of the dominance of "consumer" giving, in the past giving had far greater meaning but contrasting interpretations. On the one hand, "contract" giving, a style of giving-to-get, was based on the Greek concepts of *eros* and *philanthropia;* on the other, "charity" giving, a style of giving-because-given-to, was based on the Christian concept of *agape.* It was the latter, along with the unique Christian idea of caring that goes beyond "people like us," that gave rise to the unique Western tradition of hospitals, orphanages, leprosariums, and care for the poor.

In part 3 we will look at the rise of modern philanthropy in the nineteenth century. After examining the social conditions of the early industrial revolution, which made philanthropy necessary, we will focus on the emergence of distinctive new agencies, such as the voluntary association and the foundation, and the competing approaches to philanthropy that marked earlier centuries and lie behind modern debates.

In part 4 we will explore some major contemporary challenges to effective philanthropy, such as the way the "CNNing" of perception creates a "telescopic philanthropy" through which charity no longer "begins at home."

In part 5 we will draw together the threads of the discussion by setting out some concluding reminders of how to excel in the wise art of giving and caring.

More than two and a half centuries ago Cotton Mather proclaimed in *Bonifacius: An Essay upon the Good* that philanthropy was "sound policy, an honor, a privilege, an incomparable pleasure, and a reward in itself." As such, he urged the members of his community, they should "do good with as much application of mind as the wicked employ in doing evil." Giving and caring are still the same today and so must our reflection and applications be if a great tradition is to witness a much-needed renewal. Only then will giving and caring play their unique role, not just in supporting free societies, but in reaching out in care to human need and in creativity toward a better tomorrow.

PERSPECTIVE

"What I spent, is gone.
What I kept, is lost.
But what I gave
Will be mine for ever."

—epitaph on a tombstone

"The great use of life is to spend it for something that outlasts it."

—William James

"He is no fool who gives away what he cannot keep to gain what he cannot lose."

—Jim Elliot,
martyr and missionary to the Auca Indians,
Ecuador, 1956

ONE
MONEY—MEDIUM OF EXCHANGE OR MAMMON?

ONE OF THE GREAT ODDITIES OF PHILANTHROPY IS THAT MANY PEOPLE TRY TO UNDERSTAND the meaning of giving without understanding the meaning of money. Giving, it is true, goes back earlier than both money and the ancient barter system. But now that money has assumed a dominant position, especially within the ruling empire of capitalism, no one can begin to understand giving without understanding money.

Giving, it is also true, entails far more than simply giving money, just as wealth encompasses abundance of all kinds. But most major, modern giving includes giving money, so the trails return again to its meaning.

Money, money, money. Along with sex and power, money is a little word but a gigantic force. The place it occupies in our lives and in our culture provides a measure of who we are. No society has ever made the money factor more pervasive and more decisive than we do as proponents of democratic capitalism. In a means-oriented society, money is the ultimate means without which the modern world would slow and stop.

The story of the rise of philanthropy in Western civilization is a response to two leading questions about money: First, whose is it? And second, what is the problem?

Beguilingly simple, perhaps, these two questions have traditionally elicited very different responses with different effects in society. Our concern here is the influence on the rise of a culture of giving and caring. But the answers to these two questions help us to see whether money is simply a medium of exchange—an instrumental and neutral means—or whether it is also an end, even a dangerous end, and worth giving away for that reason alone.

MERE MONEY?

"Whether you like it or whether you do not, money is money and that is all there is about it."

—Gertrude Stein, *Saturday Evening Post,* July 13, 1936

"Money is nothing. It's just something to make bookkeeping convenient."

—H. L. Hunt, Texas oil billionaire

Trying to solve the problem of money through tinkering with the economic system or switching systems altogether will always be a failure.

The truth is, as the classical writers knew well, it is a monumental mistake to see money only as an economic issue. It was, and is, a spiritual issue. Trying to solve the problem of money through tinkering with the economic system or switching systems altogether will always be a failure. Money is money regardless of whether it is working in a free or centralized market and first needs to be understood as such. In an obvious sense we take money too seriously today. But in a less obvious sense we only do so because we don't take it seriously enough—to understand it.

POINT TO PONDER:

Money and Property—Whose Is It?

The distinctive Western tradition of giving and caring is the child of Jewish and Christian beliefs. But the biblical perspective was only one of antiquity's three major views of money—Jewish/Christian, Greek, and Roman—and each gave a distinctive answer to the question underlying money and property: Whose is it?

One view, represented by an influential if minority stream of Greek thinkers, most notably Plato and the followers of Pythagoras, was that money should be shared because its ownership is (or rather, was) common. Unlike Marxists, who place the golden age of sharing in the future, the Greeks put it in the past. They believed in an earlier age of community when all was shared, so in today's ideal society all should be held in common again—at least by those with the responsibilities of leadership (Plato's "guardians").

This first view, it must be said, was not universal among the Greeks— the comic playwright Aristophanes pilloried Plato mercilessly, and Aristotle strongly disagreed with his master. But Plato was expressing an old and powerful Greek tradition. The idea of redistribution of land in the name of equality, for instance, was prevalent even in the constitutions of Sparta and Crete. The utopian element and the drive toward justice viewed as redistribution are unmistakable. However, so too is the tendency toward despotic consequences because the gap between the real and the ideal must eventually be bridged by coercion.

A second view, represented by the Romans speaking almost unanimously, was that individuals had absolute rights over their money and property. Property, by an old definition, is a right of action. It is an expression of the human will acted out over things and people, so the concept of property without an actor has no meaning. (This line of thinking is seen today, for example, in the current slogan, "A woman has a right to her own body.")

The strength of this position is striking. For Romans, ownership in the full sense included the right to use, to enjoy, and even to abuse one's property (jus utendi, jus fruendi, jus abutendi). This was the backbone of the Roman system. A farmer could burn down his farmhouse with impunity. The father of a family (paterfamilias), acknowledged to have power of life and death over his family, could kill his children with impunity at any time. The horrible practice of maiming children to raise their potential as beggars was common in

This view tends toward an unbridled, winner-takes-all mentality that is careless of limits and deaf to weakness and need.

Rome. So also was the evil of exposing unwanted babies, mostly girls, to die.

Such a view of absolute property rights is obviously congenial to elements of today's capitalistic, even libertarian, climate. But the potential ruthlessness should be noted too. This view tends toward an unbridled, winner-takes-all mentality that is careless of limits and deaf to weakness and need. The Roman view also led to a characteristic hypocrisy. Such writers as Seneca were striking for having great personal wealth and yet producing eloquent passages disparaging it.

The third view, represented by Jews and Christians, was that human beings have a qualified right over money and property. Or, put more precisely, God has the ultimate ownership but we have stewardship of money, property, and our talents. The resources of the earth are held in trust for a divine purpose. Thus our relationship to money and property may by custom or law be defined as ownership but is really a conditional form of trusteeship. In the true sense of the Old English word "steward," we are responsible for the prudent management of an estate that is not our own.

The contrast with the other two views is profound and the differences very practical. One example was the Jewish harvest custom of not gleaning fields to the edges to create a margin for the care of the poor.

John D. Rockefeller Sr. stood clearly in this stewardship tradition when he voiced what Andrew Carnegie, despite his generosity, could never have said, "The good Lord gave me the money." It would be easy, of course, to turn such a statement into a pious cant. But there is no question that, historically, this response to "Whose is it?" was an important motivation for the generous giving that gave rise to philanthropy.

LANDLORD OR TENANT? IT MAKES A DIFFERENCE

"Let us go back to the man who says that a thing cannot be wrong unless it hurts some other human being. He quite understands that he must not damage the other ships in the convoy, but he honestly thinks that what he does to his own ship is simply his own business. But does it not make a great difference whether his ship is his own property or not? Does it not make a great difference whether I am, so to speak, the landlord of my own mind and body, or only a tenant, responsible to the real landlord? If somebody else made me, for his own purposes, then I shall have a lot of duties which I should not have if I simply belonged to myself."

—C. S. Lewis, *Mere Christianity*

❋THE GREEKS❋
Common Ownership

Plato (about 427–347 B.C.), along with his mentor Socrates and his disciple Aristotle, is a giant of the mind and a leading shaper of Western civilization and its intellectual tradition. Born a year after the death of Pericles, Plato came from a family that was prominent in Athenian politics. He, however, refused to enter politics after he became disgusted by the corruption and violence of Athenian democracy—culminating in the execution of Socrates in 399 B.C. Living in troubled times, he sought his cure from the ills of society in philosophy, not politics. He became convinced that justice would not arrive "until either real philosophers gain political power or politicians become by some miracle true philosophers."

The excerpt beginning on the next page is from Plato's most important dialogue, The Republic, an imagined conversation between Socrates and a student. In this excerpt, Socrates describes his ideal society. A class of people called the "Guardians" are the ones from whom he hopes to groom his Philosopher-Rulers. Socrates argues that to meet the Guardians' needs and encourage their devotion to the community, they must share all money and property communally. "Oneness in spirit" is to be created by "oneness of possession." By holding all goods in common, they escape the corrupting power of the quest for material goods.

It was because of passages such as this one that Karl Popper in The Open Society and Its Enemies argued that Plato was the founder of authoritarianism in the West because of his view that society must limit human freedom in the name of utopian ideals. The two paragraphs from Aristophanes and Aristotle at the end of the reading represent Plato's strongest critics.

YOURS, MINE, OURS

"The first-best society, then, that with the best constitution and code of law, is one where the old saying is most universally true of the whole society. I mean the saying that 'friends' property is indeed common property.'"

—Plato, *The Laws*

❋ Plato ❋

The Republic

"It would therefore be reasonable to say that, besides being so educated, they [the leaders of the republic] should be housed and their material needs provided for in a way that will not prevent them being excellent Guardians, yet will not tempt them to prey upon the rest of the community."

"That is very true."

"Well then," I said, "if they are to have these characteristics, I suggest that they should live and be housed as follows. First, they shall have no private property beyond the barest essentials. Second, none of them shall possess a dwellinghouse or storehouse to which all have not the right of entry. Next, their food shall be provided by the other citizens as an agreed wage for the duties they perform as Guardians; it shall be suitable for brave men living under military training and discipline, and in quantity enough to ensure that there is neither a surplus nor a deficit over the year. They shall eat together in messes and live together like soldiers in camp. They must be told that they have no need of mortal and material gold and silver, because they have in their hearts the heavenly gold and silver given them by the gods as a permanent possession, and it would be wicked to pollute the heavenly gold in their possession by mixing it with earthly, for theirs is without impurity, while that in currency among men is a common source of wickedness. . . . [O]ur purpose in founding our state was not to promote the particular happiness of a single class, but, so far as possible, of the whole community. . . .

"It follows from what we've said, and from our whole previous argument—"

"What follows?"

"—that our men and women Guardians should be forbidden by law to live together in separate households, and all the women should be common to all the men; similarly, children should be held in common, and no parent should know its child, or child its parent. . . ."

"As law-giver, you have already picked your men Guardians. You must now pick women of as nearly similar natural capacities as possible to go with them. They will live and feed together, and have no private home or property. They will mix freely in their physical exercises and the rest of their training, and their natural instincts will necessarily lead them to have sexual intercourse. . . ."

"We must, if we are to be consistent, and if we're to have a real pedigree herd, mate the best of our men with the best of our women as often as possible, and the inferior men with the inferior women as seldom as possible, and bring up only the offspring of the best. And no one but the Rulers must know what is happening, if we are to avoid dissension in our Guardian herd."

"That is very true."

"So we must arrange statutory festivals in which our brides and bride-grooms will be brought together. There will be religious sacrifices and our poets will write songs suitable to the occasion. The number of unions we will leave to the Rulers to settle. Their aim will be to keep numbers constant, allowing for wastage by war and disease and the like, and, so far as they can, to prevent our state becoming too large or too small."

"Quite right."

"And we shall have to devise an ingenious system of drawing lots, so that our inferior Guardian can, at each mating festival, blame the lot and not the Rulers."

"That will certainly be necessary."

"And among the other honors and rewards our young men can win for dis-tinguished service in war and in other activities, will be more frequent opportunities to sleep with women; this will give us a pretext for ensuring that most of our children are born of that kind of parent."

"Quite right."

"Each generation of children will be taken by officers appointed for the purpose, who may be men or women or both—for men and women will of course be equally eligible for office—"

"Yes, of course."

"These officers will take the children of the better Guardians to a nursery and put them in charge of nurses living in a separate part of the city: the chil-dren of the inferior Guardians, and any defective offspring of the others, will be quietly and secretly disposed of."

From Plato, *The Republic,* trans. Desmond Lee (London: Penguin Books, 1987). © 1953, 1974, 1987 by H.D.P. Lee. Reprinted by permission.

ARISTOPHANES ON PLATO

"BLEPYROS:

But if a man's yearning to insinuate

His kisses abed with some wench, where's the bait?

He gets a mere share of the common estate. . . .

A fraction of kisses, a ration of legs

Deducted from breakfast—desires's dirty dregs!

PRAXAGORA:

Don't forget how much easier henceforth to mate is.

The whole city of girls are your wives now, and gratis!

Whoever's inclined to make mothers of any

Just catches them up, and it costs not a penny."

—Aristophanes, *Ecclesiazusae* or *The Assembly of Women*

ARISTOTLE ON PLATO

"There is further harm in the doctrine: the greater the number of owners, the less the respect for common property. People are much more careful of their personal possessions than of those owned communally; they exercise care over common property only in so far as they are personally affected. Other reasons apart, the thought that someone else is looking after it tends to make them careless of it. (This is rather like what happens in domestic service: a greater number of servants sometimes does less work than a smaller.) Each citizen acquires a thousand sons, but these are not one man's sons; any one of them is equally the son of any person, and as a result will be equally neglected by everyone. . . .

"There are two impulses which more than all others cause human beings to cherish and feel affection for each other: 'this is my own,' and 'this is a delight.' Among people organized in this manner no one would be able to say either. . . .

"But even if one were to fix a moderate amount of all, that would still be no use: for it is more necessary to equalize appetites than possessions, and that can only be done by adequate education under the laws."

—Aristotle, *Politics*

QUESTIONS FOR THOUGHT AND DISCUSSION

1. How does Socrates plan to set up the Guardian class? What are his goals in doing so? What are some of the potential dangers he foresees if the Guardians don't have his desired attitude toward possessions?

2. Practically speaking, how does Socrates see the Guardians living? Why? What will be the explanation to the Guardians for this lifestyle?

3. At the end of the second full paragraph, he gives them his inspirational rationale—"they have no need of mortal and material gold and silver" and so on. How would you describe his appeal? Do you find it convincing?

4. Socrates says the "purpose in founding our state was not to promote the particular happiness of a single class, but . . . of the whole community." What are the implications of this for individuals?

5. Is he consistent in his reasoning for the setup of the society? Why or why not?

6. How does Socrates plan for men and women to interact? To marry? What role do women and children play in the Guardian class? Do you see any conflicting purposes?

7. Socrates never describes the society in terms of "family." What is striking about how he portrays the interaction of men, women, and children? Who ultimately is in charge of these relationships? What would be the consequences for society?

8. What overtones do you hear in such references as "our Guardian herd," "mating festival," "defective offspring," and so on?

9. What part does deception play in making the Guardian class a reality? Why is deception necessary?

10. What is the link between utopianism and despotism in these readings? Is it a stretch to go from developing a "Guardian class" to purifying the "Aryan race"? How do both go back to the underlying view of possessions?

11. What do you think of Aristophanes' and Aristotle's attacks on Plato? How far would they apply to the modern forms of communism, such as Marxism?

12. What sort of giving, if any, would this Greek view be likely to encourage?

THE EARTH BELONGS TO US ALL

"The first man who, having enclosed a piece of ground, bethought himself of saying 'this is mine,' and found people simple enough to believe him, was the real founder of civil society. From how many crimes, wars, and murders, from how many horrors and misfortunes might not anyone have saved mankind, by pulling up the stakes, or filling up the ditch, and crying to his fellows, 'Beware of listening to this imposter; you are undone if you once forget that the fruits of the earth belong to us all, and the earth itself to nobody.'"

—Jean-Jacques Rousseau, *The Social Contract*

"Those who will not even admit the Capitalist problem deserve to get the Bolshevist solution."

—G. K. Chesterton

❧THE ROMANS❧
Absolute Individual Ownership

Marcus Tullius Cicero (106–43 B.C.) was a Roman statesman who attained such eminence that he was given the title Pater patriae *("Father of his country") by the Roman Senate. He has been considered a master of oratory and persuasion throughout Western history and is often quoted today. Born into a wealthy family, he enlisted in the army at age sixteen and then entered the Roman Senate. At age forty-three he was elected consul and attained acclaim for foiling the plot of Cataline. He left behind several works of philosophy and rhetoric. Called the "conservative par excellence," Cicero spent much energy debating against agrarian reforms, such as land redistribution, proposed by other senators. His influence on Roman life was incalculable.*

The excerpt below is taken from one of his longest works, De Officiis, *or "Duty." In stark contrast to the utopian-communist visions of Plato, it portrays the typical Roman attitudes on property and relations with the state: absolute ownership rights for landowners (who were the upper class) and no taxes except in cases of national emergency. As stated earlier, ownership in the absolute sense included the right to use, enjoy, and even abuse one's property.*

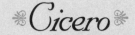

❧*Cicero*❧

De Officiis ✍

The man in an administrative office, however, must make it his first care that every one shall have what belongs to him and that private citizens suffer no invasion of their property rights by act of the state. It was a ruinous policy that

Philippus proposed when in his tribuneship he introduced his agrarian bill. However, when his law was rejected, he took his defeat with good grace and displayed extraordinary moderation. But in his public speeches on the measure he often played the demagogue, and that time viciously, when he said that "there were not in the state two thousand people who owned any property." That speech deserves unqualified condemnation, for it favored an equal distribution of property; and what more ruinous policy than that could be conceived? For the chief purpose in the establishment of constitutional state and municipal governments was that individual property rights might be secured. For although it was by Nature's guidance that men were drawn together into communities, it was in the hope of safeguarding their possessions that they sought the protection of cities. . . .

For the chief purpose in the establishment of constitutional state and municipal governments was that individual property rights might be secured.

But they who pose as friends of the people, and who for that reason either attempt to have agrarian laws passed, in order that the occupants may be driven out of their homes, or propose that money loaned should be remitted to the borrowers, are undermining the foundations of the commonwealth: first of all, they are destroying harmony, which cannot exist when money is taken away from one party and bestowed upon another; and second, they do away with equity, which is utterly subverted, if the rights of property are not respected. For, as I said above, it is the peculiar function of the state and the city to guarantee to every man the free and undisturbed control of his own particular property.

Reprinted by permission of the publishers and the Loeb Classical Library from *Cicero: Volume XXI*, trans. Walter Miller, (Cambridge, MA: Harvard University Press, 1913).

IF IT'S ABSOLUTELY MINE . . .

"Look over the livestock and hold a sale. Sell your oil, if the price is satisfactory, and sell the surplus of your wine and grain. Sell worn-out oxen, blemished cattle, blemished sheep, wool, hides, an old wagon, old tools, an old slave, a sickly slave, and whatever else is superfluous."

—Cato, *On Agriculture*

"Monstrous offspring we destroy; children too, if weak and unnaturally formed from birth, we drown. It is not anger, but reason, thus to separate the useless from the sound."

—Seneca, *On Anger*

QUESTIONS FOR THOUGHT AND DISCUSSION

1. What does Cicero say is the main purpose of the Roman governments and primary responsibility of a state official? Who is the focus?

2. Why does Cicero call Philippus's agrarian bill "ruinous policy"? What are his concerns of such a bill passing?

3. What do his criticisms say of his own view of property? Of his view of community?

4. Cicero speaks of "harmony" and "equity" being destroyed by the broader distribution of property, but can these qualities be present for all in the existing society?

5. How is injustice prevented in a society such as this? Who puts limits on owners?

6. What is the link between this absolute view of property rights and the callousness in Cato's instructions and Seneca's comments (see box p. 45)? Who determines the value of a possession, be it one's child, a slave, a cow, or a tool?

7. What sort of giving would this Roman view be likely to encourage? Who would almost certainly not be helped?

❦ JEWS AND CHRISTIANS ❦
Ownership Is God's; Stewardship Is Ours

Like the Romans, the Jews attached great significance to their land. But unlike the Romans, this attachment was not primarily based on the fact that their ancestors were buried there. Nor did it give them absolute property rights as landowners. The land was sacred because it was God's land. They had possession of it, but in a qualified sense only—really it was God's. Their possession was one of stewardship; his was one of ownership.

This perspective was far more than pious rhetoric. On the one hand, it led to the concept of "the righteous rich"—such people as Abraham and Job who were both rich and righteous. On the other hand, it set limits to what people could do with their property. Negatively, Jewish law forbade the abuse of property, whether animals, land, or slaves. For instance, humans were to rest every seven days and land to lie fallow every seven years. Positively, Jewish law created space for the care of the poor. Among other things, the poor, the widow, and the orphan had a right to a portion of every crop, as harvesting—unlike Rome's—was not to be a matter of maximized, right-to-the-edges efficiency. (We will see more on this in part 2.) Equally the poor could gather as food whatever the untended ground produced on its own. Whatever the poor did not take was left for the wild animals.

Out of this system the word tzedakah, *originally meaning "righteousness," came to carry the robust modern Jewish notion of charity. But behind everything is the ruling principle that God, as Creator, owns absolutely everything. We humans are always and only stewards. This Old Testament concept carries over strongly into the New Testament and then decisively shapes early Christian attitudes toward wealth and poverty.*

Leviticus 25:23

"The land must not be sold permanently, because the land is mine and you are but aliens and my tenants."

Deuteronomy 23:24-25

"If you enter your neighbor's vineyard, you may eat all the grapes you want, but do not put any in your basket. If you enter your neighbor's grainfield, you may pick kernels with your hands, but you must not put a sickle to his standing grain."

Psalm 50:9-12

"I have no need of a bull from your stall or of goats from your pens, for every animal of the forest is mine, and the cattle on a thousand hills. I know every bird in the mountains, and the creatures of the field are mine. If I were hungry I would not tell you, for the world is mine, and all that is in it."

1 Chronicles 29:11-14

"Yours, O LORD, is the greatness and the power
    and the glory and the majesty and the splendor,
    for everything in heaven and earth is yours.
Yours, O LORD, is the kingdom;
    you are exalted as head over all.

Wealth and honor come from you;
    you are the ruler of all things.

In your hands are strength and power
    to exalt and give strength to all.
Now, our God, we give you thanks,
    and praise your glorious name.

"But who am I, and who are my people, that we should be able to give as generously as this? Everything comes from you, and we have given you only what comes from your hand."

St. John Chrysostom

John Chrysostom (A.D. 347–407) was a bishop of the early church who later was appointed, against his will, Patriarch of Constantinople. As a priest in Antioch from A.D. 386–398, he delivered a series of sermons on several New Testament books that has established him among the greatest Christian preachers and expositors. "Chrysostom" means "golden-tongued." His sermons portrayed profound spiritual insight into the Scriptures and provided his listeners and readers with immediate practical application. In Constantinople, he preached zealously for moral reform and against the abuse of riches. Displeased with this, the empress and other enemies brought him to trial on false charges. He was forced into exile and was later deliberately killed by being forced to travel on foot in dangerous weather.

On the Social Function of Property

This parable [of the faithful servant, Matthew 24:45–47] applies not to money only but also to speech, power, gifts, and every stewardship wherewith each is entrusted. It would suit rulers in the state also, for everyone is bound to make full use of what he has for the common good. If it is wisdom that you have, or power, or wealth, or whatever, let it not be for the ruin of your fellow-servants nor for your own ruin. . . .

If it is wisdom that you have, or power, or wealth, or whatever, let it not be for the ruin of your fellow-servants nor for your own ruin. . . .

Let us who have money listen to these things as well. For Christ speaks not only to teachers but also to the rich. For both have been entrusted with riches: the teachers with the more necessary wealth, the rich with the inferior one. While the teachers are giving out the greater wealth, you are not willing to show forth your generosity even in the lesser, or rather not generosity but honesty (for you are in fact giving things that belong to others), what excuse will you have?

. . . For you too are stewards of your own possessions, no less than he who dispenses the alms of the Church. Just as he has no right to squander at random and at hazard the things given by you for the poor, since they were given for the maintenance of the poor, so you may not squander your own. For even though you have received an inheritance from your father, and have in this way come to possess everything you have, still everything belongs to God. . . . Therefore though he could have taken these possessions away from you, God left them so that you may have the opportunity to show forth virtue. Thus, bringing us into need one of another, he makes our love for one another more fervent. . . .

For, if in worldly matters no man lives for himself, but artisan, soldier, farmer, and merchant, all of them contribute to the common good, and to their neighbor's advantage, much more ought we to do this in spiritual things. For this is most properly to live. He who lives for himself only and overlooks all others, is useless, he is not even a man, he does not belong to the human race.

Message of the Fathers of the Church: Social Thought, Homily LXXVII, Volume 20, trans. Peter C. Phan (Collegeville, MN: The Liturgical Press, 1984), © 1984 by The Order of St. Benedict, Inc.

NOT OURS BUT HIS

"Whenever I get confused about my money and how to deal with it, I get a lot of clarity and perspective when I stop and think that it's not my money. Instead I view myself as a spiritual aspirant who has been entrusted with a large sum of money by God, and that my work is to learn how to utilize this money in a way that is both beneficial of my own spiritual development and of service to humanity."

—wealthy heir in *We Gave Away a Fortune*

QUESTIONS FOR THOUGHT AND DISCUSSION

1. When God says in the Scripture passages, "the land is mine and you are . . . my tenants" and "the world is mine," do you think he is speaking literally or figuratively? How would your understanding of these passages affect your perspective on ownership?

2. According to Chrysostom, how would rulers having a stewardship view of ownership benefit everyone in a society? How should this view affect their perspective on the people of the state? What is notable about the way he refers to the citizens?

3. Clearly Chrysostom did not equate giving with giving money. What is the significance of his view of other forms of wealth, such as the ability to teach?

4. Why does Chrysostom equate generosity with "honesty" in speaking to the rich on giving? What does he mean by "you are in fact giving things that belong to others"? How does this echo the statement made in the passage from 1 Chronicles?

5. How does Chrysostom reason that an inheritance is an "opportunity to show forth virtue"? How would seeing God as the owner of all that we own change the way we see those in need? Why do you think he says, "He who lives for himself only and overlooks all others, is useless, he is not even a man"?

6. Do you view Chrysostom's blunt teaching (the last sentence, for example) as tough-minded principle or pious rhetoric? What is the evidence for your view?

7. Of these three ancient views of money, which comes closest to the views of your friends and colleagues today? Which is closest to your own?

POINT TO PONDER: _____

Money—Why Is There a Problem?

Comedian Jack Benny loved to tell the story of a mugger who accosted him and said, "Your money or your life!" After an appreciable silence, the mugger says, "Well?" And Benny replies, "Don't rush me. I'm thinking, I'm thinking!"

Of course, the more that money becomes our life, the harder the choice becomes. And today, a defining feature of our modern society is wanting money above all else. As Jacob Needleman writes in Money and the Meaning of Life, *"In other times and places, not everyone has wanted money above all else; people have desired salvation, beauty, power, strength, pleasure, propriety, explanations, food, adventure, conquest, comfort. But now and here, money—not necessarily even the things money can buy, but money—is what everyone wants. The outward expenditure of mankind's energy now takes place in and through money."*

Significantly, the dominant place of money in our capitalist society coincides with a diminishing repugnance toward the fifth deadly sin of avarice. Thus we have no consensus on "financial obesity" that parallels social attitudes on physical obesity. You can never be too rich or too thin, as the saying goes. The result is a situation about which investor Warren Buffett quipped: "You won't encounter much traffic taking the high road on Wall Street."

What this modern shortsightedness overlooks is a realistic appraisal of the problem of money. In contrast, while people throughout the ages have had very different explanations of why money was a problem, they were united in believing that it was.

We look first at the two main problems with money, as tradition understood them, and then examine the two most important explanations of the problem.

❋INSATIABILITY❋

The first of the two generally acknowledged problems of money is insatiability. As we pursue money and possessions, the pursuit at a certain point grows into a never-satisfied desire described by the Bible as "a chasing after wind," by Buddhists as "craving," and by the seven deadly sins as "avarice." The Hebrew word for money (kesef) comes from a verb meaning "to desire" or "languish after something." Thus the spiritual character of money has been stressed from the very beginning.

Avarice is often confused with a Scrooge-like stinginess in hoarding but is better described as a form of spiritual dropsy or insatiable thirst. The more we seek to slake our thirst, the more it grows. The insatiability touches two areas — getting what we do not yet have and clutching onto what we do. It ends in the subservience of being to having and the valuing of things over people and time. Life ends before we actually can enjoy living, the people in our lives, or the money we have.

Avarice breeds a host of consequences, including loneliness, anxiety, waste, crime, injustice, restless unease, and neglect of the poor. It has generally been observed to be a masculine rather than a feminine sin. The avaricious does not give himself to an object as a woman gives herself in loving, but wants to have it and hold it in his hands like a man. This is the profane, secular, masculine sin whose aim is mastery, domination, and control.

The insatiable love of money always points to another need — for power, protection, approval, and so on. Howard Hughes, for example, had an extraordinary need to possess people and places without using them. He hired a man to spend months in a motel room waiting for a call that never came. And he kept at least five young starlets in mansions, with cars, chauffeurs, guards, and restaurant charge accounts — and although he never visited them, he hired private detectives to make sure no one else did. But money never buys love, or ourselves, or eternity, or God. It is the wrong means, the wrong road, the wrong search. That is why it is insatiable — and vanity.

But money never buys love, or ourselves, or eternity, or God. It is the wrong means, the wrong road, the wrong search.

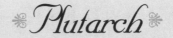 *Plutarch*

Plutarch (about A.D. 46–120) is one of the most famous chroniclers of the ancient world, best known for his book The Lives of the Noble Grecians and Romans. *Born in Boeotia, he studied in Athens and traveled extensively, including trips to Rome where his lectures attracted great attention. He lived most of his life in Greece, serving as a leader in his hometown as well as officiating as a priest of Apollo. Deeply concerned about the moral life, he was a follower of the great theories and ethics of his fellow Greeks, Plato and Aristotle. Plutarch here criticizes those who own and pursue more possessions than they need and describes the obscene and self-defeating nature of acquisitiveness.*

BEING OR HAVING?

"The greatest wealth is to live content with little."

—Plato

"Wealth obviously is not the good we seek, for the sole purpose it serves is to provide the means of getting something else."

—Aristotle

"Good God! How small a portion of the earth we hold by nature, yet we covet the whole world!"

—Philip of Macedon, on being thrown in wrestling, as he turned and saw the imprint of his body

"The longer the rich man extends his colonnades, the higher he lifts his towers, the wider he stretches out his mansions, the deeper he digs his caverns for summer, the huger loom the roofs of the banquet-halls he rears, so much the more there will be to hide heaven from his sight."

—Seneca

"Accordingly, we find no vice so irreclaimable as avarice; and though there scarcely has been a moralist or philosopher, from the beginning of the world to this day, who has not levelled a stroke at it, we hardly find a single instance of any person's being cured of it."

—David Hume

"Money never made a man happy yet, nor will it. There is nothing in its nature to produce happiness. The more a man has, the more he wants. Instead of its filling a vacuum, it makes one. If it satisfies one want, it doubles and triples that want another way."

—Benjamin Franklin

On Wealth

When some persons praised a tall fellow with a long reach as having the makings of a fine boxer, the trainer Hippomachus remarked: "Yes, if the crown were hung up and to be got by reaching." So too we can say to those who are dazzled by fine estates, great houses, and large sums of money and regard them as the greatest of blessings: "Yes, if happiness were for sale and to be got by purchase." But money cannot buy peace of mind, greatness of spirit, serenity, confidence, and self-sufficiency.

Having wealth is not the same as being superior to it, nor is possessing luxuries the same as feeling no need of them. From what other ills then does wealth deliver us, if it does not even deliver us from the craving for it? Nay, drink allays the desire of drink, and food is a remedy for hunger; . . . but neither silver nor gold allays the craving for money, nor does the greed of gain ever cease from acquiring new gains.

. . . Finding us in want of a loaf, a house, a modest protection from the weather, and whatever comes to hand to supplement our loaf, wealth infects us with the desire for gold and silver and ivory and emeralds and hounds and horses, diverting our appetite from the necessities of life to what is difficult, rare, hard to procure, and useless. Indeed in what suffices no one is poor; and no one has ever borrowed money to buy barley meal, a cheese, a loaf, or olives. Rather one man has run into debt for a splendid house, another for an adjoining olive plantation, another for fields and vineyards. . . . And then, as those who drink when no longer thirsty, or eat when no longer hungry, vomit up with the surfeit the rest as well that was taken to satisfy hunger or thirst, so those who seek the useless and superfluous do not even retain the necessary. Such then is the condition of one sort of lover of wealth.

Those on the other hand who part with nothing, though they have great possessions, but always want greater, would strike one who remembered what Aristippus said as even more absurd. "If a man eats and drinks a great deal," he used to say, "but is never filled, he sees a physician, inquires what ails him, what is wrong with his system, and how to rid himself of the disorder; but if the owner of five couches goes looking for ten, and the owner of ten tables buys up as many again, and though he has lands and money in plenty is not satisfied but bent on more, losing sleep and never sated by any amount, does he imagine that he does not need someone who will prescribe for him and point out the cause of his distress?"

Certainly in the case of sufferers from thirst you would expect the one who had had nothing to drink to find his thirst relieved after drinking, while we assume that the one who drinks on and on without stopping needs to relieve, not stuff, himself, and we tell him to vomit, taking his trouble to be caused not by any shortage in anything but by the presence in him of some unnatural pungency or heat.

So too with money-getters: he who is in want and destitute would perhaps call a halt once he got an estate or discovered a hidden treasure or was helped by a friend to pay his debt and get free from his creditor; whereas he who has more than enough and yet hungers for still more will find no remedy in gold or silver or horses and sheep and cattle, but in casting out the source of mischief and being purged. For his ailment is not poverty, but insatiability and avarice, arising from the presence in him of a false and unreflecting judgment; and unless someone removes this, like a tapeworm, from his mind, he will never cease to need superfluities—that is, to want what he does not need. . . .

Another peculiarity of the love of money is this: it is a desire that opposes its own satisfaction.

Reprinted by permission of the publishers and the Loeb Classical Library from *Plutarch: Moralia, Volume VII*, trans. Phillip H. De Lacy and Benedict Einarson (Cambridge, MA: Harvard University Press, 1959).

The Hebrew and Christian Scriptures

The biblical teaching agrees that the problem is insatiability, but also emphasizes the outcome as well as the drive and craving. What do we possess in our possessions? What do we gain by our gains? Vanity, emptiness, futility, says the Old Testament, a mere chasing the wind. Loss, says the New Testament, a stupid loss that shows us for the fools we are when we chase after money and possessions.

Ecclesiastes 2:1-11; 5:10

I thought in my heart, "Come now, I will test you with pleasure to find out what is good." But that also proved to be meaningless. "Laughter," I said, "is foolish. And what does pleasure accomplish?" I tried cheering myself with wine, and embracing folly—my mind still guiding me with wisdom. I wanted to see what was worthwhile for men to do under heaven during the few days of their lives.

I undertook great projects: I built houses for myself and planted vineyards. I made gardens and parks and planted all kinds of fruit trees in them. I made reservoirs to water groves of flourishing trees. I bought male and female slaves and had other slaves who were born in my house. I also owned more herds and flocks than anyone in Jerusalem before me. I amassed silver and gold for myself, and the treasure of kings and provinces. I acquired men and women singers, and a harem as well—the delights of the heart of man. I became greater by far than anyone in Jerusalem before me. In all this my wisdom stayed with me.

I denied myself nothing my eyes desired;
    I refused my heart no pleasure.
My heart took delight in all my work,
    and this was the reward for all my labor.
Yet when I surveyed all that my hands had done
    and what I had toiled to achieve,

everything was meaningless, a chasing after the wind;
    nothing was gained under the sun.
Whoever loves money never has money enough;
    whoever loves wealth is never satisfied with his income.
This too is meaningless.

RESTLESS HEARTS

"One cannot defend production as satisfying wants if that production creates the wants. . . . Production only fills a void that it has itself created."

—John Kenneth Galbraith, *The Affluent Society*

"If we eliminated all the *contrived* wants generated by either helpful or greedy producers, the squirrel cage would no doubt turn at a much slower pace, but it would not come to a halt. Consumerism is a creation of capitalism. Insatiability is not; capitalism only capitalizes on it.

"The rootedness of insatiability in human nature leads to a very simple but fundamental insight: the economic problem *cannot be solved by economic means alone,* not even in a hundred years. . . .

"The only proper 'object' of human insatiability is the mystery of the infinite God. . . . In God, in whom nothing worth preserving is lost, everything worth enjoying can be enjoyed."

—Miroslav Wolf, *Rethinking Materialism*

Matthew 16:26 ᔕᕓ

"What good will it be for a man if he gains the whole world, yet forfeits his soul? Or what can a man give in exchange for his soul?"

Luke 12:15-21 ᔕᕓ

Then [Jesus] said to them, "Watch out! Be on your guard against all kinds of greed; a man's life does not consist in the abundance of his possessions." And he told them this parable: "The ground of a certain rich man produced a good crop.

"He thought to himself, 'What shall I do? I have no place to store my crops.'

"Then he said, 'This is what I'll do. I will tear down my barns and build bigger ones, and there I will store all my grain and my goods. And I'll say to myself, "You have plenty of good things laid up for many years. Take life easy; eat, drink and be merry."'

"But God said to him, 'You fool! This very night your life will be demanded from you. Then who will get what you have prepared for yourself?'

"This is how it will be with anyone who stores up things for himself but is not rich toward God."

WHEN AVARICE WAS POLITICALLY INCORRECT

"In 1635 a Puritan merchant named Robert Keayne left London to take up residence in the new settlement at Boston. From humble circumstances, he had risen through hard work and careful planning to a position of some prominence. In the New World he prospered further. But four years later his ship of fortune ran aground. The elders of the First Church in Boston, of which he was a member, brought charges against him for dishonoring the name of God. Soon after, he was tried and found guilty by the General Court of the Commonwealth as well. Writing his memoirs some fourteen years later, he was still stung by the disgrace of the event. His sin was greed. He had sold his wares at a six percent profit, two percent above the maximum allowed."

—Robert Wuthnow, *God and Mammon in America*

Leo Tolstoy

Leo Tolstoy (1828–1910) was a Russian novelist and social reformer, famous for his novels War and Peace *and* Anna Karenina. *But after writing the latter he renounced his literary ambitions, believing them to be incompatible with his deepest convictions. His numerous works thereafter were on religious and moral subjects. The following reading is the concluding sections of his famous moral tale, "How Much Land Does a Man Need?"*

A Russian farmer named Pahóm buys and sells land to increase his holdings but is never satisfied. Learning of an incredibly good deal, he travels to the east, where the nomadic Bashkirs offer to sell him as much land as he can circumnavigate on foot in a day. The question is how much of his attempt to cover the ground represents an entrepreneurial spirit and how much is driven by an insatiable desire to possess.

MORE, MORE

"Just a little bit more."

—John D. Rockefeller Sr.,
when asked how much money it takes to make a man happy

"I kept saying, Sam, we're making a good living. Why go out, why expand so much more? The stores are getting farther and farther away. After the seventeenth store, though, I realized there wasn't going to be any stopping it."

—Sam Walton's wife, Helen

"1. Acquire, acquire, acquire.
 2. When the game is over, everything goes back in the box."

—Grandmother's Two Rules of "Monopoly"

"I want men that are vicious, grasping, and lusting for power."

—speaker at an American Management Association conference,
quoted in Max DePree, *Leadership Is an Art*

"It's a sickness I have in the face of which I am helpless."

—Ivan Boesky,
explaining his zeal to accumulate

"No matter how much money he had, *he was always poor in his own mind*."

—colleague of a Texas oil billionaire

"The artist Delacroix once asked James Rothschild, of the great banking family, to pose for a painting of a beggar, since he had 'exactly the right hungry expression.' Rothschild, who was a friend of the artist, agreed, and appeared the next day, suitably garbed in a disreputable costume. The masquerade was so convincing that a passerby gave him money."

—cited in Philip Slater, *Wealth Addiction*

". . . THEN I'LL BE SATISFIED."

". . . I reminded [Netscape founder Jim] Clark that he had said that once he became a real after-tax billionaire he'd retire. He said, without missing a beat, 'I just want to make more money than Larry Ellison. Then I'll stop.'

". . . I . . . asked the obvious question: 'What happens after you have more than Larry Ellison? Would you want to have more money than, say, Bill Gates?' 'Oh, no,' Clark said. . . . 'That'll never happen.' A few minutes later, . . . he came clean. 'You know,' he said, 'just for one moment, I would kind of like to have the most. Just for one tiny moment.'

"... Just a few months before, when he was worth a mere $600 million, Clark had said, 'I just want to have a billion dollars, after taxes. Then I'll be satisfied.' Back further, before he started Netscape, he'd told Mark Grossman, [at Silicon Graphics] something similar. Grossman recalled, 'Jim came into my office just before he left to start Netscape and said SGI is okay but I'd really like to have a $100 million.' Back even further, before he'd started Silicon Graphics, he'd told Tom Davis, 'that what he really wanted was to have ten million dollars.' The numbers! They kept moving! ... What Clark meant when he said, 'I'd really like to have,' was 'I will do what I need to do to get.' ...

"Why do people perpetually create for themselves the condition for their own dissatisfaction?"

—Michael Lewis, *The New New Thing*

How Much Land Does a Man Need? ❧

VIII

The Chief came up to Pahóm and, stretching out his arm towards the plain, "See," said he, "all this, as far as your eye can reach, is ours. You may have any part of it you like."

Pahóm's eyes glistened: it was all virgin soil, as flat as the palm of your hand, as black as the seed of a poppy, and in the hollows different kinds of grasses grew breast high.

The Chief took off his fox-fur cap, placed it on the ground and said:

"I'm not a machine, Deboroah. I can't just turn my greed on and off."

"This will be the mark. Start from here, and return here again. All the land you go round shall be yours."

Pahóm took out his money and put it on the cap. Then he took off his outer coat, remaining in his sleeveless under-coat. He unfastened his girdle and tied it tight below his stomach, put a little bag of bread into the breast of his coat, and tying a flask of water to his girdle, he drew up the tops of his boots, took the spade from his man, and stood ready to start. He considered for some moments which way he had better go—it was tempting everywhere.

"No matter," he concluded, "I will go towards the rising sun."

"This will be the mark. Start from here, and return here again. All the land you go round shall be yours."

"I must lose no time," he thought, "and it is easier walking while it is still cool."

The sun's rays had hardly flashed above the horizon, before Pahóm, carrying the spade over his shoulder, went down into the steppe.

Pahóm started walking neither slowly nor quickly. After having gone a thousand yards he stopped, dug a hole, and placed pieces of turf one on another to make it more visible. Then he went on, and now that he had walked off his stiffness he quickened his pace. After a while he dug another hole.

. . . It was growing warmer; he took off his under-coat, flung it across his shoulder, and went on again. It had grown quite warm now; he looked at the sun, it was time to think of breakfast.

"The first shift is done, but there are four in a day, and it is too soon yet to turn. But I will just take off my boots," said he to himself.

He sat down, took off his boots, stuck them into his girdle, and went on. It was easy walking now.

"I will go on for another three miles," thought he, "and then turn to the left. This spot is so fine that it would be a pity to lose it. The further one goes, the better the land seems."

"This spot is so fine that it would be a pity to lose it. The further one goes, the better the land seems."

He went straight on for a while, and when he looked round, the hillock was scarcely visible and the people on it looked like black ants, and he could just see something glistening there in the sun.

"Ah," thought Pahóm, "I have gone far enough in this direction, it is time to turn. Besides I am in a regular sweat, and very thirsty."

He stopped, dug a large hole, and heaped up pieces of turf. Next he untied his flask, had a drink, and then turned sharply to the left. He went on and on; the grass was high, and it was very hot.

Pahóm began to grow tired; he looked at the sun and saw that it was noon.

"Well," he thought, "I must have a rest."

He sat down and ate some bread and drank some water, but he did not lie down, thinking that if he did he might fall asleep. After sitting a little while, he went on again. At first he walked easily: the food had strengthened him, but it had become terribly hot and he felt sleepy, still he went on, thinking: "An hour to suffer, a life-time to live."

He went a long way in this direction also and was about to turn to the left again, when he perceived a damp hollow. "It would be a pity to leave that out," he thought. "Flax would do well there." So he went on past the hollow, and dug a hole on the other side of it before he turned the corner. Pahóm looked towards the hillock. The heat made the air hazy: it seemed to be quivering, and through the haze the people on the hillock could scarcely be seen.

"Ah!" thought Pahóm, "I have made the sides too long; I must make this one shorter." And he went along the third side, stepping faster. He looked at the sun: it was nearly half-way to the horizon, and he had not yet done two miles of the third side of the square. He was still ten miles from the goal.

"No," he thought, "though it will make my land lopsided, I must hurry back in a straight line now. I might go too far, and as it is I have a great deal of land."

So Pahóm hurriedly dug a hole and turned straight towards the hillock.

IX

Pahóm went straight towards the hillock, but he now walked with difficulty. He was done up with the heat, his bare feet were cut and bruised, and his legs began to fail. He longed to rest, but it was impossible if he meant to get back before sunset. The sun waits for no man, and it was sinking lower and lower.

"Oh dear," he thought, "if only I have not blundered trying for too much! What if I am too late?"

He looked towards the hillock and at the sun. He was still far from his goal, and the sun was already near the rim.

Pahóm walked on and on; it was very hard walking but he went quicker and quicker. He pressed on but was still far from the place. He began running, threw away his coat, his boots, his flask, and his cap, and kept only the spade which he used as a support.

"What shall I do?" he thought again. "I have grasped too much and ruined the whole affair. I can't get there before the sun sets."

And this fear made him still more breathless. Pahóm went on running, his soaking shirt and trousers stuck to him and his mouth was parched. His breast was working like a blacksmith's bellows, his heart was beating like a hammer, and his legs were giving way as if they did not belong to him. Pahóm was seized with terror lest he should die of the strain.

Though afraid of death, he could not stop. "After having run all that way, they will call me a fool if I stop now," thought he. And he ran on and on, and drew near and heard the Bashkírs yelling and shouting to him, and their cries inflamed his heart still more. He gathered his last strength and ran on.

The sun was close to the rim, and cloaked in mist looked large, and red as blood. Now, yes now, it was about to set! The sun was quite low, but he was

Though afraid of death, he could not stop. "After having run all that way, they will call me a fool if I stop now," thought he.

also quite near his aim. Pahóm could already see the people on the hillock waving their arms to hurry him up. He could see the fox-fur cap on the ground and the money on it, and the Chief sitting on the ground holding his sides. And Pahóm remembered his dream.

"There is plenty of land," thought he, "but will God let me live on it? I have lost my life, I have lost my life! I shall never reach that spot!"

Pahóm looked at the sun, which had reached the earth: one side of it had already disappeared. With all his remaining strength he rushed on, bending his body forward so that his legs could hardly follow fast enough to keep him from falling. Just as he reached the hillock it suddenly grew dark. He looked up—the sun had already set! He gave a cry. "All my labor has been in vain," thought he and was about to stop, but he heard the Bashkírs still shouting and remembered that though to him, from below, the sun seemed to have set, they on the hillock could still see it. He took a long breath and ran up the hillock. It was still light there. He reached the top and saw the cap. Before it sat the Chief laughing and holding his sides. Again Pahóm remembered his dream, and he uttered a cry: his legs gave way beneath him, he fell forward and reached the cap with his hands.

"Ah, that's a fine fellow!" exclaimed the Chief. "He has gained much land!"

Pahóm's servant came running up and tried to raise him, but he saw that blood was flowing from his mouth. Pahóm was dead!

The Bashkírs clicked their tongues to show their pity.

His servant picked up the spade and dug a grave long enough for Pahóm to lie in and buried him in it. Six feet from his head to his heels was all he needed.

His servant picked up the spade and dug a grave long enough for Pahóm to lie in and buried him in it. Six feet from his head to his heels was all he needed.

Excerpt from Leo Tolstoy, "How Much Land Does a Man Need?" trans. Louise and Aylmer Maude (1886).

FASTER, FASTER

"Everything that is not nailed down is mine, and anything I can pry loose is not nailed down."
                    —Collis P. Huntington, California railroad magnate

"It is the pursuit of wealth that enlivens life. The dead game, the fish caut [sic] become offensive in an hour."

                                        —Andrew Carnegie

"Couldn't the old man be satisfied with his $75,000 a year and rest? No! The frontage of the store must be widened to 400 feet. Why? That beats everything, he says. In the evening when his wife and daughter read together, he wants to go to bed. Sunday he looks at the clock every five minutes to see when the day will be over—What a futile life!"

—Max Weber, describing a German émigré to the United States

"Just as Napoleon drove his soldiers on with the slogan that every footsoldier carried a marshall's baton in his knapsack, so Carnegie had taught his men to believe that every worker carried a partnership in his lunch pail. . . . There were rewards all along the track and the promise of a splendid prize at the goal, it is true, but the goal never seemed to be reached. It was always 'more, more, faster, faster.' The race went on and on and the casualties were heavy. But still they ran, with Carnegie alternately cheering and cursing them on."

—Joseph Frazier Wall, *Andrew Carnegie*

"If only we would all agree to stop. But we can't, because for each individual, the best situation is the one in which everyone stops but him. And the situation to be feared and avoided is the one in which he, and only he, stops. It's like being in a crowded football stadium, watching the crucial play. A spectator several rows in front stands up to get a better view. A chain reaction follows. Soon everyone is standing, just to be able to see as well as before. Everyone is standing rather than sitting, but no one's position has improved. And if someone, unilaterally and resolutely, refuses to stand, he might just as well not be at the game at all."

—Barry Schwartz, *The Costs of Living*

QUESTIONS FOR THOUGHT AND DISCUSSION

1. In Plutarch's essay, "On Wealth," he says "Having wealth is not the same as being superior to it, nor is possessing luxuries the same as feeling no need of them." How do you understand this? What two types of lovers of money does he address?

2. How can wealth change our view of our "needs" and "desires"? What can happen when we lose a healthy perspective?

3. In comparing craving money to hungering for food and drink, what physical illness and remedy does Plutarch describe? Why does avarice act "like a tapeworm"?

4. What ironies does Plutarch note in describing the love of money? Do you find this true in your life or the lives of others?

5. In the Ecclesiastes passage, where is Solomon, the writer, focusing in all his busyness? What connection does his resulting feeling of meaninglessness have with Jesus' assessment of the rich man at the end of the Luke passage? How was the rich man's pursuit of wealth meaningless?

6. In Tolstoy's "How Much Land Does a Man Need?" each time Pahóm thinks to turn to mark his boundaries, he pushes himself further on for a while. What is the incentive? How does he rationalize his suffering?

7. On his way back to the group, his body is crying out urgently. Why doesn't he listen? Is this a universal problem? Why do we lose objectivity with ourselves?

8. What are the features of "insatiability" common to all these perspectives?

9. Why does it become so hard to stop, however strong our critique of the problems of others? How do you "audit" yourself in practice?

❊ COMMODIFICATION ❊

The second of the two generally acknowledged problems of money is "commodification." This rather forbidding word describes the process whereby money assumes such a dominant place in human thinking that everything (and everyone) is seen as a commodity to be bought and sold.

The term is a modern one, but as the Greek legend of Midas shows, the problem is not new. Among the celebrated incidences of commodification in the past are the moneychangers in the Jerusalem temple and the papal selling of indulgences by Johann Tetzel in the medieval era. The first occasioned the vehement overturning of their wares by Jesus and the second triggered Martin Luther's outraged protest that led to his Ninety-Five Theses and the Reformation. Another example is Simon Magus, who attempted to buy spiritual powers from the apostles John and Peter, and from whose name we get the word "simony." But the supreme biblical examples are the selling of Joseph in the Old Testament and the selling of Jesus in the New—hence the scandal of the sale that shamed all selling—"They sold the Righteous One."

The negative connotations of commodification are not a criticism of the marketplace itself—buying, selling, merchandising, and marketing are all legitimate in their place. But not everything can or should be given a market price. The sign of a good society is the level and number of things that are acknowledged to be beyond market values—and thus appreciated for their own sake and not for extrinsic, especially financial, rewards. The line drawn between "For Sale" and "Not for Sale" is a key indication of a nation's values.

The sign of a good society is the level and number of things that are acknowledged to be beyond market values—and thus appreciated for their own sake and not for extrinsic, especially financial, rewards.

WE BECOME WHAT WE WORSHIP

"But their idols are silver and gold, made by the hands of men. . . . Those who make them will be like them, and so will all who trust in them."

—Psalm 115:4,8

THE LEGEND OF KING MIDAS

"And you, my worthy Midas, you deserve a reward: ask what you will, you shall have it."

Midas was a rich man, but like many rich men, he wanted to be richer; so he said at once, "I ask that everything I touch may turn into gold!"

Dionysus could not help thinking this was a greedy wish; but he had promised, and he said, "Be it so: everything you touch shall turn into gold."

Midas went off delighted. He plucked a twig from a tree—twig, leaves, and all turned into gold. He touched a stone—the stone turned into gold. He patted his favorite dog—the dog at once froze into gold, and stood there, a golden image! Midas did not know whether to be glad or sorry at that, but he kept his fingers from his attendants, for fear they might turn into gold too.

When he came home, he had recovered his spirits a little, and he said, "Let us have a grand feast tonight, to celebrate this occasion." He was careful to eat nothing meanwhile, so that he might have more room for the feast when it came.

The feast was ready, the courtiers were in their places, and Midas began by taking up a goblet of wine, to drink their health. "Your good health, gentlemen!" he cried, and raised it to his lips. The goblet was gold already; but as soon as the wine touched his lips, it turned into liquid gold. He did not like this at all, and spat out the drop he had taken. "What's this!" he cried, but nobody else knew what it was; they only looked at him in surprise. He sat down, and took up a piece of bread—it turned into gold. He passed a bit of game to his lips—it turned into gold. The guests were eating and drinking away comfortably, and did not notice the King, until he suddenly said, "Look here, all my food is turning into gold, and I shall starve!"

How they all stared at him, and tried not to laugh. They gave him tidbits with their own hands, but no sooner did the food touch his lips, than it was gold. The King left the table, and went to his room, and spent a very unhappy night.

Next day things were no better, and he went off post-haste to Dionysus. When he found the god, Midas looked so pale and unhappy, that Dionysus asked, "Why, what is the matter?"

Midas said, "Your gift!"

Dionysus said, "What is the matter with my gift? Didn't it come off?"

"Only too well!" said Midas. "All my food turns to gold, and I shall just starve to death!"

"Well," said Dionysus, "I gave you what you asked, so don't blame me."

—*Gods, Heroes, and Men of Ancient Greece* by W.H.D. Rouse
(New York: New American Library, 1985), pp. 82–83.

Suzanne W. Stout

Suzanne Stout is a writer who lives with her family in Greenwich Village, New York. Her article below was published in The New York Times. *Stout's seven-year-old boy has an innocence that forces us to see how much commodification has become a fact of life to which we adults have become inured.*

A Mom's Plea to a Ballplayer

Baseball is our little boy's passion and Gregg Jefferies, the rookie second-baseman for the Mets, is his first, and beloved, hero. A photograph plaque of Gregg Jefferies hangs in a position of honor, alone on the wall over his bed. On his seventh birthday, my son solemnly placed a Gregg Jefferies baseball card in the center of his birthday cake.

So, when we heard that Mr. Jefferies would be signing autographs in a toy shop in New Jersey, it was not a question of would we go, but of how?

However, as we investigated, we realized that Mr. Jefferies would not simply be visiting with kids and signing autographs. No, he would be *selling* his autograph, which required buying a $10 ticket, advance purchase advised.

I called the toy shop to ask if we really needed to buy a ticket in advance. The owner said that 800 had already been sold and they were expecting to sell 2,000. I was stunned. . . . I bought three.

Expectation kept our son in a state of frenzy. The night before the event, he couldn't sleep. He greeted us at dawn in his Mets uniform, ready to go.

When we arrived at the toy shop . . . hundreds of families were there, with many mini-Mets in uniforms just like our son. The toy shop had taken over the adjacent vacant store for the day, and sold Gregg Jefferies photographs, baseball cards, and other items for him to sign. The line moved fast, and before we knew it, we were standing in front of Gregg Jefferies.

He sat with his cute girlfriend at a table, signing his name as fast as he could. Gregg did not look up when he signed our son's picture. He never saw our son's face go white, his eyes pleading to make contact. This was an assembly-line operation. Ninety seconds after we had entered the shop, we stood outside, autographs in hand.

As we drove back, our son sat staring sadly at the autograph. Exasperated by his misery, I snapped: "What's wrong? You got to see Gregg Jefferies and you got his autograph. . . . "

"But Mom, he didn't even look at me."

"Well," I said, "the format wasn't right for a visit or eye contact."

"Yeah, but Mom, he's my guy. My all time top guy. You don't understand, Mom. He's my hero."

My husband and I slumped in our seats. Now we all felt terrible. But what had we expected? I suppose we had hoped to meet a hero: a symbol of possibility for our son, a whole-hearted man who excels at playing his part on a team in a game with rules. And more: A man with enough respect for his craft, the game and his role not to merchandise his signature.

After a bit, our son's mood lifted. "Mom, if there were 2,000 people out there, that means Gregg Jefferies made $20,000. And he made it in three hours. Does the toy shop get some? How's Gregg spending that money, Mom? Is he helping the homeless?" I told him I didn't know. My son begged me to find out.

"Because," he continued, "if I know how much money he needs to make for three hours work, maybe I can save up enough to pay him to come to our house for dinner."

"Hold it," I wailed. "We are not paying anybody anything to come to our house for dinner."

"But Mom, that's what Gregg Jefferies wants: *money.*"

We've had this same conversation many times since that day. My husband

and I are saddened and bewildered. We just read that José Canseco and Roger Clemens feel no guilt about selling their autographs. They believe the kids are purchasing their autographs for resale at a profit. But the kids we saw in New Jersey that day were just like our son: little Mets, dressed in the cloth of their hero, straining for a glimpse of Gregg Jefferies, the man they all hoped to become.

I did call the toy shop on behalf of my son. The owner's wife would not disclose the finances, but she offered some advice: "In today's world, it's never good to get too close to your heroes. Better to view them from afar." But I don't want today's world to be like that. And I wish Gregg Jefferies would take his signature off the market.

Suzanne W. Stout, "A Mom's Plea to a Ballplayer," *The New York Times,* 25 June 1989. Reprinted by permission of the author.

WHAT DOES AN ECONOMIST ECONOMIZE ON?

"Money is like a government agency—continually trying to enlarge its jurisdiction. Just as TV, which exists for the purpose of entertaining us, tends to convert everything to entertainment, even the news, so money, which exists to create a common standard of value, tends to reduce everything to that standard, even life and death."

—Philip Slater, *Wealth Addiction*

"For $10 million, 25 percent of those surveyed would abandon their friends, leave their church, become a prostitute for a week, or undergo a sex change operation."

—survey of U.S. residents in Bernice Kanner's *Are You Normal?,* 1996

"What does an economist economize on? Economist D. H. Robertson asked this question about fifty years ago. His answer: 'The economist economizes on love.' What he meant by this was that a competitive-market system gets people to serve one another's interests out of a desire for personal gain, for profit. Love is not required. So we can get by as a society with less love under a market system than under any other. The market economizes on love."

—Barry Schwartz, *The Costs of Living*

"Several of my economist colleagues tell me that the single concept that is most difficult to convey to beginning economics students is the concept of *opportunity cost.* The opportunity cost of some activity is the gain that we would realize by doing something else. If working on a legal brief at night instead of being with friends would have gotten us a $500 bonus, then that $500 bonus foregone is the opportunity cost of our decision to be with friends. What the concept of opportunity cost does is put a literal price on everything we do."

—Barry Schwartz, *The Costs of Living*

THE OLDEST PROFESSION

"The word prostitution should either not be used at all, or else applied impartially to all persons who do things for money that they would not do if they had other assured means of livelihood."

—George Bernard Shaw

"Autograph hounds and worshipful kids take note. In an unprecedented combination of hubris and marketing savvy, Green Bay Packers quarterback Brett Favre has registered his name, signature and, yes, even his face with the Wisconsin Secretary of State's office."

—*Sky*, February 1998

"I don't wake up for less than $10,000 a day."

—Linda Evangelista

"The challenge of the American newspaper is not to stay in business, it is to stay in journalism."

—Harold Evans, former editor, London's *Sunday Times*

QUESTIONS FOR THOUGHT AND DISCUSSION

1. What is the meaning of the Midas legend (see box p. 68)? What is the significance of Midas not being able to eat? Of his frustration with the success of the gift?

2. In the article, "A Mom's Plea to a Ballplayer," how does each of the parties involved—the boy, his parents, and Jefferies—see the autographing event? What are their expectations?

3. Before the event, the boy considers Jefferies his hero. Does his status change after the boy's disappointment? How is the boy's understanding of "hero" redefined by Jefferies? What kind of "hero" was his mother hoping to see? What is he looking for when the boy asks, "Is he helping the homeless?"

4. What is wrong with the little boy's quick lesson in capitalism that "maybe I can save up enough to pay him to come to our house for dinner?"

5. What do you think of the advice from the toy shop owner's wife: "it's never good to get too close to your heroes"?

6. In the box "What Does an Economist Economize On?" Barry Schwartz describes economics students being taught "opportunity cost." Where can this reasoning lead? What happens when we apply a monetary value to everything we do and the people we do it with?

7. Examples of commodification abound, such as the time-is-money commercialization of law and the lawyers' "billable hours" or the money-is-respect scale by which our society shows its appreciation of people by the amount it pays them. Which examples of commodification cause you concern?

❊ EXCESS ❊

If there is a general acknowledgment of the two main problems with money—insatiability and commodification—there are important differences in explanations of the cause. One major view, strongly represented by the Greeks and Romans, sees the problem simply as one of excess. "Moderation in all things" is the watchword, but good things taken to excess become bad things. Therefore the challenge is to have enough, but not too much, money.

This first view has wide support and appeal. For instance, it is one strand of the biblical perspective, even though the biblical outlook goes far beyond the "excess" view. Thus the writer of Proverbs prays: "Give me neither poverty nor riches, but give me only my daily bread. Otherwise I may have too much and disown you and say, 'Who is the Lord?' Or I may become poor and steal and so dishonor the name of my God." And as we saw earlier, Andrew Carnegie defined philanthropists as administrators of "surplus wealth."

This view is helpful as far as it goes but has an obvious snag. Who defines moderation? Who is to say when "enough is enough"? One person's moderation is another person's excess, for nothing is more human than for each of us to see ourselves as moderates in the middle and everyone who disagrees with us as the extremes. In short, this view is highly vulnerable to rationalization and self-deception. Tolstoy's question "How much land does a man need?" can be answered in two ways: "Just a little bit more" or "Whatever it takes to be buried in."

KEEP WITHIN BOUNDS

"Gaius Caesar, whom, as it seems to me, Nature produced merely to show how far supreme vice, when combined with supreme power could go, dined one day at a cost of ten million sesterces; and though everybody used their ingenuity to help him, yet he could hardly discover how to spend the tribute-money from three provinces on one dinner! . . . He, therefore, who keeps himself within the bounds of nature will not feel poverty; but he who exceeds the bounds of nature will be pursued by poverty even though he had unbounded wealth."

—Seneca, "Letter from exile to his mother, Helvia"

"It was for this reason that the godlike Lycurgus gave directions in certain *rhetrae* [unwritten laws] that the doors and roofs of houses should be fashioned by saw and ax alone and no other tool should be used— not of course because he had a quarrel with gimlets and adzes and other instruments for delicate work. It was because he knew that through such rough-hewn work you will not be introducing a gilded couch, nor will you be so rash as to bring silver tables and purple rugs and precious stones into a simple house. The corollary of such a house and couch and table and cup is a dinner which is unpretentious and a lunch which is truly democratic; but all manner of luxury and extravagance follow the lead of an evil way of life 'As a new-weaned foal beside her mother runs.'"

—Plutarch, "On the Eating of Flesh"

IF WEALTH RISES, GOODNESS FALLS?

"The rich are useless and always grasping for more. The poor without livelihood are dangerous and always full of envy, ready to sting the rich and are tricked by the tongues of evil leaders. But the middle class in between, the middle ones save the state, they who keep the order which the state decrees."

—Euripides, *Suppliants*

"Much good is there to the middle ones; I would wish to be midmost in a city."

—Phocylide

"The accumulation of wealth in private hands is what destroys timocracy [a state governed on principles of honor and military glory]. The men find ways to become extravagant, and for this reason pervert the law and disobey it, and the women follow their example."

"That's all likely enough."

"And mutual observation and jealousy stamps the same character on the ruling class as a whole."

"Likely again."

"The further they go in the process of accumulating wealth, the more they value it and the less they value goodness. For aren't wealth and goodness related like two objects in a balance, so that when one rises the other must fall?"

"Emphatically yes."

"So the higher the prestige of wealth and the wealthy, the lower that of goodness and good men will be."

"Obviously."

—Plato, *The Republic*

Aristotle

Aristotle (384–322 B.C.) was a student of Plato, tutor of Alexander the Great, founder of the Lyceum, and one of the world's greatest and most influential thinkers. He explored, discovered, argued, and taught in fields as diverse as logic, metaphysics, theology, history, politics, aesthetics, ethics, psychology, anatomy, biology, zoology, botany, astronomy, and the ancient equivalents of physics and chemistry. This passage from his The Politics is an admirable statement of the virtue of moderation.

The Politics ☙

If we were right when in our *Ethics* we stated that virtue is a mean, and that the happy life is a life without hindrance in its accordance with virtue, then the best life must be the middle life, consisting in a mean which is open to men of every kind to attain. And the same principles must be applicable to the virtue or badness of constitutions and states. For the constitution of a state is in a sense the way it lives.

In all states there are three state-sections: the very well-off, the very badly off, and thirdly those in between. Since therefore it is agreed that moderation and a middle position are best, it is clear that, in the matter of the goods of fortune also, to own a middling amount is best of all. This condition is most easily obedient to reason, and following reason is just what is difficult both for the exceedingly rich, handsome, strong and well-born, and for their opposites, the extremely poor, the weak, and those grossly deprived of honor. The former incline more to arrogance and crime on a large scale, the latter are more than averagely prone to wicked ways and petty crime. The unjust deeds of the one class are due to an arrogant spirit; the unjust deeds of the other to wickedness. Add the fact that it is among the members of the middle section that you find least reluctance to hold office as well as least eagerness to do so; and both these attitudes, eagerness and reluctance, are detrimental to states. . . .

It is the middle citizens in a state who are the most secure: they neither covet, like the poor, the possessions of others, nor do others covet theirs as the poor covet those of the rich. So they live without risk, not scheming and not being schemed against. Phocylides' prayer was therefore justified when he wrote, "Those in the middle have many advantages; that is where I wish to be in the state."

It is clear then both that the best partnership in a state is the one which operates through the middle people, and also that those states in which the middle element is large, and stronger if possible than the other two together, or at any rate stronger than either of them alone, have every chance of having a well-run constitution.

For the addition of its weight to either side will turn the balance and prevent excess at the opposing extremes. For this reason it is a most happy state of affairs when those who take part in the constitution have a middling, adequate amount of property; since where one set of people possess a great deal and the other nothing, the result is either extreme democracy or unmixed oligarchy, for a tyranny due to the excesses of either. For tyranny often emerges from an over-enthusiastic democracy or from an oligarchy, but much more rarely from intermediate constitutions or from those close to them. . . .

As for major crimes, men commit them when their aims are extravagant, not just to provide themselves with necessities. Who ever heard of a man making himself a dictator in order to keep warm?

It is the middle citizens in a state who are the most secure: they neither covet, like the poor, the possessions of others, nor do others covet theirs as the poor covet those of the rich. So they live without risk, not scheming and not being schemed against.

Aristotle, *The Politics*, Translation © the Estate of T. A. Sinclair, 1962. Revised translation © Trevor J. Saunders, 1981 (Penguin, 1962, 1981).

SPREAD IT AROUND

"Poverty, when measured by the natural purpose of life, is great wealth, but unlimited wealth is great poverty."

—Epicurus, *Fragments*, No. XXV

"Riches is a good handmaid but the worst mistress.
Money is like muck, not good except to spread around."

—Sir Francis Bacon

"Wealth in the gross is death, but life diffus'd;
As Poison heals, in just proportion us'd:
In heaps, like Ambergrise, a stink it lies,
But well-dispers'd, is Incense to the Skies."

—Alexander Pope

QUESTIONS FOR THOUGHT AND DISCUSSION

1. What does Aristotle mean by "virtue is a mean"?
2. According to Aristotle, what are the natural inclinations of the rich and the poor—the extremes in society? Why?
3. What do you think of Aristotle's argument that a "middling" amount of wealth produces "a most happy state of affairs"?
4. He states that those in the middle "are the most secure: they neither covet, . . . nor do others covet theirs." Do you agree? What happens when an entire society is relatively wealthy, compared to other nations, such as in the United States? Is this still true? Or has the majority of the society become an extreme, according to Aristotle's way of thinking?
5. What do you see as the pros of Aristotle's overall argument? What are the cons?
6. How do you yourself determine what is "surplus" and when "enough is enough"? Is it by principle or with the help of friends and colleagues?

✣ THE IDOLATRY OF MAMMON ✣

If the first position views the cause of the problems of money as excess, the second is deeper and more dynamic. According to this view, money can assume an inordinate place in our lives until it becomes an idol—a personal, spiritual, godlike force that rules us. In a word, it becomes what Jesus called Mammon.

Jesus' use of "Mammon" is unique—he gave it a strength and precision that the word (Aramaic for wealth) never had before. He did not usually personify things, let alone deify them. And neither the Jews nor the nearby pagans knew a god by this name. But what Jesus says in speaking of Mammon is that money is a power—and not in a vague sense, as in the "force" of words. Rather, money is a power in the sense that it is an active agent with decisive spiritual power and is never neutral. It is a power before we use it, not simply as we use it or whether we use it well or badly. As such, Mammon is a genuine rival to God. The recurring biblical demand confronts us: "You shall not worship the work of your hands."

At least three things follow from this view. First, this position confronts people with a decisive choice. Jesus challenged his hearers to choose one master or another—God or Mammon. Either we serve God and use money or we serve money and use God. Ultimately we follow what we have loved most intensely to its natural destination—eternity or death—"for where your treasure is, there will your heart be too."

> *Rather, money is a power in the sense that it is an active agent with decisive spiritual power and is never neutral.*

WHO? WHOM?

"In a shipwreck one of the passengers fastened a belt about him with two hundred pounds of gold in it, with which he was afterward found at the bottom. Now, as he was sinking—had he the gold? Or had the gold him?"

—John Ruskin

Second, money can never be treated as a purely economic issue. It is always a spiritual and moral issue first. Precisely to pretend that money is neutral and simply a medium of exchange is to leave ourselves vulnerable to its power as something more—an idol to which we can become enslaved.

Third, there are two roads toward slavery to money. The poor person's road is via the confusion of need with entitlement, which leads to dependency; the rich person's road is via the confusion of need with desire, which leads to the driven-ness of insatiability.

Curiously, both these explanations of the problem of money have direct impli-cations for giving, as we shall see in part 2. For those of us who see the problem of money as excess, we are to give to get rid of surplus wealth. For those of us who see the problem of money as idolatry, we are partly to give because in giving freely we decisively repudiate the power of money. But this is a secondary, not a primary, motive. As the New Testament puts it, "The Lord loves a cheerful giver." In other words, God loves a person so freed from the grip of Mammon as to thumb his or her nose at it and thus to give with a carefree abandon that is oblivious of its hold.

YOU GOTTA SERVE SOMEBODY (BOB DYLAN)

"As for property and material wealth, these you should ever hold in fear."

—Leonardo da Vinci

"Man must have an idol—the amassing of wealth is one of the worst species of idolatry—no idol more debasing than the worship of money."

—Andrew Carnegie, personal memorandum, 1868

"I have tried hard to like Carnegie, but it is pretty difficult. There is no type of man for whom I feel a more contemptuous abhorrence than for one who makes a god of mere money-making."

—President Theodore Roosevelt, 1905

"**Mammon,** *n.* The god of the world's leading religion. His chief temple is in the holy city of New York."
"**Gold,** *n.* A yellow metal greatly prized for its convenience in the various kinds of robbery known as trade. The word was formerly spelled 'God'—the *l* was inserted to distinguish it from the name of another and inferior deity."

—Ambrose Bierce, *The Devil's Dictionary*

"Alfred Krupp, of the German munitions empire, was so obsessed with work that he built his home in the middle of his steel works—the better to keep an eye on the factory at all times. He refused to go to concerts or other entertainments on the grounds that no music could be as sweet to his ears as the sounds of steel being produced."

—Philip Slater, *Wealth Addiction*

He "loved the manipulation of millions with an intensity no woman could inspire."

—friend of Andrew Mellon

Mark 10:17-25

As Jesus started on his way, a man ran up to him and fell on his knees before him. "Good teacher," he asked, "what must I do to inherit eternal life?"

"Why do you call me good?" Jesus answered. "No one is good—except God alone. You know the commandments: 'Do not murder, do not commit adultery, do not steal, do not give false testimony, do not defraud, honor your father and mother.'"

"Teacher," he declared, "all these I have kept since I was a boy."

Jesus looked at him and loved him. "One thing you lack," he said. "Go, sell everything you have and give to the poor, and you will have treasure in heaven. Then come, follow me."

At this the man's face fell. He went away sad, because he had great wealth.

Jesus looked around and said to his disciples, "How hard it is for the rich to enter the kingdom of God!"

The disciples were amazed at his words. But Jesus said again, "Children, how hard it is to enter the kingdom of God! It is easier for a camel to go through the eye of a needle than for a rich man to enter the kingdom of God."

Luke 16:13

"No servant can serve two masters. Either he will hate the one and love the other, or he will be devoted to the one and despise the other. You cannot serve both God and Money."

1 Timothy 6:10

For the love of money is a root of all kinds of evil.

NEEDLING THE RICH

"Now, perhaps some one of you will remark with good reason: 'Every day you preach about covetousness.' Would that it were possible to speak of it every night also! Would that I might follow you in the marketplace and at table. Would that wives and friends and children and servants and husbandmen and neighbors, and the very pavement and walls might be able to shout forth this word that we might then cease for at least a little while. This contagion has seized upon the whole world, and the great tyranny of mammon possesses the souls of all men. We have been redeemed by Christ and become the slaves of gold. We proclaim the rule of one Master and obey another. Moreover, we listen with eagerness to whatever the latter ordains and on his account forget everything: race, friendship, nature, laws. No one looks to heaven; no one thinks of the life to come."

—St. John Chrysostom, *Homilies on the Gospel of John, LXXVI*

"Only the Christian church can offer any rational objection to a complete confidence in the rich. For she has maintained from the beginning that the danger was not in man's environment, but in man. . . . I know that the most modern manufacture has been really occupied in trying to produce an abnormally large needle. I know that the most recent biologists have been chiefly anxious to discover a very small camel. But if we diminish the camel to his smallest, or open the eye of the needle to its largest—if, in short, we assume the words of Christ to have meant the very least that they could mean, His words must at the very least mean this—that rich men are not very likely to be morally trustworthy. Christianity even when watered down is enough to boil all modern society to rags. The mere minimum of the church would be a deadly ultimatum to the world. For the whole modern world is absolutely based on the assumption, not that the rich are necessary (which is tenable), but that the rich are trustworthy, which (for a Christian) is not tenable."

—G. K. Chesterton, *Orthodoxy*

"If you would know what the Lord God thinks of money, you have only to look at those to whom he gives it."

—Maurice Baring

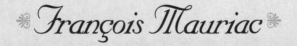

François Mauriac

François Mauriac (1885–1970) was a French novelist, essayist, and dramatist. He served in the medical corps during World War I and was active in the French Resistance during World War II. Awarded the Nobel Prize for Literature in 1952,

Mauriac was a devout Catholic who presents the attempts and failures of people who seek full satisfaction in money, property, and love.

In Mauriac's short but profound novel Viper's Tangle *(1932), Louis, a wealthy landowner in his late sixties, is dying. He has spent his entire life nursing an overwhelming hatred for his family, intensified by the death of his favorite daughter. As his children greedily wait for him to die, Louis tries to find a way to leave them penniless. In a final desperate move, he seeks out his illegitimate son, Robert, in hopes that he will be worthy of the inheritance. Robert, however, betrays Louis's scheme to his other children. It is only at this point that Louis realizes that he is hopelessly trapped by his lifetime of hatred, vengeance, resentment—and greed.*

Viper's Tangle

For years I had dreamt of this unknown son of mine. All through my poor life, I had never lost the feeling that he existed. Somewhere there was a child born of me, whom I could find again and who, perhaps, would comfort me.

The fact that he was of humble condition made him all the closer to me. It was pleasant to me to think that he would be in no way like my legitimate son. I endowed him at one and the same time with that simplicity and that power of attraction which are not rare among the common people.

Finally I had played my last card. I knew that, after him, I had nothing left to expect from anybody, and that there would be nothing for me to do but curl up and turn my face to the wall. For forty years I had believed that I accepted hatred: that which I inspired, that which I felt. But, like other people, I cherished a hope, and I had deceived my hunger, as best I could, until I was reduced to my last resource. Now it was finished.

There did not remain to me even the frightful pleasure of laying plans to disinherit those who had wronged me. Robert had put them on the track. They would certainly end by discovering my safes, even those which were not in my own name.

Think of something else? Oh, if only I could go on living, and have the time to spend it all—and die, and leave them with not enough to find to pay for a pauper's burial! But after a whole life of saving, when I had made myself a slave to my passion for economy for years, how was I to learn, at my age, the ways of the prodigal?

Besides, the children were watching me, I said to myself. I should never be able to do anything in that direction without its becoming a formidable weapon in their hands. . . . I should have to ruin myself furtively, little by little. . . .

Alas! I should never be able to ruin myself. I should never succeed in losing my money. If only it were possible to take it with me into the grave, to go back to earth holding that gold, those notes, those securities in my arms! If only I could give the lie to those who preach that this world's riches do not follow us into death!

If only it were possible to take it with me into the grave, to go back to earth holding that gold, those notes, those securities in my arms! If only I could give the lie to those who preach that this world's riches do not follow us into death!

There were "good works"—"good works" are pitfalls which swallow up everything. Could I not send anonymous gifts to the Board of Charity, to the Little Sisters of the Poor? Could I not, in short, think of others—others besides my enemies?

But the horror of old age is that it is the sum-total of a life—a sum-total of which one cannot change a figure. I have spent sixty years creating this old man dying of hatred. I am what I am. I should have to become somebody else. Oh God, oh God—if only You existed! . . .

From François Mauriac, *Viper's Tangle*, trans. Warren B. Wells (Carroll & Graf, 1987). Originally published in French as *Le Noued de Vipères* © 1932 by Les Editions Bernard Grasset. Reprinted by permission of Georges Borchardt Inc.

HE WHO LAUGHS LAST

"Probably nobody will miss me. Not even a dog like Bella will shed a tear for me. Yet she would probably be the most honest of all, since she would not go poking around for gold left behind. Besides, in that respect, my dear people will be awfully disappointed. I am taking the great delight in advance in all the widened eyes and curses the absence of money will cause."

—Alfred Nobel

LACKING IN POETRY

"The manner of this lust for power has changed through the centuries, but its source is still the same volcano. . . . What we once did 'for the sake of God' we now do for the sake of money. . . . This is what at present gives the highest feeling of power."

—Friedrich Nietzsche, *The Dawn*

"Any life directed toward money is death."

—Albert Camus, *Journal*

"It's true that there's no money in poetry, but there's no poetry in money, either."

—Robert Graves,
to a friend asking why he had not chosen a more lucrative profession

"Money doesn't talk, it swears."

—Bob Dylan

QUESTIONS FOR THOUGHT AND DISCUSSION

1. Look at the story of Jesus and the rich man (Mark 10:17-25). Note that in listing the commandments, Jesus did not mention all ten of them. Which did he significantly omit (Exodus 20:1-17)? What point was he making to the man? How does his point connect with his words, "One thing you lack, . . . Go, sell everything"?

2. What did Jesus mean when he said, "It is easier for a camel to go through the eye of a needle than for a rich man to enter the kingdom of God"? Do you think he intended for everyone to give away his or her wealth?

3. In *Viper's Tangle,* what had been Louis's last hope? How had his imagination distorted his judgment? Why do you think this was so?

4. What are the strategies Louis considered for dispersing his wealth? Why did he realize that none of them would work? What does his realization say about him?

5. What did Louis mean by "the horror of old age is that it is the sum-total of a life—a sum-total of which one cannot change a figure"? What is the significance of his last words, "Oh God, oh God—if only You existed"?

6. What do you think are the effects on you of your lifetime habits in dealing with money—perhaps in particular, of your own lifetime race for money, position, and power?

TWO
GIVING—EMPOWERING OR ENSLAVING?

HENRY DAVID THOREAU ONCE OBSERVED THAT "PHILANTHROPY IS ALMOST THE ONLY *virtue which is sufficiently appreciated by mankind." But such a rosy view of giving is not borne out by the facts. In contrast, the Greek historian Polybius was too cynical when he argued that "Nobody ever gives anything of his own willingly to anybody." But it is harder to argue with Seneca, who wrote, "There is no beneficent act so perfect as to defy the carping of the cynic." And a traditional Chinese saying captures the bogey that bedevils giving on the inside—the potentially torturous relationship that giving creates between the one who gives and the one who receives. As the Chinese put it tartly, "Why do you hate me? I have never given you anything."*

A CYNIC'S VIEW

"**Beg,** *v.* To ask for something with an earnestness proportioned to the belief that it will not be given.

"**Beggar,** *n.* A pest unkindly inflicted upon the suffering rich.

"**Benefactor,** *n.* One who makes heavy purchases of ingratitude.

"**Bequeath,** *v. t.* To generously give to another that which can no longer be denied to *somebody.*

"**Distance,** *n.* The only thing that the rich are willing for the poor to call theirs, and to keep.

"**Philanthropist,** *n.* A rich (and usually bald) old gentleman who has trained himself to grin while his conscience is picking his pocket."

—Ambrose Bierce, *The Devil's Dictionary*

Democratic societies can no more afford a naïve view of giving than they can a naïve view of money. And nothing is more false than the sentimental notion that giving is simple to do and easy to understand—a free, voluntary surrender of resources with an overriding motive of benevolence.

Of course, we all give at times in ways that go against our better judgments. Probably there is no more honest-humorous account of this than Benjamin Franklin's famous story of succumbing to George Whitefield's appeal.

SOFTENING AGAINST HIS BETTER JUDGMENT

"I did not disapprove of the design [of Whitefield's proposed orphanage in Georgia], but, as Georgia was then destitute of materials and workmen, and it was proposed to send them from Philadelphia at a great expense, I thought it would have been better to have built the house here, and brought the children to it. This I advis'd; but he was resolute in his first project, rejected my counsel, and I therefore refus'd to contribute.

"I happened soon after to attend one of his sermons, in the course of which I perceived he intended to finish with a collection, and I silently resolved he should get nothing from me. I had in my pocket a handful of copper money, three or four silver dollars, and five pistoles in gold. As he proceeded I began to soften, and concluded to give the coppers. Another stroke of his oratory made me asham'd of that, and determin'd me to give the silver; and he finish'd so admirably, that I empty'd my pocket wholly into the collector's dish, gold and all.

"At this sermon there was also one of our club, who, being of my sentiments respecting the building in Georgia, and suspecting a collection might be intended, had, by precaution, emptied his pockets before he came from home. Towards the conclusion of this discourse, however, he felt a strong desire to give, and apply'd to a neighbour, who stood near him, to borrow some money for the purpose. The application was unfortunately [made] to perhaps the only man in the company who had the firmness not to be affected by the preacher. His answer was, '*At any other time, Friend Hopkinson, I would lend to thee freely; but not now, for thee seems to be out of thy right senses.*'"

—Benjamin Franklin, *Autobiography*

We therefore turn to ask questions about the meaning of giving and caring, as we did the meaning of money. In particular, why give? And why care for the poor and needy? What emerges in the exploration is that different responses to these questions lead to very different conceptions of philanthropy and of society. We see that ideas have consequences. How we think is the measure of how, why, and with what results we give; some motives for giving lead in one direction and others in another. And some kinds of giving truly empower while others equally enslave.

POINT TO PONDER:

Why Give?

In 1905, Dr. John R. Mott, leader of the Student Volunteer Movement, gave a clarion call: "We in America have a choice," he said. "We can give from our abundance and make an investment by sending 1,000 missionaries to Japan, or within fifty years we will be forced to send 200,000 of our boys with guns and bayonets."

As historians later pointed out, America in fact sent fewer than a dozen missionaries; the war was only thirty-six, not fifty years coming; the United States eventually sent a million young men, not 200,000; and they took not only guns and bayonets but an atomic bomb.

But regardless of the details, Mott's is an open appeal to giving as a form of investment. Why give? Several fundamental motives are cited as the leading reasons: compassion for the needy, self-interested altruism, community spirit. Most important of all, however, is reciprocity, the principle that we repay the good done to us by the good we do to others. Reciprocity can be seen as "passing it on," a form of giving that keeps on giving. Thus Andrew Carnegie built free public libraries around the world in gratitude for Colonel James Anderson of Allegheny, who shared his library and "opened to me the intellectual wealth of the world."

PASS IT ON

"I will charge thee with nothing but the promise that thee will help the next man thee finds in trouble."

—Mennonite proverb

Many people do not realize the central place of reciprocity in giving and of giving to the story of money in human society. Rather than our money-society being preceded by a moneyless society based on barter, the truth is that both money and barter were preceded by gifts. In the earliest societies most goods were transferred through cycles of obligatory returns of gifts.

Put differently, the subtle dynamics of giving and its fundamental place in the development of human societies have been obscured by the dominant form of giving today in a capitalistic society — "consumer giving." We therefore need to understand the centrality and power of consumer giving today before we examine the two earlier visions of reciprocal giving that are critical to the rise of a culture of giving and caring.

One earlier view could be called "contract giving." Whole societies were once based on elaborate systems of exchanging gifts as if by unspoken contract. Some might automatically think of the Potlatch festivals of the Indians in Northwest America or the Kula Rings of the Trobriand islanders in the South Pacific. We should not dismiss these practices as purely primitive; the same mentality was evident in attitudes toward giving in the great civilizations of Egypt, Greece, and Rome. And it is also resurgent in modern philanthropy, lying behind the fateful split between "philanthropy" as community enhancement and "charity" as caring for the needy.

There are numerous benefits of contract giving. When it works well, the system of cycling gifts forms the heart and soul of a society. It reinforces the concept of honor in giving, sharpens competition in doing good, balances inequalities, circulates goodwill, confirms relationships and strengthens the bonds of community, and so on. But what matters is its core principle — Do ut des, "I give so that you may give." Or more simply, "give-to-get." Contract giving is giving based on a stated or unstated quid pro quo.

Interestingly, this mentality underlies not only one kind of philanthropy, where the giving-to-get is a pursuit of honor, but most non-biblical forms of sacrificing to the gods. Vedic sacrifice in ancient Hindu culture, for example, is openly a contract sacrifice with the gods, a giving-to-get in order to buy divine appeasement.

Generous donors in classical times were not reticent about what they desired to get through their giving. As thousands of inscriptions testify, they were remarkably, and even brazenly, open about the honors they wished to receive in return for their largesse. The same quest for recognition lingers on in modern appeals to major donors. What matters, however, is the mentality. From the perspective of contract giving, "There are no free gifts." All giving is a giving-to-get, however unstated or "respectable" the calculated returns.

The other earlier view was "charity giving." Derived from the Latin word caritas, charity originally had a freshness (long since lost) because of at least two vital elements. First, it grew from a sense of grace — God's unmerited favor that is his stunningly surprising response to our human predicament and a total reversal of all human logic and rules. Second, it was rooted in a willingness to go to costly lengths even where the price was exorbitant.

Thus reciprocity operates in both cases, but where "contract giving" is give-to-get or give-to-be-given-to, "charity giving" is give-because-given-to. In the former there are "no free gifts." In the latter there is only pure gift.

Thus reciprocity operates in both cases, but where "contract giving" is give-to-get or give-to-be-given-to, "charity giving" is give-because-given-to. In the former there are "no free gifts." In the latter there is only pure gift.

In other words, whereas "contract giving" was based on the Greek ideal *of eros, a love in which reciprocity was required and central, "charity giving" was based on Jesus' revolutionary principle of agape, a love in which reciprocity was triggered but not required and sacrifice was voluntary. For the Greeks, eros was a desire, yearning, and appetite aroused by the attractive qualities of the object of its desire (whether honor, beauty, love, or God). For Christians, agape was a love born only of the nature of love, independent of any motivation, stimulus, or reward outside itself.*

Needless to say, both types of giving are important and together complete the picture of philanthropy. But the differences between the two are not just word games; they make an enormous, practical difference in the contrasting types of society they produce. The fruits of contract giving can be seen as clearly in the magnificent buildings of the Parthenon or the buildings Herodes Atticus donated all over the Greek world, just as the fruits of charity giving can be seen in the explosion of hospitals, orphanages, leprosariums, and projects to help the poor that accompanied the spread of the gospel of Jesus in the ancient world.

❊ CONSUMER GIVING ❊

At the end of one of his stand-up routines, Woody Allen used to tell a final joke. He would take out an old, gold pocket watch, check the time, and say: "It's an old family heirloom. . . . [pause] My grandfather sold it to me on his deathbed."

The joke worked because of the incongruity between a market exchange and a family heirloom at the threshold of death. But it also highlights a clash of cultures. A vital difference between a gift and a commodity exchange is the bond a gift creates or confirms between two people. A sale leaves no such connection.

This is why the contemporary marriage of commerce and celebration is so foreign from the standpoint of history. Christmas today stands out as the peak consumer festival of what social scientist Thorstein Veblen called "devout consumption." (According to one estimate, American gift-giving at Christmas amounts to nearly $40 billion, which is bigger than the gross national product of Ireland.) But commercial ingenuity in exploiting such other national days as Mother's Day, Father's Day, and St. Valentine's Day does not lag far behind. As author and Princeton University professor Leigh Eric Schmidt argues, "So deeply enmeshed are commerce and the calendar in American culture that most holidays would be scarcely recognizable without the trappings of the market." Consumerism is refashioning giving.

According to one estimate, American gift-giving at Christmas amounts to nearly $40 billion, which is bigger than the gross national product of Ireland.

DEVOUT CONSUMPTION

"We suit our religion to our business, not our business to our religion."

—*Millinery Trade Review,* 1886

"1776 rang liberty to America. 1899 rings your liberty from high prices."

—Fourth of July slogan in *Advertising World,* 1899

"In a *Family Circus* cartoon . . . two little boys are in a shopping mall surveying various Easter commodities—baskets, candies, rabbits, eggs, and other novelties of the season. The slightly older boy says to his little brother, 'This may be Good Friday, but Sunday's going to be even gooder.'"

—Leigh Eric Schmidt, *Consumer Rites*

"A sign in a show window at 'Jack's department store' reads, 'COLUMBUS DAY * SALE * ALL MERCHANDISE MARKED UP 200% BECAUSE, LET'S FACE IT, COLUMBUS WAS A GREEDY LITTLE OPPORTUNIST JUST LIKE JACK IS.'"

—1992 editorial cartoon, cited in *Consumer Rites*

Leigh Eric Schmidt

Leigh Eric Schmidt (born 1961) is Associate Professor of Religion at Princeton University. Born in Redlands, California, he graduated from the University of California at Riverside and earned his Ph.D. from Princeton. The passage from his Consumer Rites *portrays what happens to holiday giving when (inevitably, it seems) it gets wrapped up in a commercial culture that puts its Midas touch on everything. In the case of the African American festival Kwanzaa, the irony is all the stronger because the festival was founded to counter white American/Christian styles of celebrating Christmas.*

Consumer Rites

A week-long celebration stretching from the day after Christmas to New Year's, [the African American festival] Kwanzaa is relatively new, having been invented in 1966 by the sociologist Maulana Karenga. . . . Founded as a counter-cultural celebration of racial solidarity and self-determination, the festival was intended, the young Al Sharpton explained to a group of Harlem school-children in 1971, as a "way of de-whitizing" the festivities of winter. To Karenga himself, Kwanzaa was set up in direct opposition to "the high-priced hustle and bustle of Christmas buying and selling"; it was an explicit alter-native to the "European cultural accretions of Santa Claus, reindeer, mistletoe, frantic shopping, [and] alienated gift-giving."

    Yet as observance of the festival has spread more widely in the African American community, it has taken on increasingly consumerist form. At a Kwanzaa Holiday Expo . . . in 1993, three hundred exhibitors were on hand with everything from "Kwanzaa cards and wrapping paper" to "teddy bears in African garb." Such corporate giants as Anheuser-Busch, Hallmark, J.C. Penney, and Pepsi-Cola sent representatives. Hearing of the trade extravaganza, Karenga remarked in angry tones that Anna Jarvis [the disillusioned founder of Mother's Day] would have appreciated: "This is a capitalistic society where they rent wombs and sell bodies. One can expect they will try to commodicize. The challenge of the African people is to avoid the problems of commercialization that they've learned from other holidays like Christmas." African American entrepreneurs at the trade show were more sanguine: "Black people need not be embarrassed about making money," one woman noted. "That is what pays the rent and that is what makes America tick." The issues in the debate are old, but with Kwanzaa, as with Christmas, they are proving no less contested for that grizzled familiarity.

Certainly many have felt about commercial ingenuity much as this African American businessperson does: It is what makes America tick, and the holidays are none the worse for this entrepreneurial merchandising. As the *American Florist* argued in sweeping terms in 1914, "The American people are a money-making people, and it does not detract from the sacredness of an occasion for them to make money out of it."

Leigh Eric Schmidt, *Consumer Rites: The Buying & Selling of American Holidays.* © 1995 by Princeton University Press.

MAKE A BUCK, MAKE A BUCK

"Easter, in common with the other great festivals of the year, has already been recognized as a basis of trade attraction, and, while it commemorates an event which is sacred to many, yet there is no legitimate reason why it should not also be made an occasion for legitimate merchandising."

—*Dry Goods Chronicle*, February 1900

"Yea, there's a lot of bad isms floating around this world, but one of the worst is commercialism. Make a buck, make a buck. Even in Brooklyn it's the same: Don't care what Christmas stands for. Just make a buck, make a buck."

—Alfred the janitor, in *Miracle on Thirty-Fourth Street*, 1947

"In Japan, these events [Christmas, Halloween, St. Valentine's Day, and even St. Patrick's Day] have no religious meaning at all. We just take the form and use it to sell."

—Tokyo merchant, cited in *Consumer Rites*

QUESTIONS FOR THOUGHT AND DISCUSSION

1. Think of a holiday you care about. What are the effects of commercialization on that holiday? Has the meaning of Kwanzaa been lost for African Americans because of its commercialization, or do you agree with the exhibitors' view?

2. What do you think of the *American Florist* statement, "it does not detract from the sacredness of an occasion for them to make money out of it"?

3. Consumers enjoy acquiring and merchandisers enjoy profits. What are the dangers of mixing these motives with the giving of gifts?

4. Of the problems outlined in part 1 (insatiability, commodification, excess, and idolatry), which would you say could lie behind consumer giving?

❋CONTRACT GIVING❋

❋ Bronislaw Malinowski ❋

Bronislaw Malinowski (1884–1942) was a Polish-born Englishman who became a father of modern social anthropology. He was elected to the first chair in that field at the London School of Economics and in 1938 moved to the United States and taught at Yale. But it was his earlier study of an island people group and its culture that influenced anthropology the most. When World War I broke out, Malinowski found himself confined to the Trobriand Islands off the eastern tip of New Guinea. Thanks to this experience he carried out a scientific first: By living with the islanders and participating in their day-to-day lives and rituals, he originated modern ethnographic fieldwork. His book Argonauts of the Western Pacific *set new standards for ethnographic description.*

In the excerpt below, the islanders display a form of contract giving common to many earlier civilizations. Paradoxically, possession of the gifts is genuine but temporary, and their exchange is voluntary but customary. This reciprocal giving creates and nourishes the bonds of trust between tribes.

Argonauts of the Western Pacific 🐚

The Kula is a form of exchange, of extensive, inter-tribal character; it is carried on by communities inhabiting a wide ring of islands, which form a closed circuit. This circuit can be seen on the map on the following page, where it is represented by the lines joining a number of islands to the North and East of the East end of New Guinea. Along this route, articles of two kinds, and these two kinds only, are constantly traveling in opposite directions. In the direction of the hands of a clock, moves constantly one of these kinds—long necklaces of red shell, called soulava. In the opposite direction moves the other kind—bracelets of white shell called mwali. Each of these articles, as it travels in its own direction on the closed circuit, meets on its way articles of the other class, and is constantly being exchanged for them. Every movement of the Kula articles, every detail of the transactions is fixed and regulated by a set of traditional rules and conventions, and some acts of the Kula are accompanied by an elaborate magical ritual and public ceremonies. . . .

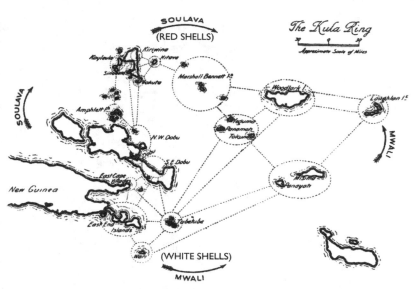

Now we pass to another rule of the Kula, of the greatest importance. As just explained the armshells and shellstrings always travel in their own respective directions on the ring, and they are never, under any circumstances, traded back in the wrong direction. Also, they never stop. It seems almost incredible at first, but it is the fact, nevertheless, that no one ever keeps any of the Kula valuables for any length of time. Indeed, in the whole of the Trobriands there are perhaps only one or two specially fine armshells and shell necklaces permanently owned as heirlooms, and these are set apart as a special class, and are once and for all out of the Kula. "Ownership" therefore, in Kula, is quite a special economic relation. A man who is in the Kula never keeps any article for longer than, say, a year or two. Even this exposes him to the reproach of being niggardly, and certain districts have the bad reputation of being "slow" and "hard" in the Kula. On the other hand, each man has an enormous number of articles passing through his hands during his life time, of which he enjoys a temporary possession, and which he keeps in trust for a time. This possession hardly ever makes him use the articles, and he remains under the obligation soon again to hand them on to one of his partners. But the temporary ownership allows him to draw a great deal of renown, to exhibit his article, to tell how he obtained it, and to plan to whom he is going to give it. And all this forms one of the favorite subjects of tribal conversation and gossip, in which the feats and the glory in Kula of chiefs or commoners are constantly discussed and re-discussed. Thus every article moves in one direction only, never comes back, never permanently stops, and takes as a rule some two to ten years to make the round.

Bronislaw Malinowski, *Argonauts of the Western Pacific: An Account of Native Enterprise and Adventure in the Archipelagoes of Melanesian New Guinea* (New York: E.P. Dutton & Company, 1922). Reprinted by permission of Routledge and Penguin Putnam Inc.

PASS IT ON

"Giving and returning is that which binds men together in their living."

—Aristotle

"What's given to friends is outside fortune's grasp:
Your gifts will prove the only wealth to last."

—Martial, Roman writer, A.D. 40–104

"Those who exchange presents with one another
Remain friends the longest . . .
A present given always expects one in return."

—"Havamal," one of the poems of the ancient Scandinavian *Edda*

"If money goes, money comes. If money stays, death comes."

—Urdu proverb

"A folk tale from Kashmir tells of two Brahmin women who tried to dispense with their alms-giving duties by simply giving alms back and forth to each other. They didn't quite have the spirit of the thing. When they died, they returned to earth as two wells so poisoned that no one could take water from them."

—Lewis Hyde, *The Gift*

"There should not be any free gifts. What is wrong with the so-called free gift is the donor's intention to be exempt from return gifts coming from the recipient. Refusing requital puts the act of giving outside any mutual ties."

—Mary Douglas, anthropologist

"There is not a more erroneous belief than that one good turn deserves another. In repaying a kindness you degrade it to the level of barter."

—Ambrose Bierce

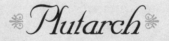

Plutarch

Plutarch was introduced previously in part 1. The following reading is from his finest work, The Lives of the Noble Grecians and Romans. *His description of Pericles, Athens' greatest leader in Athens' greatest era, clearly shows the sort of community-enhancing, honor-seeking "contract giving" that lay behind the construction of the*

Parthenon and other great public works. The Parthenon, it should be stressed, was constructed at public — not private — expense. But Pericles' honor-seeking motivation emerges clearly in his response to the complaint that it was costing the public funds too much.

A PLATINUM-CIRCLE DONOR

"Whereas Aurelius Marcus, son of Theobulus, is a man by family tradition munificent to the people and a benefactor to each and all, who on no occasion ever fails with public spirit nobly and amply to relieve the needs pressing upon his native town, . . . and now with unstinting generosity more than requiting the people for their praises of him, he has further given for public distribution and festivities a corn-purchase fund, so that through the munificence of this great gift the festival of Happiness-day will year by year make a braver show; therefore the people, mindful of these and of his other acts of kindness, have by general and popular vote decreed the erection in his honor, on the most conspicuous spot, of a statue with suitable inscription, so that his children and descendants may jointly and severally enjoy this honor in perpetuity by contemplating the gratitude of his native town enduring and worthily expressed."

—A decree from Phrygia, A.D. 237

Pericles

That which gave most pleasure and ornament to the city of Athens, and the greatest admiration and even astonishment to all strangers, and that which now is Greece's only evidence that the power she boasts of and her ancient wealth are no romance or idle story, was his construction of the public and sacred buildings. . . .

[I]t was good reason, that, now the city was sufficiently provided and stored with all things necessary for the war, they should convert the overplus of its wealth to such undertakings as would hereafter, when completed, give them eternal honor, and, for the present, while in process, freely supply all the inhabitants with plenty. With their variety of workmanship and of occasions for service, which summon all arts and trades and require all hands to be employed about them, they do actually put the whole city, in a manner, into state-pay; while at the same time she is both beautiful and maintained by herself. For as those who are of age and strength for war are provided for and maintained in the armaments abroad by their pay out of the public stock, so, it being his desire and design that the undisciplined mechanic multitude that stayed at home should not go without the share of public salaries, and yet should not have them given them for sitting still and doing nothing, to that end he thought fit to bring in among them, with the approbation of the people, these vast projects of buildings and designs of work, that would be of some continuance before they were finished, and would give employment to numerous arts, so that the part of the people that stayed at home might, no less than those that were at sea or in garrisons or on expeditions, have a fair and just occasion of receiving the benefit and having their share of the public moneys.

The materials were stone, brass, ivory, gold, ebony, cypresswood; and the arts or trades that wrought and fashioned them were smiths and carpenters, molders, founders and braziers, stone-cutters, dyers, goldsmiths, ivory-workers, painters, embroiderers, turners; those again that conveyed them to the town for use, merchants and mariners and ship-masters by sea, and by land cartwrights, cattle-breeders, waggoners, rope-makers, flax-workers, shoe makers and leather-dressers, road-makers, miners. And every trade in the same nature, as a captain in an army has his particular company of soldiers under him, had its own hired company of journeymen and laborers belonging to it banded together as in array, to be as it were the instrument and body for the performance of the service. Thus, to say all in a word, the occasions and services of these public works distributed plenty through every age and condition.

"Ms. Jones, I seem to be suffering from an image problem. Please send out a large anonymous contribution to a charitable organization, then notify the newspapers!"

As then grew the works up, no less stately in size than exquisite in form, the workmen striving to outvie the material and the design with the beauty of their workmanship, yet the most wonderful thing of all was the rapidity of their execution. . . .

When the orators, who sided with Thucydides and his party, were at one time crying out, as their custom was, against Pericles, as one who squandered away the public money, and made havoc of the state revenues, he rose in the open assembly and put the question to the people, whether they thought that he had laid out much; and they saying, "Too much, a great deal," "Then," said he, "since it is so, let the cost not go to your account, but to mine; and let the inscription upon the buildings stand in my name." When they heard him say thus, whether it were out of a surprise to see the greatness of his spirit or out of emulation of the glory of the works, they cried aloud, bidding him to spend on, and lay out what he thought fit from the public purse, and to spare no cost, till all were finished. . . .

However, there is a story that [the renowned philosopher] Anaxagoras himself, while Pericles was taken up with public affairs, lay neglected, and that, now being grown old, he wrapped himself up with a resolution to die for want of food; which being by chance brought to Pericles's ear, he was horror-struck, and instantly ran thither, and used all the arguments and entreaties he could to him, lamenting not so much Anaxagoras's condition as his own, should he lose such a counselor as he had found him to be; and that, upon this, Anaxagoras unfolded his robe, and showing himself, made answer: "Pericles," said he, "even those who have occasion for a lamp supply it with oil."

"Then," said he, "since it is so, let the cost not go to your account, but to mine; and let the inscription upon the buildings stand in my name."

Plutarch, *The Lives of the Noble Grecians and Romans,* trans. John Dryden, revised by Arthur Hugh Clough (New York: Modern Library, 1864).

FOR THE SAKE OF HONOR

"I desired that it might be well with me in the great god's presence."

—from the tomb of an Egyptian nobleman of about 2300 B.C., next to the list of his charitable contributions, explaining why he had given them

"It is quite clear that most people are generous in their gifts not so much by natural inclination as by reason of the lure of honor—they simply want to be seen as beneficent."

—Cicero

"I wish to confer my gracious gift . . . on the stated conditions, which are to be published upon three marble stones; of these, one should be erected in the temple of the Caesars, close by the gates, and one in the gymnasium, so that to citizens and non-citizens alike at Gytheion my philanthropic and kindly act may be evident and well known."

—Classical era donor

"We are hopeful of receiving still more lavish gifts hereafter from a man of whose high worth we have been conscious in the past and therefore we co-opt Rutilius Viator as patron."

—third-century resolution bestowing the status of "patron" to Rutilius Viator at Beneventum

"You pour forth statues and inscribe sculptured images and have your honorary epitaphs, reading 'to the eternal memory of. . . .' Why, as far as it lies in your power, you yourselves provide a kind of resurrection for the dead!"

—Tertullian, early Christian writer commenting on the motives of the pagans

Again, there is nothing new in renouncing one's riches and giving them in charity to the poor or to one's fatherland. Many did this before the Savior's coming, some to have leisure for the pursuit of dead wisdom, others to gain empty fame and vainglory."

—Clement of Alexandria

"Pride and vanity have built more hospitals than all the virtues together."

—Bernard Mandeville, *The Fable of the Bees*, 1714

"Never before in the history of plutocratic America had any one man purchased by mere money so much social advertising and flattery. . . . He would have given millions to Greece had she labeled the Parthenon 'Carnegopolis.'"

—Poultney Bigelow, commentary on Andrew Carnegie

"We believe that what is called being charitable is a particularly mean form of self-glorification—mean because, while it pretends to aid, it really hurts. The giver to charity gets a certain cheap satisfaction out of being regarded as a kind and generous man."

—Henry Ford

"The economy of nature is competitive from beginning to end. . . . No hint of genuine charity ameliorates our vision of society once sentimentalism has been laid aside. . . . Scratch an altruist and watch a hypocrite bleed."

—Michael Ghiselin, Darwinian biologist

"These new super-rich [America's multibillionaires] won't loosen their wads because they're afraid they'll reduce their net worth and go down the list. That's their Super Bowl. . . . My hands shook when I signed the papers [for charitable gifts] because I knew I was taking myself out of the running for richest man in America."

—Ted Turner, *New York Times*, 1996

GETTING GIVING GOING

The Preacher of Dubno was once asked why it was that a rich man would sooner give alms to a blind man or to a cripple than to a needy scholar.

"If the rich man prefers to aid a cripple or a blind man," explained the Preacher, "it is because of selfishness. Seeing them, he is frightened at the thought that he himself might someday become a cripple or blind. So he gives them alms, but actually he gives it to himself. On the other hand, why should he give aid to a poor scholar? He knows very well that not even when the dead will rise again can he ever hope to become one himself!"

—*The Treasury of Jewish Humor*

A direct-mail campaign at the Jewish National Fund last year attracted three times as many new donors as previous mailings and boosted the average contribution to $126, from $46.

Was it philanthropy, or was it the miles?

The JNF was the first charity to buy American Airlines frequent-flier miles and offer donors one mile for every dollar contributed. Donors, by a ratio of 10 to 1, opted for miles over other incentives, including T-shirts and mugs. "Everyone's a mileage junkie," says Stuart Paskow, a fund-raising consultant for the JNF.

—Scott McCartney,
"Free Airline Miles Become a Potent Tool for Selling Everything,"
The Wall Street Journal, April 15, 1996

"People in our world are swimming in money but in order to get the city's rich to give a lousy thousand dollars to the poor who are drowning in front of their eyes you have to . . . give them party favors."

—Felix Rohatyn, commentary on charity balls

QUESTIONS FOR THOUGHT AND DISCUSSION

1. What are the practical rules of the Kula that Malinowski notes?
2. How is the community enhanced because of the Kula?
3. How is temporary ownership a source of honor? What happens if you keep the Kula for too long?
4. In the first two paragraphs of Plutarch's passage on Pericles, he sets the stage for why the statesman started such an expensive public building campaign. What are some of the reasons he gives?
5. What is Pericles' response to the complaint that he was spending too much on the building campaign? Why do his critics then encourage rather than discourage the spending? How is seeking honor evident on both sides?
6. How does a "giving-to-get" approach to giving affect how Pericles responds to the demise of Anaxagoras? What does Anaxagoras mean by "even those who have occasion for a lamp supply it with oil"?
7. What are the consequences of give-to-get, honor-seeking forms of "contract giving"?
8. Have you ever given something and later been aware of an element of "giving to get" within it, perhaps with disappointing or calamitous results? What went wrong?

❊ CHARITY GIVING ❊

Jewish Tzedakah

Charity giving is different from contract giving not only in terms of why it is done but who is included. Where contract giving has focused on public enrichment or reciprocity, charity giving has focused on the poor and needy. For the Jews, the leading motive for this was "righteousness," with the Hebrew word for righteousness, tzedakah, *becoming the Jewish term for charity. For the Christians, the leading motive was love, understood as* agape *rather than* eros, *with the Latin word for love,* caritas, *becoming the Christian word for charity. A notable feature of both Jewish* tzedakah *and Christian* caritas, *which often has been lost, is the insistence on the dignity of the recipient. Whatever straits the poor and needy are in, they are still fellow human beings who are made in the image of God, and all giving must acknowledge this reality.*

Whatever straits the poor and needy are in, they are still fellow human beings who are made in the image of God, and all giving must acknowledge this reality.

Deuteronomy 26:12-13

When you have finished setting aside a tenth of all your produce in the third year, the year of the tithe, you shall give it to the Levite, the alien, the fatherless and the widow, so that they may eat in your towns and be satisfied. Then say to the LORD your God: "I have removed from my house the sacred portion and have given it to the Levite, the alien, the fatherless and the widow, according to all you commanded. I have not turned aside from your commands nor have I forgotten any of them."

Isaiah 58:6-7

"Is not this the kind of fasting I have chosen:
    to loose the chains of injustice
    and untie the cords of the yoke,

to set the oppressed free
    and break every yoke?
Is it not to share your food with the hungry
    and to provide the poor wanderer with shelter—
when you see the naked, to clothe him,
    and not to turn away from your own flesh and blood?"

❧ *Moses Maimonides* ❧

Moses ben Maimon, also known as Moses Maimonides (1135–1204) is the leading figure of medieval Judaism. Born in Moorish-controlled Cordoba, Spain, he fled persecution and eventually settled in Cairo, where he became the leader of the Jewish community and the personal doctor of Saladin, the sultan. He brought out his Mishneh Torah *in 1180, joining the long Talmudic tradition of Jewish scholars who interpret and comment on the Torah, the first five books of the Bible. This long work has had a powerful and lasting influence on Judaism. Maimonides profoundly influenced such Christian thinkers as St. Thomas Aquinas as well as Jews and Muslims.*

The passage below, from the Mishneh Torah, *describes the different degrees of* tzedakah. *It is Maimonides's commentary on the Jewish Scriptures about the best and worst kinds of giving to the needy and the degrees in between. The highest ideal is to teach and help the poor to become self-supporting. But interestingly, the next highest kind of giving is anonymous, a kind that prevents the potential abuses of a power relationship.*

NONE LIKE MOSES

"About Moses Maimonides there is an old Jewish folk saying: 'From Moses to Moses there was none like Moses.'"

—David Novak, "The Mind of Maimonides," *First Things*, February 1999

The Eight Stages of Tzedakah ✍

We are duty bound to be more needful with regard to the discharge of the commandment relating to charity than with all the other precepts of the Torah, for benevolence is the characteristic of the righteous descendants of the seed of Abraham, our father, of whom it is said, "For I know him to the end that he command his children and his household after him that they may keep the way of the Lord, to do tzedakah."

Sacred unto the Lord is the human dignity and personality of the recipient of charity, and they must not be hurt or lowered. Moreover, of greater merit than giving to the poor, is to help him to become self-supporting.

Tzedakah implies the fullest obligation that people owe to one another. Tzedakah calls for more than mere almsgiving, because in its exercise there must be kindness, tenderness, not to shame the poor or put him to disgrace. Sacred unto the Lord is the human dignity and personality of the recipient of charity, and they must not be hurt or lowered. Moreover, of greater merit than giving to the poor, is to help him to become self-supporting.

There are eight degrees of tzedakah, each one superior to the next.

(1) The highest degree, than which there is none higher, is the one who upholds the hand of an Israelite reduced to poverty by handing that person a gift or loan, or by entering into a partnership with him or her, or by finding that Israelite work, in order to strengthen that person's hand, so that she or he will have no need to beg from others. Concerning such a person it is stated, *You shall uphold that one, as a stranger and a settler shall that person live with you*—meaning, uphold that person, so that she or he will not lapse into want.

(2) Below this is one who gives alms to the poor in such a way that the giver knows not to whom the alms are sent, nor does the poor person know from whom the alms are received. This constitutes the fulfilling of a religious duty for its own sake, and for such there was a Chamber of Secrets in the Temple, where the righteous would contribute sums secretly, and where the poor of good families would draw their sustenance in equal secrecy. Close to such a person is the one who contributes directly to the charity fund. . . .

(3) Below this is the person who knows the one receiving while the poor person knows not from whom the gift comes. Such a donor is like the great among the sages who would set forth secretly, throwing money before the doors of the poor. This is an appropriate procedure, to be preferred if those administering charity funds are not behaving honorably.

(4) Below this is the instance in which the poor knows the identity of the donor, but remains unknown to the donor. The giver is thus like the great among the sages who would place money in the folded corner of a linen sheet,

throw the sheet over their shoulders, and allow the poor to come up behind them and remove the money without being subject to humiliation.

(5) Below this is the one who hands charity directly to the poor before being asked for it.

(6) Below this is the one who hands charity to the poor after the poor has requested it.

(7) Below this is the one who gives to the poor less than what is appropriate, but gives it in a friendly manner.

(8) Below this is the one who gives charity with a scowl.

The great among the sages used to hand a small coin to a poor person before praying and then to pray, as it is stated, As *for me, I shall behold Your face in righteousness.*

Quoted in Jacob Neusner, *Tzedakah: Can Jewish Philanthropy Buy Jewish Survival?* (Chappaqua, New York: Rossel Books, 1982).

THE GREATEST PLEASURE

"The greatest pleasure I know is to do a good deed by stealth, and to have it found out by accident."

—Charles Lamb

QUESTIONS FOR THOUGHT AND DISCUSSION

1. Which features of this Jewish teaching on *tzedakah* strike you the most? How does the principle of the dignity of the recipient influence the teaching throughout?

2. Why do you think the first level is the highest ideal? What kind of effect would this level of giving have on the giver? How is the commitment to give different from the other levels?

3. Do you agree with the emphasis on "anonymity" that was also pronounced in Jesus' teaching (Matthew 6:1-4)? What are the pros and cons of secrecy in giving?

4. According to the Jewish idea of *tzedakah*, how does our attitude affect the level, or the righteousness, of a gift? Does the size of the gift matter? Why do you think this would be so?

❈CHARITY GIVING❈

❈ *Christian Caritas* ❈

The Christian notion of charity giving—giving because given to—is unquestionably the strongest single influence in the rise of the West's unique tradition of giving, caring, and philanthropy. But the contrast between charity and contract giving is not absolute. There are examples of contract giving in the New Testament, though charity giving is clearly the highest and most characteristically Christian.

Putting together the biblical views of money and giving, we may say that, from a Christian perspective, there are three principal reasons for giving. First, giving reflects the character of God. As French scholar Jacques Ellul says in Money and Power, "the major characteristic of God's world is the fact that in it everything is given freely. Grace is grace precisely because it is not bought."

As French scholar Jacques Ellul says in Money and Power, *"the major characteristic of God's world is the fact that in it everything is given freely. Grace is grace precisely because it is not bought."*

Second, giving reciprocates the gift of grace in Christ. Christian teaching notes that only once does God buy and sell rather than give—in redeeming sinners. Again Ellul: "God pays a price. He accepts the exchange that Satan demanded, and Satan can claim to have put God under his own law, the law of selling." But God's only way of dealing with human beings is through giving, so when God has paid the price, he freely gives his son in order to give liberty. Thus the world of grace is a world where the deepest things are not for sale; those who live in that world are to live in that way.

Thus the world of grace is a world where the deepest things are not for sale; those who live in that world are to live in that way.

Third, giving repudiates the power of Mammon, the idolatry of money. As we saw earlier, "The Lord loves a cheerful giver." Giving is the test, for how we give reflects how we see grace. The cheerful giver is the one for whom the power of Mammon has lost its grip. In cheerful giving we profane Mammon, debunking its idolatrous character and bringing money back to its simple role as a created thing and a medium of exchange. The idol is destroyed. Thus Christian charity giving aims to be self-giving without being self-serving, and to go beyond the natural boundaries of family, tribe, and nation to embrace the neighbor in need wherever he or she is.

A TIME TO DEBUNK

"There is only one act par excellence which profanes money by going directly against the law of money, an act for which money is not made. This act is *giving*."

—Jacques Ellul, *Money and Power*

Matthew 5:42-45

"Give to the one who asks you, and do not turn away from the one who wants to borrow from you.

"You have heard that it was said, 'Love your neighbor and hate your enemy.' But I tell you: Love your enemies and pray for those who persecute you, that you may be sons of your Father in heaven. He causes his sun to rise on the evil and the good, and sends rain on the righteous and the unrighteous."

Luke 14:12-14

Then Jesus said to his host, "When you give a luncheon or dinner, do not invite your friends, your brothers or relatives, or your rich neighbors; if you do, they may invite you back and so you will be repaid. But when you give a banquet, invite the poor, the crippled, the lame, the blind, and you will be blessed. Although they cannot repay you, you will be repaid at the resurrection of the righteous."

1 John 3:16-18

This is how we know what love is: Jesus Christ laid down his life for us. And we ought to lay down our lives for our brothers. If anyone has material possessions and sees his brother in need but has no pity on him, how can the love of God be in him? Dear children, let us not love with words or tongue but with actions and in truth.

2 Corinthians 8:1-15

[Paul earlier has asked the churches in Greece to give to the churches in Palestine, which are experiencing severe drought and famine.]

Out of the most severe trial, their overflowing joy and their extreme poverty welled up in rich generosity.

And now, brothers, we want you to know about the grace that God has given the Macedonian churches. Out of the most severe trial, their overflowing joy and their extreme poverty welled up in rich generosity. For I testify that they gave as much as they were able, and even beyond their ability. Entirely on their own, they urgently pleaded with us for the privilege of sharing in this service to the saints. And they did not do as we expected, but they gave themselves first to the Lord and then to us in keeping with God's will. So we urged Titus, since he had earlier made a beginning, to bring also to completion this act of grace on your part. But just as you excel in everything—in faith, in speech, in knowledge, in complete earnestness and in your love for us—see that you also excel in this grace of giving.

I am not commanding you, but I want to test the sincerity of your love by comparing it with the earnestness of others. For you know the grace of our Lord Jesus Christ, that though he was rich, yet for your sakes he became poor, so that you through his poverty might become rich.

"Now this $1-million contribution I made, was it a sincere gesture or just for tax purposes?"

Reprinted from The Chronicle of Philanthropy by permission of the artist, Joseph Brown.

And here is my advice about what is best for you in this matter: Last year you were the first not only to give but also to have the desire to do so. Now finish the work, so that your eager willingness to do it may be matched by your completion of it, according to your means. For if the willingness is there, the gift is acceptable according to what one has, not according to what he does not have.

Our desire is not that others might be relieved while you are hard pressed, but that there might be equality. At the present time your plenty will supply what they need, so that in turn their plenty will supply what you need. Then there will be equality, as it is written: "He who gathered much did not have too much, and he who gathered little did not have too little."

IMPOSSIBLE LOVE?

"There is no deed, not a single one, not even the best, of which we dare to say unconditionally: he who does this thereby unconditionally demonstrates love. It depends upon *how* the deed is done. . . One can perform works of love in an unloving, yes, even in a self-loving way. . . . Alas, Luther is supposed to have said that not once in his life had he prayed entirely undisturbed by any distracting thoughts. In the same way the honest man confesses that never, however often he has willingly and gladly given charity, that never has he done it except in frailty . . . perhaps to save face . . . perhaps seeking alleviation by giving charity. . . ."

—Søren Kierkegaard, *Works of Love*

Fyodor Mikhailovich Dostoyevsky (1821–1881) was a Russian novelist, unarguably one of the most influential writers of modern literature and possibly the greatest novelist of all time. Born in Moscow the son of a doctor, he went to the Military Engineering College in St. Petersburg, but he soon resigned from the army and took up his lifelong occupation as a writer.

In 1848, Dostoyevsky became involved with a group of young intellectuals who were suspected of politically subversive activities. Arrested, imprisoned for eight months, condemned to death, and then reprieved at the last second, he was shaped forever by this shattering experience. Throughout his life Dostoyevsky also was plagued by epileptic attacks, proneness to gambling, and chronic financial worries. Despite all this, his books such as Notes from Underground, Crime and Punishment, The Idiot, and The Brothers Karamazov secured his eminent reputation, which since his death has grown steadily everywhere except in his own country.

During Dostoyevsky's prison term, the only book he was allowed was the New Testament. He read it constantly until its perspectives shaped his whole life, as is clear from this passage from The Brothers Karamazov. Father Zossima the Elder is a beloved monk of the local monastery and is thought to be one in whom the Christian ideal of love is lived out.

In the passage below, Father Zossima explains the Christian concept of love, *which he calls "active love," to a visitor. Active love, he says, involves obstinacy, hard work, and sometimes even frightening force but ultimately is not limited by human capabilities and desires. His visitor is a high-strung, histrionic woman who professes a great need to know for sure whether or not God exists. Father Zossima begins by assuring the woman that though one cannot prove God's existence, one can be convinced of it—by practicing "love in action." As the story develops, it becomes clear that Father Zossima is not so foolish as to think that "love in action" is easy. Only when the woman sees the bankruptcy of "love in dreams" does she get to the end of her own efforts and become open to a very different kind of love.*

LOVE FOR ONE

"Without thinking what he was doing, he took another drink of brandy. As the liquid touched his tongue he remembered his child, coming in out of the glare: the sullen unhappy knowledgeable face. He said, 'Oh God, help her. Damn me, I deserve it, but let her live for ever.' This was the love he should have felt for every soul in the world: all the fear and the wish to save concentrated unjustly on the one child. He began to weep; it was as if he had to watch her from the shore drown slowly because he had forgotten how to swim. He thought: This is what I should feel all the time for everyone. . . . "

—Graham Greene, *The Power and the Glory*

The Brothers Karamazov ᔫ

"How?"

> *In as far as you advance in love you will grow surer of the reality of God and of the immortality of your soul.*

"By the experience of active love. Strive to love your neighbour actively and indefatigably. In as far as you advance in love you will grow surer of the reality of God and of the immortality of your soul. If you attain to perfect self-forgetfulness in the love of your neighbor, then you will believe without doubt, and no doubt can possibly enter your soul. This has been tried. This is certain."

"In active love? There's another question—and such a question! You see, I so love humanity that—would you believe it?—I often dream of forsaking all that I have, leaving Lise, and becoming a sister of mercy. I close my eyes and think and dream, and at that moment I feel full of strength to overcome all obstacles. No wounds, no festering sores could at that moment frighten me. I would bind them up and wash them with my own hands. I would nurse the afflicted. I would be ready to kiss such wounds."

"It is much, and well that your mind is full of such dreams and not others.

Some time, unawares, you may do a good deed in reality."

"Yes. But could I endure such a life for long?" the lady went on fervently, almost frantically. "That's the chief question — that's my most agonizing question. I shut my eyes and ask myself, 'Would you persevere long on that path? And if the patient whose wounds you are washing did not meet you with gratitude, but worried you with his whims, without valuing or remarking your charitable services, began abusing you and rudely commanding you, and complaining to the superior authorities of you (which often happens when people are in great suffering)—what then? Would you persevere in your love, or not?' And do you know, I came with horror to the conclusion that, if anything could dissipate my love to humanity, it would be ingratitude. In short, I am a hired servant, I expect my payment at once — that is, praise, and the repayment of love with love. Otherwise I am incapable of loving anyone."

She was in a very paroxysm of self-castigation, and, concluding, she looked with defiant resolution at the elder.

"It's just the same story as a doctor once told me," observed the elder. "He was a man getting on in years, and undoubtedly clever. He spoke as frankly as you, though in jest, in bitter jest. 'I love humanity,' he said, 'but I wonder at myself. The more I love humanity in general, the less I love man in particular. In my dreams,' he said, 'I have often come to making enthusiastic schemes for the service of humanity, and perhaps I might actually have faced crucifixion if it had been suddenly necessary; and yet I am incapable of living in the same room with anyone for two days together, as I know by experience. As soon as anyone is near me, his personality disturbs my self-complacency and restricts my freedom. In twenty-four hours I begin to hate the best of men: one because he's too long over his dinner; another because he has a cold and keeps on blowing his nose. I become hostile to people the moment they come close to me. But it has always happened that the more I detest men individually the more ardent becomes my love for humanity.'"

"But what's to be done? What can one do in such a case? Must one despair?"

"No. It is enough that you are distressed at it. Do what you can, and it will be reckoned unto you. Much is done already in you since you can so deeply and sincerely know yourself. If you have been talking to me so sincerely, simply to gain approbation for your frankness, as you did from me just now, then, of course, you will not attain to anything in the achievement of real love; it will all get no further than dreams, and your whole life will slip away like a phantom. In that case you will naturally cease to think of the future life too, and will of yourself grow calmer after a fashion in the end."

"You have crushed me! Only now, as you speak, I understand that I was really only seeking your approbation for my sincerity when I told you I could not endure ingratitude. You have revealed me to myself. You have seen through me and explained me to myself!"

Above all, avoid falsehood, every kind of falsehood, especially falseness to yourself.

"Are you speaking the truth? Well, now, after such a confession, I believe that you are sincere and good at heart. If you do not attain happiness, always remember that you are on the right road, and try not to leave it. Above all, avoid falsehood, every kind of falsehood, especially falseness to yourself. Watch over your own deceitfulness and look into it every hour, every minute. Avoid being scornful, both to others and to yourself. What seems to you bad within you will grow purer from the very fact of your observing it in yourself. Avoid fear, too, though fear is only the consequence of every sort of falsehood. Never be frightened at your own faint-heartedness in attaining love. Don't be frightened overmuch even at your evil actions. I am sorry I can say nothing more consoling to you, for love in action is a harsh and dreadful thing compared with love in dreams. Love in dreams is greedy for immediate action, rapidly performed and in the sight of all. Men will even give their lives if only the ordeal does not last long but is soon over, with all looking on and applauding as though on the stage. But active love is labor and fortitude, and for some people too, perhaps, a complete science. But I predict that just when you see with horror that in spite of all your efforts you are getting farther from your goal instead of nearer to it—at that very moment I predict that you will reach it and behold clearly the miraculous power of the Lord who has been all the time loving and mysteriously guiding you."

From Fyodor Dostoyevsky, *The Brothers Karamazov*, Book II, chapter 4, trans. Constance Garnett (1912).

GIVING TILL YOU FEEL IT

"Let thine alms sweat in thy hands, until thou knowest to whom thou shouldst give."

—*The Didache*, second century

"The family has given away something like a billion dollars, but obviously, as any observer could see, it has not caused any great sacrifice to the family. They've done it because they've been interested to do it, and I believe they've done a lot of good works with it. But it certainly hasn't been a sacrifice. Giving away a million dollars when you've got a hundred million really doesn't make you a better person than others."

—Steven Rockefeller, great-grandson of John D. Rockefeller Sr.

"ANYWAY"

"People are unreasonable, illogical, and self-centered,
LOVE THEM ANYWAY

If you do good, people will accuse you of selfish, ulterior motives,
DO GOOD ANYWAY

If you are successful, you win false friends and true enemies,
SUCCEED ANYWAY

The good you do will be forgotten tomorrow,
DO GOOD ANYWAY

Honesty and frankness make you vulnerable,
BE HONEST AND FRANK ANYWAY

What you spent years building may be destroyed overnight,
BUILD ANYWAY

People really need help but may attack you if you help them,
HELP PEOPLE ANYWAY

Give the world the best you have and you'll get kicked in the teeth,
GIVE THE WORLD THE BEST YOU'VE GOT ANYWAY."

—Sign on a wall of a children's home in Calcutta,
cited by Mother Teresa

QUESTIONS FOR THOUGHT AND DISCUSSION

1. What are the distinctive features of an agape-inspired Christian charity as mentioned in the Scripture passages? In striking contrast to "contract giving," why in the Luke passage does Jesus tell his host to "invite the poor, the crippled, the lame, the blind" to a banquet?

2. In the passage from 2 Corinthians, Paul is raising money for the poor believers in Jerusalem. What is notable about the Macedonian church and their giving? What did the Macedonians do first that allowed them to give so freely and generously?

3. Why is Paul mentioning the Macedonians to the Corinthians, a wealthy church in Greece? What does he want to encourage the Corinthians to do? Is he simply being manipulative or is there a deeper concern here? What does Paul say he desires? What is his reasoning?

4. When Father Zossima explains to the woman how "active love" or "love in action" proves God's existence, what does he say must happen for her to have no doubt? Where is her focus presently? What does Father

Zossima mean when he says, "Some time, unawares, you may do a good deed in reality"?

5. Would you say the woman's concerns about becoming a sister of mercy are realistic? What is keeping her from acting on her dream? What "pay" would she expect in such a life of free service?

6. What three things does Father Zossima tell the woman to avoid, so she might attain love? Why do these particular attitudes stand in the way of love? What differences does Father Zossima make between "love in action" and "love in dreams"?

7. How is it possible that the more the doctor (like the woman) despises men individually, he loves humanity more ardently? Do you think he is unique in his attitude? How does Father Zossima's "active love" answer this problem?

8. Examine Dostoyevsky's contrast between "love in dreams" and "love in action." How are they different? How helpful is this contrast for you?

POINT TO PONDER:

Why Care for the Poor and Needy?

Closely related to the question "Why give?" is the companion question, "Why care for anyone, especially for the poor and needy?" And the same decisive ideas that divide contract giving from charity giving make their weight felt here too.

Our word "philanthropy" is derived from the Greek word that literally means "love of humankind." The term originally signified the benevolence of the gods for human beings, although it slowly softened into the more general sense of kindness and friendliness in social relationships. Yet what is startling is that philanthropy among the Greeks and Romans ("contract giving") never took the form of private charity or of personal concern for those in need.

There are several reasons why. First, the benevolence, whether of the gods to humans or rulers to their subjects, always had a strain of condescension of the superior to the inferior that precluded any sense of solidarity or sympathy.

Second, the very give-to-get character of contract giving that requires reciprocity was bound to bias giving toward one's peers rather than toward the poor. After all, the poor could never reciprocate, so gifts to them were a "waste."

PROPER COURSE

"When you find a man starving, the least you can do is to loan him your umbrella. That is the proper course."

—Ambrose Bierce

Third, unlike the God of the Hebrew and Christian Scriptures, the Greek and Roman gods showed little concern for the poor, for only the rich and powerful could offer worthy sacrifices. Even the very Latin words for "poor" implied people who were dishonest and undeserving.

Fourth, pity as an emotion was regarded as inappropriate for the poor. Stoics were suspicious of pity because they saw it as purely emotional, irrational, and self-centered. Others did advocate pity, but of a very limited sort. They reserved it for their own affinity group, those whom Aristotle calls "people like us"—for the upper classes who experienced poverty as a grand reversal of their previous fortune. The poor, after all, had never fallen into misfortune; it was their normal lot. And if the rich were ever to fall themselves, it would be other wealthy people—certainly not the poor—who might reciprocate their earlier generosity.

Fifth, the seeking of honor in return for public benefaction was part and parcel of Greek and Roman city-state life. A community's financial burdens were shouldered either by those holding public office (at considerable personal expense) or by appeals to the wealthy for a public subscription. The triple motives for such appeals were philotimia *("love of honor"),* philodoxia *("love of glory"), or simply shame. For example, as an act of munificence, the Athenian citizen Herodes Atticus gave a water supply to the city of Troas, a theatre to Corinth, a stadium to Delphi, an aqueduct for Canusium in Italy, and baths for Thermopylae.*

JULIUS CAESAR'S WILL

"*Antony:* Here is the will, and under Caesar's seal:

To every Roman citizen he gives,

To every several man, seventy-five drachmas.

2nd Plebeian: Most noble Caesar! We'll revenge his death.

3rd Plebeian: O royal Caesar!

Antony: Hear me with patience.

All: Peace, ho!

Antony: Moreover he hath left you all his walks,

His private arbours and new-planted orchards,

On this side Tiber; he hath left them for you,

And to your heirs for ever, common pleasures,

To walk abroad and recreate yourselves.

Here was a Caesar! When comes such another?"

—William Shakespeare, *Julius Caesar,* Act III, scene ii

Such factors meant that classical Greek and Roman philanthropy in the form of contract giving was civic, not personal. As Diogenes Laertius says in a phrase cited to Aristotle, "Our gift is not to a man but to mankind." Historians Sir William Tarn and G. T. Griffith conclude: "Broadly speaking, pity for the poor had little place in the normal Greek character, and consequently for the poor, as such, no provision usually existed; the idea of democracy and equality was so strong that anything done must be done for all alike; there was nothing corresponding to our mass or privately organized charities and hospitals."

Charity giving, by contrast, was generous but expected nothing in return. Like the Good Samaritan, it went beyond the boundaries of "people like us" and was distinctive for its passion for the poor and needy—as individuals. A general love of humanity was never a motive. So although the Greek word philanthropy was rarely used by early Christian writers, followers of Christ so infused giving with the dynamic of agape and caritas that it can be said legitimately that what we know now as "philanthropy" is a Christian product. There were, for example, pre-Christian infirmaries, but the rise of the hospital was a distinctively Christian contribution. Early Christian hospitals included separate buildings for orphans, the elderly, lepers, travelers, and pilgrims. More importantly they were open to all in need and were run on the spiritual imperative of care and compassion.

These differences between contract giving and charity giving are neither semantic nor antiquarian. Today's welfare debates raise issues of the "politics of pity" all over again. Those who follow Herbert Spencer's Social Darwinism or Friedrich Nietzsche's attack on compassion are openly contemptuous of pity, whereas other varieties of pity, such as Buddha's and Aristotle's, are severely limited. (For example, in Buddhism, care for others is valued because it means one has been successful in renouncing self. Paradoxically, the focus remains on self—on the renunciation of self—rather than on the value of the unique other person. Loving one's neighbor as oneself cannot carry the Jewish and Christian meaning because in Buddhist thinking, the individuality of both one's neighbor and oneself are illusions, and the suffering of one's neighbor is also an illusion.) Only the Jewish and Christian view could and did give rise to the Western culture of caring that we know. Anyone concerned over today's fateful divergence between "philanthropy" and "charity" would do well to ponder the different roots and varying consequences of the two approaches. At the very least the fate of the poor is at stake, not to mention the character of a generous, caring society.

🕸 GREEKS AND ROMANS 🕸
Concern for Humankind

Plato was introduced earlier in part 1. This short paragraph from The Republic *is an early form of welfare and healthcare debate and shows plainly how individuals were viewed in a day when scarcity was a real problem and the group overshadowed the importance of the individual.*

The Republic 🕸

Let us say, then, that Asclepius too knew all this, and therefore introduced medical treatment for those who have a good constitution and lead a healthy life. If they get some specific disease, he gets rid of it by drugs or surgery, but tells them to go on leading their normal life so as not to make them less useful to the community. But he makes no attempt to cure those whose constitution is basically diseased by treating them with a series of evacuations and doses which can only lead to an unhappy prolongation of life, and the production of children as unhealthy as themselves. No, he thought that no treatment should be given to the man who cannot survive the routine of his ordinary job, and who is therefore of no use either to himself or society.

From Plato, *The Republic*, trans. Desmond Lee (London: Penguin Books, 1987). © 1953, 1974, 1987 by H.D.P. Lee.

Aristotle

Aristotle, too, was introduced in part 1. The following passage is from his Rhetoric, *where he is discussing human emotions and their part in effective writing and public speaking. To Aristotle, pity is caused by a prior concern for ourselves, not foremost by a concern for others. The application of this view of pity (limited to "people like us") to the treatment of the poor is noteworthy, although from our perspective deeply understandable.*

NOT THE MAN, BUT HUMANITY

"When someone accused [Aristotle] of having given a subscription to a dishonest man — for the story is also told in this form — 'It was not the man,' said he, 'that I assisted, but humanity.'"

—Diogenes Laertius, "Aristotle"

On Pity

Pity may be defined as a feeling of pain caused by the sight of some evil, destructive or painful, which befalls one who does not deserve it, and which we might expect to befall ourselves or some friend of ours, and moreover to befall us soon. In order to feel pity, we must obviously be capable of supposing that some evil may happen to us or some friend of ours, and moreover some such evil as is stated in our definition or is more or less of that kind. It is therefore not felt by those completely ruined, who suppose that no further evil can befall them, since the worst has befallen them already; nor by those who imagine themselves immensely fortunate — their feeling is rather presumptuous insolence, for when they think they possess all the good things of life, it is clear that the impossibility of evil befalling them will be included, this being one of the good things in question. Those who think evil *may* befall them are such as have already had it befall them and have safely escaped from it; elderly men, owing to their good sense and their experience; weak men, especially men inclined to cowardice; and also educated people, since these can take long views. Also those who have parents living, or children, or wives; for these are our own, and the evils mentioned above may easily befall them. And those who are neither moved by any courageous emotion such as anger or confidence (these emotions take no account of the future), nor by a disposition to presumptuous insolence (insolent men, too, take no account of the possibility that something evil will happen to them), nor yet by great fear (panic-stricken people do not feel pity, because they are taken up with what is happening to themselves); only those feel pity who are between these two extremes. In order to feel pity we must also believe in the goodness of at least some people; if you think nobody good, you will believe that everybody deserves evil fortune. And, generally, we feel pity whenever we are in the condition of remembering that similar misfortunes have happened to us or ours, or expecting them to happen in future.

. . . Again, we feel pity when the danger is near ourselves. Also we pity those who are like us in age, character, disposition, social standing, or birth; for in all these cases it appears more likely that the same misfortune may befall us also. Here too we have to remember the general principle that what we fear for ourselves excites our pity when it happens to others.

From Aristotle, *Rhetoric*, trans. W. Rhys Roberts, Book II, chapter 8, Modern Library, 1954.

THE CARELESS SOCIETY

"Give to those who are 'worthy.'"

—Cicero

"It is a mistake if anyone thinks that it is an easy thing to give. . . . To certain people I shall not give, even though there is need, because there will still be a need, even if I do give."

—Seneca

"My love is something valuable to me which I ought not to throw away without reflection. . . . If I love someone, he must deserve it some way. . . . But if he is a stranger to me and if he cannot attract me by any worth of his own or any significance that he may already have acquired for my emotional life, it will be hard for me to love him. Indeed, I should be wrong to do so, for my love is valued by all my own people as a sign of my preferring them, and it is an injustice to them if I put a stranger on a par with them. . . . What is the point of a precept enunciated with so much solemnity if its fulfillment cannot be recommended as reasonable? Nothing runs so strongly counter to the original nature of man."

—Sigmund Freud, **commenting on the words of Jesus, "Love your enemies."**

In Aristotle there is "an almost complete absence of what may be called benevolence or philanthropy. The sufferings of mankind, in so far as he is aware of them, do not move him emotionally; he holds them, intellectually, to be an evil, but there is no evidence that they cause him unhappiness except when the sufferers happen to be his friends."

—Bertrand Russell

"The Oriental attitude to the sick and the poor is notoriously indifferent, because caste, rank, wealth and health are pre-ordained by the laws of Karma. Welfare work in the slums and care of the poor in general was, and still is, a monopoly of the Christian missions in Asia. Gandhi's crusade for the Untouchables and Vinoba's crusade for the landless are modern developments under Western influence — Gandhi himself acknowledged that he was inspired by Christianity, Tolstoy, Ruskin and Thoreau."

—Arthur Koestler, *The Lotus and the Robot*

"Brotherly love in the literal sense comes at the expense of brotherly love in the biblical sense; the more precisely we bestow unconditional kindness on relatives, the less of it is left over for others."

—Robert Wright, *The Moral Animal*

"Pity and compassion, to the Greeks, were comprehensible only if they served pride and the drive for fame. To ancient philosophers, from Plato in the fourth century B.C. to Marcus Aurelius in the second century A.D., gratuitous pity 'was a defect of character unworthy of the wise and excusable only in those who have not yet grown up. It was an impulsive response based on ignorance. Plato had removed the problem of beggars from his ideal state by dumping them over the borders.' . . . The Roman historian Tacitus condemned the Jewish teaching that infanticide and abortion were sinful as a 'sinister and revolting' doctrine. Nor was this sentiment only theory; it was put into practice on an enormous scale. In 1991, archaeologists digging in the Hellenistic port city of Ashkelon found bones 'of nearly 100 little babies apparently murdered and thrown into the sewer.' Laws of both Athens and Rome assumed that weak or deformed infants would be routinely exposed to die."

—David Gress, *From Plato to NATO*

QUESTIONS FOR THOUGHT AND DISCUSSION

1. What is striking about Plato's assessment of who receives medical treatment? Who is in and who is out? What is the decisive criterion? Where do you see this line of thinking today?
2. What are the separate components in Aristotle's definition of pity? What categories of people are likely to feel pity? Who is the object of their pity? Why? What will be the social effect of limiting pity to "people like us"?

3. Overall, how would you describe Greek and Roman attitudes to the poor and needy?

4. What do you think of their counsel about giving only to "the useful" and deserving? How does this bear on modern welfare debates about "the undeserving poor"?

5. Read Bertrand Russell's comment on Aristotle in the box at the top of the previous page. How fair do you think his observation is?

❋JEWS AND CHRISTIANS❋

❋Compassion for All Human Beings❋

The dignity of all human beings, not just "those like us," is a defining feature of Jewish caring. But through the teaching, life, and death of Jesus of Nazareth this view became a revolutionary new force in the first century and is the strongest single influence behind the distinctive Western culture of giving and caring.

In fact, historians view the Christian practice of caring as a prime reason why an obscure, marginal movement on the fringe of the Roman Empire rose to dislodge classical paganism and became the dominant faith of Western civilization and the world's first universal religion.

A very practical example of caring in action was the Christian response to the catastrophic plagues of A.D. 165 and 260. In the former, from a quarter to a third of the population of the Roman Empire died, including Marcus Aurelius, the emperor. Generally speaking, pagans fled from such epidemics because they were powerless. Christians, however, stayed and provided both a better theoretical explanation of the disasters and a better practical demonstration of caring. No testimony to the difference made is more striking than that of the Emperor Julian, who tried, unavailingly, to get his pagan priests to match Christian caring.

Leviticus 19:15; 25:35-37 ༄

Do not pervert justice; do not show partiality to the poor or favoritism to the great, but judge your neighbor fairly. . . .

If one of your countrymen becomes poor and is unable to support himself among you, help him as you would an alien or a temporary resident, so he can continue to live among you. Do not take interest of any kind from him, but fear your God, so that your countryman may continue to live among you. You must not lend him money at interest or sell him food at a profit.

Deuteronomy 24:17-22 ❧

Do not deprive the alien or the fatherless of justice, or take the cloak of the widow as a pledge. Remember that you were slaves in Egypt and the LORD your God redeemed you from there. That is why I command you to do this. When you are harvesting in your field and you overlook a sheaf, do not go back to get it. Leave it for the alien, the fatherless and the widow, so that the LORD your God may bless you in all the work of your hands. When you beat the olives from your trees, do not go over the branches a second time. Leave what remains for the alien, the fatherless and the widow. When you harvest the grapes in your vineyard, do not go over the vines again. Leave what remains for the alien, the fatherless and the widow. Remember that you were slaves in Egypt. That is why I command you to do this.

A SINGLE HUMAN SOUL

"If I am not for myself, who is for me?

If I care only for myself, what am I?

If not now, when?"

—Rabbi Hillel

"Our tradition says that God created us through one human being to teach us that whoever destroys a single human soul has destroyed an entire world. And whoever sustains a single human soul has sustained an entire world."

—*The New Union Prayerbook,*
Central Conference of American Rabbis, 1975

Matthew 25:44-46 ❧

"They also will answer, 'Lord, when did we see you hungry or thirsty or a stranger or needing clothes or sick or in prison, and did not help you?' He will reply, 'I tell you the truth, whatever you did not do for one of the least of these, you did not do for me.'

"Then they will go away to eternal punishment, but the righteous to eternal life."

Luke 10:25-37

On one occasion an expert in the law stood up to test Jesus. "Teacher," he asked, "what must I do to inherit eternal life?"

"What is written in the Law?" he replied. "How do you read it?"

He answered: "'Love the Lord your God with all your heart and with all your soul and with all your strength and with all your mind'; and, 'Love your neighbor as yourself.'"

"You have answered correctly," Jesus replied. "Do this and you will live."

But he wanted to justify himself, so he asked Jesus, "And who is my neighbor?"

In reply Jesus said: "A man was going down from Jerusalem to Jericho, when he fell into the hands of robbers. They stripped him of his clothes, beat him and went away, leaving him half dead. A priest happened to be going down the same road, and when he saw the man, he passed by on the other side. So too, a Levite, when he came to the place and saw him, passed by on the other side. But a Samaritan, as he traveled, came where the man was; and when he saw him, he took pity on him. He went to him and bandaged his wounds, pouring on oil and wine. Then he put the man on his own donkey, took him to an inn and took care of him. The next day he took out two silver coins and gave them to the innkeeper. 'Look after him,' he said, 'and when I return, I will reimburse you for any extra expense you may have.'

"Which of these three do you think was a neighbor to the man who fell into the hands of robbers?"

The expert in the law replied, "The one who had mercy on him."

Jesus told him, "Go and do likewise."

THE POWERLESSNESS OF THE PAGANS

"The doctors were quite incapable of treating the disease because of their ignorance of the right methods. . . . Equally useless were prayers made in the temples, consultation of the oracles, and so forth; indeed, in the end people were so overcome by their sufferings that they paid no further attention to such things."

—Thucydides, on the plague in Athens of 431 B.C.,
in his *History of the Peloponnesian War*

"The heathen behaved in the very opposite way. At the first onset of the disease, they pushed the sufferers away and fled from their dearest, throwing them into the roads before they were dead, and treated unburied corpses as dirt, hoping thereby to avert the spread and contagion of the fatal disease; but do what they might, they found it difficult to escape."

—Dionysius (died about 264), bishop of Alexandria

"The impious Galileans support not only their own poor but ours as well, everyone can see that our people lack aid from us."

—Emperor Julian (361–63), complaining that Christians cared for Christian and pagan alike

A REVOLUTIONARY NEW CARE

"It is our care of the helpless, our practice of loving kindness that brands us in the eyes of many of our opponents. 'Only look,' they say, 'look how they love one another!'"

—Tertullian, Carthaginian theologian, *Apology*

"Our compassion spends more in the streets than yours does in the temples."

—Tertullian

"How suitable, how necessary it is that this plague and pestilence, which seems horrible and deadly, searches out the justice of each and every one and examines the minds of the human race; whether the well care for the sick, whether relatives dutifully love their kinsmen as they should, whether masters show compassion for their ailing slaves, whether physicians do not desert the afflicted."

—Cyprian, bishop of Carthage

"Most of our brother Christians showed unbounded love and loyalty; never sparing themselves and thinking only of one another. Heedless of the danger, they took charge of the sick, attending to their every need and ministering to them in Christ, and with them departed this life serenely happy; for they were infected by others with the disease, drawing on themselves the sickness of their neighbors and cheerfully accepting their pains. Many, in nursing and curing others, transferred their death to themselves and died in their stead."

—Dionysius, describing Christian care for the sick during a plague

"The people being assembled together, he first of all urges on them the benefits of mercy. . . . Then he proceeds to add that there is nothing remarkable in cherishing merely our own people with the due attentions of love, but that one might become perfect who should *do something more than heathen men or publicans,* one who, overcoming evil with good, and practicing a merciful kindness like that of God, should love his enemies as well. . . . Thus the good was done to all men, not merely to the household of faith."

—Pontanius, on Cyprian's instructions to his church

"We have no longer to look on the fearful and pitiable sight of men like corpses before death, with the greater part of their limbs dead, driven from cities, from dwellings, from public places, from water-courses. Basil it was more than anyone who persuaded those who are men not to scorn men, nor to dishonor Christ the head of all by their inhumanity to human beings."

—Gregory of Nazianzus, describing a visit to the Basileias, the new hospitals-cum-poor-centers set up by Christians in about 372 in Cappadocia

"We must, then, open the doors to all the poor and all those who are victims of disasters, whatever the causes may be, since we have been told to *rejoice with those who rejoice and to weep with those who weep* (Romans 12:12). And since we are human beings, we must pay our debt of goodness to our fellow human beings, whatever the cause of their plight: orphanhood, exile, cruelty of the master, rashness of those who govern, inhumanity of tax-collectors, brutality of blood-thirsty bandits, greediness of thieves, confiscation, or shipwreck. All are equally miserable and look up to our hands in the same way as we look up to those of God whenever we stand in need of something."

—Gregory of Nazianzus, "On the Love of the Poor"

"Of all human calamities, famine is the principal one, and the most miserable of deaths is no doubt that by starvation. . . . It dries up the natural liquids, diminishes the body heat, contracts the size, and little by little drains off the strength. The flesh clings to the bones like a cobweb. The skin has no color. . . . The belly is hollow, contracted, formless, without weight, without the natural stretching of the viscera, joined to the bones of the back. Now, what punishment should not be inflicted upon the one who passes by such a body? . . . The person who can cure such an infirmity and because of avarice refuses his medicine, can with reason be condemned as a murderer."

—Basil of Caesarea, "Homilies Delivered in Times of Famine and Drought"

"For nothing can so make a man an imitator of Christ as caring for his neighbors."

—St. John Chrysostom, *Homily XXV*

The Christian faith introduced "the most revolutionary and decisive change in the attitude of society toward the sick. . . . The social position of the sick man thus became fundamentally different from what it had been before. He assumed a preferential position which has been his ever since."

—Henry Sigerist, *A History of Medicine*

It was the Christians' success in creating a community that cared both for its own and for others that was "a major cause, perhaps the strongest single cause, of the spread of Christianity."

—E. R. Dodds, *Pagan and Christian in an Age of Anxiety*

Saint Francis of Assisi

Francis of Assisi (1181–1226) is one of the best known and most loved saints in Christian history. Born in Assisi, the son of a rich cloth merchant, Francis was high-spirited and generous. But after converting dramatically and being publicly disowned by his father, he took a vow of poverty and dedicated his life to serving the poor and restoring both churches and the Church. As the founder of the Franciscan Order and its companion society for women under St. Clare, his life, preaching, and travels made him an enormous force for the "evangelical ideal" of "living after the gospel."

Francis's passionate devotion to God, his simple and unaffected faith, and his deep generosity and compassion to those suffering are all clearly evident in the famous incident of his kissing the leper. It was the year of his conversion and he was still the rich, young son of a nobleman. The following description is from a biography, Saint Francis of Assisi, *by the Danish scholar Johannes Jörgensen. This was truly a kiss that echoed around the world, rejuvenating the early Christian dedication to the poor, the sick, the suffering, and the outcast.*

Kissing the Leper

The lepers occupied a very particular position among the sick and poor of the Middle Ages. Based on a passage in the Prophet Isaiah (53:4) the lepers were looked upon as an image of the Redeemer, more than all other sufferers. As early as the days of Gregory the Great we find the story of the monk, Martyrius, who met a leper by the wayside, who from pain and weariness was fallen to the ground and could drag himself no further. Martyrius wrapped the sick man in his cloak and carried him to his convent. But the leper changed in his arms to Jesus himself, who rose to heaven as he blessed the monk, and said to him: "Martyrius, thou wert not ashamed of me on earth; I will not be ashamed of thee in heaven!"

. . . And so the lepers were more than any others an object for pious care during the Middle Ages. For them was founded a special order of knights—Knights of Lazarus—whose whole office was to take care of the lepers. So too there were erected all over Europe the numerous houses of St. George, where the lepers were taken care of in a sort of cloistered life. Of these lepers' homes there were 19,000 in the thirteenth century. But in spite of everything the life of the leper was sad enough; they were repulsed by the rest of humanity, and they were hedged in by severe laws isolating them and hemming them in on all sides.

As with all other cities, there was also in the vicinity of Assisi a lepers' hospital — the lepers were in fact the first real hospital patients and in some languages their name expresses this fact. The hospital lay midway between Assisi and Portiuncula. . . .

On his walks in this place, Francis now and then passed by the hospital, but the mere sight of it had filled him with horror. He would not even give an alms to a leper unless someone else would take it for him. Especially when the wind blew from the hospital, and the weak, nauseating odor, peculiar to the leper, came across the road, he would hurry past with averted face and fingers in his nostrils.

It was in this that he felt his greatest weakness, and in it he was to win his greatest victory.

For one day, as he was as usual calling upon God, it happened that the answer came. And the answer was this: "Francis! Everything which you have loved and desired in the flesh it is your duty to despise and hate, if you wish to know my will. And when you have begun thus, all that which now seems to you sweet and lovely will become intolerable and bitter, but all which you used to avoid will turn itself to great sweetness and exceeding joy."

These were the words which at last gave Francis a definite program, which showed him the way he was to follow. He certainly pondered over these words in his lonely rides over the Umbrian plain and, just as he one day woke out of reverie, he found the horse making a sudden movement, and saw on the road before him, only a few steps distant, *a leper,* in his familiar uniform.

Francis started, and even his horse shared in the movement, and his first impulse was to turn and flee as fast as he could. But there were the words he had heard within himself, so clearly before him — "what you used to abhor shall be to you joy and sweetness." . . . And *what* had he hated more than the lepers? Here was the time to take the Lord at His word — to show his good will. . . .

And with a mighty victory over himself, Francis sprang from his horse, approached the leper, from whose deformed countenance the awful odor of corruption issued forth, placed his alms in the outstretched wasted hand — bent down quickly and kissed the fingers of the sick man, covered with the awful disease, whilst his system was nauseated with the action. . . .

When he again sat upon his horse, he hardly knew how he had got there. He was overcome by excitement, his heart beat, he knew not whither he rode.

But the Lord had kept his word. Sweetness, happiness, and joy streamed into his soul—flowed and kept flowing, although his soul seemed full and more full—like the clear stream which, filling an earthen vessel, keeps on pouring and flows over its rim, with an ever clearer, purer stream. . . .

The next day Francis voluntarily wandered down the road he had hitherto always avoided—the road to San Salvatore delle Pareti. And when he reached the gate he knocked, and when it was opened to him he entered. From all the cells the sick came swarming out—came with their half-destroyed faces, blind inflamed eyes, with club-feet, with swollen, corrupted arms and fingerless hands. And all this dreadful crowd gathered around the young merchant, and the odor from their unclean swellings was so strong that Francis against his will for a moment had to hold his breath to save himself from sickness. But he soon recovered control of himself, he drew out the well-filled purse he had brought with him, and began to deal out his alms. And on every one of the dreadful hands that were reached out to take his gifts he imprinted a kiss, as he had done the day before.

From Johannes Jörgensen, *St. Francis of Assisi*, trans. T. O'Conor Sloane (Garden City, New York: Image Books, 1955). © 1912 by Longmans, Green & Co., Inc.; © 1939 by T. O'Conor Sloane.

BEGGARLY TO BEGGARS?

"I happen to think the whole modern attitude toward beggars is entirely heathen and inhuman. . . . Everyone would expect to have to help a man to save his life in a shipwreck; why not a man who has suffered a shipwreck of his life?"

—G. K. Chesterton

WESLEY'S RULE

"Do all the good you can,
By all the means you can;
In all the ways you can,
In all the places you can,
At all the times you can,
To all the people you can,
As long as ever you can."

—John Wesley

"What is nobody's business is my business."

—Clara Barton, founder, American Red Cross

QUESTIONS FOR THOUGHT AND DISCUSSION

1. What separate motivations for compassion to the poor do you see in the readings from Leviticus, Deuteronomy, Matthew, and Luke? How are these motives different from what you read in the writings of the Greeks and the Romans?

2. What are the practical ways for caring for "the alien, the fatherless, and the widow" as mentioned in the Scriptures? Who else in need is mentioned? What is the connection to remembering Egypt?

3. Why do you think God emphasizes justice when speaking of caring for the poor and needy?

4. Jesus responded to the lawyer's question, "Who is my neighbor?" with a parable. What was the point of the story? Why do you think Jesus specifically mentioned a priest, a Levite, and a Samaritan?

5. How was Francis of Assisi able to conquer his "greatest weakness"? What are the differences between his first encounter with a leper and the second? Why do you think the second encounter was easier for him? What do you think was behind this "weakness" of his?

Rembrandt van Rijn, Beggars Receiving Alms at the Door of a House. Reproduced by permission of the National Gallery of Art, Washington, Rosenwald Collection.

6. In kissing the lepers, not just handing them alms, what did Francis give them? What did he give himself in this act?

7. What lessons can we learn from this story of Francis? Who are the "lepers" of our day?

8. Francis of Assisi was the most famous proponent of the vow-of-poverty approach to human need. What dimensions of this older approach have been lost in the shift to our modern vow-of-wealth approach?

THREE
THE RISE OF MODERN PHILANTHROPY

WHETHER PROVIDENTIAL OR COINCIDENTAL, THE YEAR 1776 WITNESSED BOTH THE BIRTH *of the United States and the publication of Adam Smith's* The Wealth of Nations. *Modern capitalism simultaneously found its champion and its herald.*

The rise of modern capitalism proved decisive for philanthropy too. In general terms it caused the shift from the "vow of poverty" approach of the medieval world to the "vow of wealth" approach of the modern world. More particularly, it created the astonishing wealth that made modern forms of philanthropy possible and led to the rise of highly original modern innovations—the voluntary association and the foundation.

But for all the unquestionable strengths and profound contributions of our modern approaches, we must not be uncritical. There is evidence, for example, that the foundation movement is showing signs of betraying the vision of its founders, just as the late-medieval monasteries betrayed those of St. Benedict and St. Francis. We might even see a modern equivalent of Henry VIII's dissolution of the monasteries—a contemporary uprising against the indifference to real need by those sometimes called "the elite's elite."

Our task here, however, is not to speculate. Rather it is to trace the rise of modern philanthropy, to recognize the challenges behind its

A medal issued in 1797 to commemorate The Wealth of Nations.

135

origins, to appreciate the main debates that shaped its attitudes and initiatives, and to analyze the wisdom and energies that led to its present institutional forms.

In particular, we will explore the two main innovations of the modern world (the voluntary association and the foundation) and the two main schools of thought as to the best approach to philanthropy. In their original nineteenth-century forms, these schools of thought are called the "Social Calvinists" and the "Social Universalists," but the discussion of giving and caring is far from mostly history. These positions are highly vocal and deeply consequential today. Needless to say, there were many charitable initiatives outside these two main schools—the Roman Catholic Church, for example, was prolific in its work on behalf of the poor and needy. But these two schools were the most prominent in their time and have left the most influential legacy today.

POINT TO PONDER: _____

Social Conditions

If modern capitalism made modern philanthropy possible, modern poverty made it necessary. Prior to 1800, help came to most people from one of three main sources, which formed a kind of three-legged stool—families, churches and synagogues, or neighbors. But with the convergence of capitalism, the Industrial Revolution, and the population explosion in England in the late eighteenth century, millions in Europe and North America encountered the rise of the modern world as a tearing away from their traditional communities and systems of support.

Many people who justifiably celebrate the triumphs and virtues of market capitalism today fail to acknowledge this point: A savage price and brutal uprooting were the cost of the Industrial Revolution on the first generations experiencing it.

If modern capitalism made modern philanthropy possible, modern poverty made it necessary.

THE COST OF CAPITALISM

"The early period of industrial capitalism in England, and probably in other Western countries, exacted considerable human costs, if not in an actual decline in material living standards then in social and cultural dislocation."

—Peter L. Berger, *The Capitalist Revolution*,
proposition 4 of 50 propositions about prosperity, equality, and liberty

---

Reasons of space preclude our doing justice to describing the terrible social conditions of the early Industrial Revolution. But readers of Charles Dickens on London, Friedrich Engels on the British Midlands, Victor Hugo on Paris, and Jacob Riis and Charles Loring Brace on New York can easily conjure up pictures of the grim, cruel, inhumane, "Dickensian" world that was the reverse side of early modern prosperity.

More than humanitarianism is at stake in appreciating these appalling conditions. Despite heroic and remarkably effective responses in countless ways, many people grew convinced that major responses to such dire problems were beyond the resources of private charity. The climate was created in which one answer was to develop a new view of philanthropy that sought to identify and eliminate the causes of social problems rather than just ameliorate them. The answer was to develop the rationale for the modern welfare state.

DICKENSIAN

"We have come to this absurd, this dangerous, this monstrous pass, that the dishonest felon is, in respect of cleanliness, order, diet, and accommodation, better provided for, and taken care of, than the honest pauper."

—Charles Dickens, "A Walk in a Workhouse"

"In the dark loneliness of the mines men, women, and children work in great heat and the majority of them take off most (if not all) of their clothes. You can imagine the consequences for yourself. There are more illegitimate children in the mining districts than elsewhere."

—Friedrich Engels,
The Condition of the Working-Class in England in 1844

"The *mass* of poverty and wretchedness is, of course, far greater in the English capital. There are classes with inherited pauperism and crime more deeply stamped in them, in London or Glasgow, than we ever behold in New York; but certain small districts can be found in our metropolis with the unhappy fame of containing more human beings packed to the square yard, and stained with more acts of blood and riot, within a given period, than is true of any other equal space of earth in the civilized world."

—Charles Loring Brace
The Dangerous Classes of New York, 1872

"Meanwhile the cities spiraled out of control. New York was four times as large in 1900 as it had been in 1860; Chicago was fully fifty-five times as big. Unplanned, with public funds pilfered, the cities became gigantic hellholes for the system's cheap "manpower." . . . They were literally the worst in the world. In 1894, New York's Sanitation District A included thirty-two acres on which more than 31,000 people attempted to live—a density of 986 people per acre. The highest density in Bombay, India, was 759 people per acre; Prague had only 485 per acre in what were known as the worst ghettoes in Europe."

—Harvey Wasserman, *History of the United States*

"One journalist, Oliver Dyer, calculated that if all the New York's post-Civil War liquor shops (5,500), houses of prostitution (647, by his count), gambling halls, and other low-life establishments were placed for a night on a single street, they would reach from City Hall in lower Manhattan to White Plains thirty miles away, with a robbery every 165 yards, a murder every half mile, and thirty reporters offering sensational detail."

—Marvin Olasky, *The Tragedy of American Compassion*

THE RISE OF THE
⁘VOLUNTARY ASSOCIATIONS⁘

"Americans of all ages, all conditions, and all dispositions constantly form associations. . . . Wherever at the head of a great undertaking you see the government in France, or a man of rank in England, in the United States you will be sure to find an association." Few passages from Alexis de Tocqueville are more quoted than this one, especially in our day when an "associational revolution" seems to be sweeping the world. The measure of a free society, it is often said today, is reflected in the vitality of its free associations—the freedom of citizens to organize a group to promote an idea or cause, whether new or dissenting.

This picture usually ties in with a golden view of voluntarism: volunteer fire-fighters rushing to save the blazing homes of neighbors, farmers joining together to raise a barn, collection plates passing down the aisles of countless churches and synagogues, wives and mothers going door-to-door collecting for worthy causes, and so on.

But even American voluntarism cannot be traced back simply to colonial or frontier life. Voluntary associations were few and small in America before the period of 1790 to 1820. However, the seeds of the idea were certainly there, in that freedom of association correlates to freedom of conscience. The voluntary church, with its voluntary membership and voluntary contributions, is the historical prototype of the voluntary association.

The framers, however, were actually resistant to such associations because of their fear of the power of "factions." In his Leviathan (1651), Thomas Hobbes had attacked voluntary associations and the voluntary principle. Since nothing should exist apart from state control, he maintained, voluntary associations were "worms in the entrails of Leviathan." Similarly, George Washington in his Farewell Address warned against "all combinations and associations, under whatever plausible character, with the real design to direct, counteract, or awe the regular deliberation and action of the constituted authorities."

Voluntary associations actually began flowering strongly only slightly before de Tocqueville's trip to the United States in 1831. During the 1820s and 1830s, the Second Great Awakening, a spiritual renewal emphasizing good works, was sweeping the nation and produced many voluntary associations. In particular,

Presbyterian minister Lyman Beecher issued a revolutionary call for a "society for the Suppression of Vice and the Promotion of Good Morals" in New Haven, Connecticut, in 1812. But while birthed in the Second Awakening, the voluntary associations have three principlal roots.

One root was the disintegration of ways of life and work based on the family, especially the traditional independence of subsistence farming. As people were exposed to wider market forces, they felt the need to band together in new associations. Another was the enormously successful precedent of the British abolition movement led by such evangelical leaders as William Wilberforce and his "Clapham Sect." Wilberforce, described as "Prime minister over a cabinet of philanthropists," succeeded in numerous reforms because of his many effective voluntary associations. A third influence on the voluntary movement in America was the effect of the second wave of disestablishment in the 1820s and 1830s. No longer did states have an established church—Connecticut was the last to declare that Congregationalism was no longer the state's official church. During this period, the emphasis of moral agency in public life shifted from churches as institutions to individual Christians acting as individuals in public life—in association.

As people were exposed to wider market forces, they felt the need to band together in new associations.

This history forms the backdrop of the influential speeches of Lyman Beecher and Congregationalist Leonard Bacon, who were grappling with the implications of disestablishment in Connecticut. In words that anticipate Andrew Carnegie's later call for foundations, they argued that "the benevolent institutions of these days, give to the humblest individual the power of doing good to all men, in a sense in which it was once the prerogative of princes."

Whatever the causes, volunteering and voluntary associations are now recognized as vital components of the "social capital" of all democratic societies. A number of fundamental ideas are present:

First and most obviously, individuals can do jointly what they cannot do singly. Power in a society of equals is the product of voluntary association.

Second, voluntarism as a fruit of freedom of conscience widens the sphere of liberty and deepens the wellsprings of democracy.

Third, voluntary associations provide an important "mediating" role between the small, sometimes atomistic, world of individuals and the large, often abstract and impersonal, world of the state.

Fourth, voluntary associations provide a sometimes creative, sometimes critical force that counters democracy's natural tendencies toward entropy. Simultaneously, the associations sustain a renewing stream to revitalize democracy.

For our purposes here, voluntary associations are historically important too, because they were a vital part of the early-nineteenth-century reform campaigns *against poverty. They were philanthropy's pre-political goads prodding society toward change. Or as their nineteenth-century proponents described them, they were the "disciplined moral militias" and "a mighty engine" on behalf of "the benevolent Empire"—the giving, caring, reforming culture that was the direct product of the Second Great Awakening.*

Alexis de Tocqueville

Alexis de Tocqueville (1805–1859) was a French statesman and author of the celebrated study Democracy in America. *The son of a nobleman who was imprisoned during the French Revolution, he grew up with a deep sense of the epochal, transitional character of his times. Tocqueville and his friend Gustave de Beaumont arrived in New York in May 1831. Officially, they were on a French government mission to examine American prisons. But their real purpose was to analyze the young American democracy. Nine months, seven thousand miles, hundreds of interviews, and fourteen packed notebooks later, they returned to France with their commission completed.*

The first volume of Democracy in America *was published in 1835 and the second in 1840, receiving instant, almost universal, acclaim. The study is one of the best, most accurate, and most quoted books written about the United States. At once penetrating and comprehensive, it is a wide-canvas panorama of America fifty years after the Revolution. The passage below describes a defining feature of the American experiment: that the constitutionally protected right to free association was crucial for democracy to thrive. In early America, doing good was rarely done alone.*

Democracy in America

The political associations that exist in the United States are only a single feature in the midst of the immense assemblage of associations in that country. Americans of all ages, all conditions, and all dispositions constantly form associations. They have not only commercial and manufacturing companies, in which all take part, but associations of a thousand other kinds, religious, moral, serious, futile, general or restricted, enormous or diminutive. The Americans make associations to give entertainments, to found seminaries, to build inns, to construct churches, to diffuse books, to send missionaries to the antipodes; in this manner they found hospitals, prisons, and schools. If it is proposed to inculcate some truth or to foster some feeling by the encouragement of a great example, they form a society. Wherever at the head of some new undertaking you see the government in France, or a man of rank in England, in the United States you will be sure to find an association.

Wherever at the head of some new undertaking you see the government in France, or a man of rank in England, in the United States you will be sure to find an association.

I met with several kinds of associations in America of which I confess I had no previous notion; and I have often admired the extreme skill with which the inhabitants of the United States succeed in proposing a common object for the exertions of a great many men and inducing them voluntarily to pursue it.

I have since traveled over England, from which the Americans have taken some of their laws and many of their customs; and it seemed to me that the principle of association was by no means so constantly or adroitly used in that country. The English often perform great things singly, whereas the Americans form associations for the smallest undertakings. It is evident that the former people consider association as a powerful means of action, but the latter seem to regard it as the only means they have of acting.

Thus the most democratic country on the face of the earth is that in which men have, in our time, carried to the highest perfection the art of pursuing in common the object of their common desires and have applied this new science to the greatest number of purposes. Is this the result of accident, or is there in reality any necessary connection between the principle of association and that of equality?

Aristocratic communities always contain, among a multitude of persons who by themselves are powerless, a small number of powerful and wealthy citizens, each of whom can achieve great undertakings single-handed. In aristocratic societies men do not need to combine in order to act, because they are strongly held together. Every wealthy and powerful citizen constitutes the head of a permanent and compulsory association, composed of all those who are dependent upon him or whom he makes subservient to the execution of his designs.

Among democratic nations, on the contrary, all the citizens are independent and feeble; they can do hardly anything by themselves, and none of them can oblige his fellow men to lend him their assistance. They all, therefore, become powerless if they do not learn voluntarily to help one another. If men living in democratic countries had no right and no inclination to associate for political purposes, their independence would be in great jeopardy, but they might long preserve their wealth and their cultivation: whereas if they never acquired the habit of forming associations in ordinary life, civilization itself would be endangered. A people among whom individuals lost the power of achieving great things single-handed, without acquiring the means of producing them by united exertions, would soon relapse into barbarism. . . .

Feelings and opinions are recruited, the heart is enlarged, and the human mind is developed only by the reciprocal influence of men upon one another. I have shown that these influences are almost null in democratic countries; they must therefore be artificially created, and this can only be accomplished by associations. . . .

As soon as several of the inhabitants of the United States have taken up an opinion or a feeling which they wish to promote in the world, they look out for mutual assistance; and as soon as they have found one another out, they combine. From that moment they are no longer isolated men, but a power seen from afar, whose actions serve for an example and whose language is listened to. . . .

Among the laws that rule human societies there is one which seems to be more precise and clear than all others. If men are to remain civilized or to become so, the art of associating together must grow and improve in the same ratio in which the equality of conditions is increased.

Alexis de Tocqueville, *Democracy in America*, trans. J. P. Mayer, Volume II, Chapter 5. © 1945 and renewed 1973 by Alfred A. Knopf, Inc. Reprinted by permission of the publisher.

VOLUNTARISM IN AN OPEN SOCIETY

No matter how good an idea, "if it does not incarnate, it will dissipate."

—James Luther Adams,
the leading U.S. theorist of the voluntary association

"Where two or three Americans are gathered together it is likely that a committee is being formed."

—James Luther Adams

The United States is "the association-land *par excellence*."

—Max Weber

The American people are "a nation of joiners."

—Max Lerner

"In most other developed countries, the volunteer tradition was crushed by the Welfare State. In Japan, for instance, temples and Shinto shrines were active centers of community service with strong participation by local volunteers. The 1867 Meiji Restoration 'Westernized' by making religion into a government function—and both the volunteers and the temple community services soon disappeared. In Britain, all through the nineteenth century charity was a community activity and seen as a responsibility of the well-to-do. After 1890, with the growing belief in government as the master of society, most of this disappeared. The Salvation Army (founded in London in 1878) is one of the few survivors of what was a flourishing culture of community service in Victorian times. And in France, any community action that is not organized and controlled by government has been suspect since Napoleon, and is in fact considered almost subversive."

—Peter Drucker, *Post-Capitalist Society*

"Even the church is financed by the government, and the creation of even one non-profit philanthropic organization would be a quantum jump."

—comment on Sweden in "Care and Welfare at the Crossroads,"
a study by the Swedish Secretariat for Futures Studies

"Where two or three Americans are gathered together and speaking of 'service,' you may be sure that someone is going to get 'gypped.'"

—H. L. Mencken

QUESTIONS FOR THOUGHT AND DISCUSSION

1. What differences did de Tocqueville observe in the ways English and Americans accomplished things? What was it in each society that produced these differences?
2. Why does de Tocqueville argue that democracy needs voluntary associations—not only to thrive but to survive? Why does he say that associations are necessary "if men are to remain civilized"? What is your assessment of his argument?
3. In the box, "Voluntarism in an Open Society," Peter Drucker notes the effects a welfare state has on its associations. Why would a government consider voluntary associations subversive?
4. What are the pluses and minuses in the institution of voluntary associations? Based on the voluntary associations you know from firsthand experience, how healthy do you think most are today?

❧ *Leonard Bacon* ❧

Leonard Bacon (1801–1881) was born in a log cabin on the Michigan frontier. Although he grew up poor, he graduated from Yale and Andover Theological Seminary and then attained a position as a Congregationalist clergyman with the highly influential First Church of New Haven. His mentor was Lyman Beecher, an important preacher during the Second Great Awakening. Bacon fought against slavery, wrote several books, and became a professor of theology at Yale.

This reading is from one of his most influential sermons in the 1830s — just before de Tocqueville's visit. He reminds his audience that they are stewards, not owners, of their property. Yet the responsibility for their decisions is their own, not their church's or pastor's. In urging their constructive participation in all kinds of voluntary associations, he issues a call that flowered in the energetic voluntarism of the "benevolent empire" and makes a transition from the more church-centered emphasis of earlier days to the voluntarist spirit mirrored here.

The Christian Doctrine of Stewardship in Respect to Property ❧

Every man is bound to regard all his property, and all the avails of his industry and enterprise, as belonging to God; he is to hold it all, and manage it, as a sacred trust for which he must give account to the supreme proprietor; he is to apply it and dispose of it exclusively as the Lord's servant, and in the work of the Lord. . . .

The church was not formed to manage the property of its members, or to command their charitable efforts; nor can it show any commission to that effect. You are a steward not for the church, but for God. The property which you have, or may have in possession, belongs to you; as an individual and not as a member of the church; and you as an individual, must account for it to the supreme proprietor. . . .

I have not said that your property belongs, or must be given, to the Missionary society or the Bible society, or to any or every benevolent institution.

The property which you have, or may have in possession, belongs to you; as an individual and not as a member of the church; and you as an individual, must account for it to the supreme proprietor.

I say your property is entrusted to your individual keeping, and not to the keeping of any other individual, or of any association whatever. If you wish to avail yourself of the principle of combination with others, in order to accomplish some important good which separate and unconnected efforts could not so well accomplish; you have a right to do so. And the many benevolent associations of the day, afford you abundant opportunities for the exercise of that right. . . .

And just so far as in your deliberate and conscientious judgment, you can accomplish more good by combining your contributions and your efforts with those of others, in one and another or in all of these benevolent associations, or in any other way, just so far you are bound to do so. Still, however, your property is your own. The fact, that some other man, or some association of men, might manage it better, and employ it for good ends more effectively than you can, makes it none the less yours or gives to any man, or to any association of men, any shadow of proprietorship over that which God has committed to your keeping, and for which he holds you singly responsible.

. . . You may look abroad over the wide world, you may calculate its wants; you may "take the gauge and dimensions" of its misery; and you may set yourself to work for its renovation. You may send, not your benevolent desires alone, but your actual beneficence, all round the globe. There is no land which your bounty cannot reach—I had almost said, no tribe or family which you cannot help to enlighten and to bless. You may strike off the fetters of the slave, and send him back, a glad freeman, to the land which God gave to his fathers. You may at once bear a part in taming the fierce warrior of the wilderness, and cooperate with ten thousand fellow-laborers in breaking down the idol temples of the east. You may extend the cup of salvation to him who pants beneath the tropics, and at the same time send the genial radiance of the sun of righteousness to cheer the shivering natives of the farthest north. All this is your privilege. It is the privilege of the age which other generations will mark as the era of combined and associated efforts for the salvation of the world. . . .

The benevolent institutions of these days, give to the humblest individual the power of doing good to all men, in a sense in which it was once the prerogative of princes. How many holy men of old, as they looked over the world, and, amazed at its miseries, cried, O Lord how long!—would have rejoiced at such a privilege. How would it have cheered them—how would it have made their hearts to overflow with praise—how would it have impelled them to new diligence, new self-denial, new intensity of effort, could they have seen this day. And does this privilege bring with it no proportionate responsibility? Think you that, such a price having been put into your hands, you shall not be constrained to account for it? Are you God's steward; and can you let slip such golden opportunities of applying most effectively for the advancement of his interests, that which he has entrusted to your discretion; and shall you not give a fearful account of your neglect in the day when you appear before him?

Leonard Bacon, *The Christian Doctrine of Stewardship in Respect to Property* (Sermon to the Young Men's Benevolent Society, New Haven, CT, 1832).

ENCOURAGED BY WILBERFORCE AND HIS FRIENDS

"The abolition of the Slave Trade in England, and in our own country, is a memorable exhibition of what may be done by well directed, persevering efforts. . . . It is not yet fifty years since this first effort was made, and now the victory is won. Who produced this mighty revolution? A few men at first, lifted up their voice and were reinforced by others, till the immortal work was done. . . . Other efforts of the same kind have been crowned with similar success. A society was established in London about the year 1697, to suppress vice, by promoting execution of the laws. . . .

"Similar societies have been formed in England at different times, ever since. In 1802, a very respectable society of the above description was established in London. It experienced at first most virulent opposition, but has completely surmounted every obstacle, and now commands fear and respect, and gratitude. Such has been its influence in preventing crimes, that at one annual meeting, the number of convictions reported was an hundred and seventy-eight, at the next only seventy. As it respects the observation of the Sabbath particularly, the whole city of London exhibits, to a considerable degree, a new face. A vast number of shops are closed, which used to be open on that day. The butchers of several markets have thanked the society, for compelling them to an act of which they find productive of so much comfort to themselves, and have even associated to secure that triumph, which the labours of the society had won."

—Lyman Beecher, "A Reformation of Morals," 1812

OLD GOALS, NEW GOADS

"The value of associations is to be measured by the energy, the freedom, the activity, the moral power, which they encourage and diffuse. In truth, the great object of all benevolence is to give power, activity, and freedom to others."

—William Ellery Channing, "Remarks on Associations," 1831

"It is by the constant energy and strong attraction of powerful institutions only that the needed intellectual and moral power can be applied; and the present is the age of founding them. If this work be done, and well done, our country is safe, and the world's hope is secure. The government of force will cease, and that of intelligence and virtue will take its place; and nation after nation, cheered by our example, will follow in our footsteps, till the whole earth is free."

—Lyman Beecher, "A Plea for the West," 1835

"They say ministers have lost their influence. The fact is, that they have gained. By voluntary efforts, societies, missions, and revivals, they exert a deeper influence than ever they could by queues, and shoe buckles, and cocked hats, and gold-headed canes. . . . The great aim of the Christian Church in relation to the present life is not only to renew the individual man, but also to reform human society. That it may do this needs full and free scope. The Protestantism of the Old World is still fettered by the union of the Church with the State. Only in the United States of America has the experiment been tried of applying Christianity directly to man and to society without intervention of the state."

—Lyman Beecher

"It may be said, without much exaggeration, that everything is done now by societies. Many have learned what wonders can be accomplished in certain cases by union, and seem to think that union is competent to do everything. You can scarcely name an object for which some institution has not been formed. Would men make one set of opinions, or crush another? They make a Society. Would they improve the penal code, or relieve poor debtors? They form Societies. Would one class encourage horse-racing, and another discourage traveling on Sunday? They form Societies. . . . To the philanthropist and the Christian it is exceedingly interesting, for it is a mighty engine, and must act, for good or evil, to an extent which no man can foresee or comprehend."

—Anonymous author, "Associations," 1830s

QUESTIONS FOR THOUGHT AND DISCUSSION

1. Of Bacon's first two paragraphs, one conveys traditional ideas and one has novel ones. Which is which? What lies behind the shift in the novel paragraph?

2. Who is making the decisions about how money is given and to whom? Why is this significant?

3. How does he use the ideas of stewardship and individual responsibility as primary motives for "combination with others"?

4. Read the famous paragraph beginning "You may look abroad over the wide world. . . . " What strikes you about its tone, themes, and sense of opportunities? Do you like it or view it as patronizing?

5. What types of good works does he say can be done in association? Is this different from what a church can accomplish? How and why?

6. In what ways does Bacon elevate the task of helping others? How are these incentives for pressing on?

7. Do we have the same confidence as Bacon in the capacity of "combined and associated efforts" to transform the world? What has happened since his time?

8. Read the Lyman Beecher quotations in the box "Old Goals, New Goads." What is the link between voluntary associations and the disestablishment of the church?

POINT TO PONDER: _____

Competing Schools of Philanthropy

Along with the appalling social conditions created by the early Industrial Revolution and the flowering of voluntary associations in the early 1800s, the nineteenth century was significant for a third reason: A long-running debate ensued between competing schools of philanthropy over the best philosophy and most effective approaches in attacking poverty and pauperism.

The nineteenth century saw three principal schools of philanthropy, each with its own philosophy and accompanying approach to poverty. Two schools have had an enduring influence today, although their names have disappeared. The third school, while short-lived as a philosophy, has had residual effects.

1. *Social Calvinism: This was the earliest, largest, and mostly evangelical Christian wing of philanthropy. It was known for its combination of seemingly limitless enterprise, its deep compassion, and its discriminating moral requirements of those it helped, such as "work-tests" that were set up to sort out the "deserving poor" from the "undeserving poor."*

2. *Social Universalism: This wing of nineteenth-century philanthropy blended theological liberalism with political socialism to produce a movement that grew into the dominant twentieth-century thinking. Characterized by strong universalist and utopian overtones, it relied confidently on the government.*

3. *Social Darwinism: A third nineteenth-century school has fortunately faded from the debate, though it still persists in the attitudes of many individuals. This movement was based on the theories of Charles Darwin and Herbert Spencer, especially those of natural selection and the survival of the fittest. More a school of thought in reaction to poverty, its implications for philanthropy were so hard-hearted and cruel that it was virtually "the party of anti-compassion." Fortunately, it was short-lived, but its resonance has not died completely in individual attitudes.*

The debates between the schools led at the end of the nineteenth century to the second great modern innovation—the rise of foundation-centered philanthropy. This movement, pioneered by Andrew Carnegie and John D. Rockefeller Sr., saw philanthropy as the business of "administering surplus wealth" and became the main engine of philanthropy in the twentieth century.

This development openly challenges the traditional Christian combination of "philanthropy" and "charity." Favoring philanthropy and rejecting charity, it is concerned with the enhancement of community and the future rather than the relief of suffering in the present.

The debate between these positions is not simply theoretical or historical. It held, and holds, the key to wise, effective philanthropy and responsible welfare. For at its heart lies a simple question that faces democratic societies a century later: How can a good society protect those who cannot protect themselves without being so generous that it subverts personal responsibility?

Ironically, today's arguments are an eerie echo of those in the nineteenth century. But people who know the earlier debate save themselves the trouble of reinventing the wheel. They also know that no one on any side has the final answer.

How can a good society protect those who cannot protect themselves without being so generous that it subverts personal responsibility?

❊ SOCIAL CALVINISM ❊

The Social Calvinists, composed mainly of evangelical Christians, were the earliest and largest wing of nineteenth-century initiators in philanthropy. Despite the name, most were not Calvinist in theology because of the meltdown and dismissal of Calvinism in the Second Awakening. But in their combination of warmheartedness and hard-headedness, they represented a throwback to earlier Calvinist thought.

Above all, the Social Calvinists believed that just as the Christian gospel was to be preached to all, knowing that only "the elect" would respond, so should they reach out in compassion to all in need, knowing that in the process "the deserving poor" would winnow themselves out from the undeserving through such means as work-tests. Thus the Social Calvinists were marked by deep compassion, tireless enterprise, and a willingness to give themselves and their time and money. But they were also distinctive for several reasons:

- *their drawing a line between poverty and pauperism*
- *their mistrust of "indiscriminate charity"*
- *their critical discernment of the giving process*
- *their requirement of moral responsibility in those they helped*
- *their belief that individual change was an irreplaceable part of social change*
- *their reluctance to rely on government*
- *their commitment to coalitions of charities*

Several examples were typical of this Social Calvinist school: Thomas Chalmers, who practically solved the problem of poverty in his parish in Glasgow, Scotland (and was a Calvinist in every sense of the word); Charles Loring Brace, who led the "Children's Aid Society" in New York; and the philanthropy readings in the McGuffey Eclectic Readers. Surveying the combined work, writer Josiah Strong commented in 1893, "Probably during no hundred years in the history of the world have there been saved so many thieves, gamblers, drunkards, and prostitutes as during the past quarter of a century."

Today the Social Calvinist arguments are championed by those, mainly conservative, who want to cut back the role of the government. But whether now or then, the decisive question facing this position is: Given the enormity of the needs arising out of the modern social crisis, can there be any hope of solutions relying on the independent sector alone? Does not the very scale of the problem make some form of private-public partnership inescapable?

Given the enormity of the needs arising out of the modern social crisis, can there be any hope of solutions relying on the independent sector alone?

BIBLICAL REALISM

"For even when we were with you, we gave you this rule: 'If a man will not work, he shall not eat.'"

—2 Thessalonians 3:10

"If anyone does not provide for his relatives, and especially for his immediate family, he has denied the faith and is worse than an unbeliever."

—1 Timothy 5:8

"The poor that can't work are objects for your liberality. But the poor that *can* work and *won't,* the best liberality to them is to *make* them."

—Cotton Mather, 1698

"Instead of exhorting you to augment your charity, I will rather utter an exhortation . . . that you may not *abuse* your charity by misapplying it."

—Cotton Mather

"Put yourself in the place of every poor man and deal with him as you would God deal with you."

—John Wesley

❈ S. Humphreys Gurteen ❈

The Reverend Stephen Humphreys Villiers Gurteen (1840–1898) was an Anglican minister who founded the Buffalo Charity Organization Society (COS) in 1877, the first in America to imitate the model of London's successful COS. Among many other functions, the various COSs investigated the backgrounds of those they helped (so as not to be taken in by "sob stories"), kept track of all applicants for funds (thereby preventing the nineteenth-century equivalent of "welfare queens"), and shared the information with all charities in the city. Social Calvinists often acted like those who today call themselves "social entrepreneurs"—using their resources creatively to help the poor find work, gain an education, and maintain a stable home.

The following reading from Gurteen's Handbook *shows his blend of compassion and practical realism. The three great principles of Social Calvinism stand out plainly: (1) Coordinate, (2) Investigate, and (3) Reconnect (the rich and the poor). Anyone tempted to dismiss the Social Calvinists for their hard-headedness should remember the monumental generosity and sacrificial quality of what they did. These were not just words.*

A Handbook of Charity Organization ᴊꙮ

One thing is certain; look where we will, there is not a single system, however well considered, which is found to be working beneficially. On the contrary, the cry comes from all sides that the wisest municipal systems are only aggravating the evil; are helping still more to pauperize the poor, and are virtually raising up an army of paupers. Take, as an example, the following statement from a report made by some of the ablest men in Scotland on the operation of the Poor-law in Edinburgh in 1868:

"It makes the industrious support the idle.

"It makes no distinction between poverty resulting from misfortune and poverty resulting from vice.

"It diminishes industry, frugality, and provident habits.

"It lessens the sympathy of the wealthier for the poorer classes.

"It destroys sympathy between the poor. . . .

"It tends to increase enormously the number and expense of the poor."

During the last fifty years we have entered upon the *fourth* stage in the method of dealing with Pauperism and Poverty, viz.: that of voluntary organization, when the people, the citizens, taking the matter in hand, and seeking to co-operate with the Church, the State and the Municipality, have endeavored to show what can be done in this matter of checking the curse of indiscriminate alms-giving, by the diffusion of sound, practical views and the adoption of wise, discriminating action. . . .

The avowed aim of this [London Charity Organization] Society was thus nothing less than the complete organization or banding together of all the charities, official and private, of a city of nearly four millions of people, and boasting of a greater number and a greater variety of charitable agencies than existed, perhaps, in any other city in the world. The leaders in this movement—the most prominent of England's statesmen and philanthropists—stated that their

During the last fifty years we have entered upon the fourth stage in the method of dealing with Pauperism and Poverty, viz.: that of voluntary organization, when the people, the citizens, taking the matter in hand, and seeking to co-operate with the Church, the State and the Municipality, have endeavored to show what can be done in this matter of checking the curse of indiscriminate alms-giving, by the diffusion of sound, practical views and the adoption of wise, discriminating action.

object was to sift out the helpless poor from the worthless pauper by means of thorough and searching investigation — to expose and prosecute impostors and fraudulent charitable societies — to stop street begging and vagrancy, and to better the condition of the honest poor. . . .

The necessity of good works is a cardinal point of Christianity. Accordingly, keeping our view fixed on the large cities, we see Charity moving from two different directions upon the outworks of Pauperism, with its army of gloomy retainers, and attacking, with varying success, the strongholds of the enemy. There is *official* charity, with its mechanical movement, in which the hand moves while the heart is untouched, taking note of naught save the bare fact of destitution, and but too often relieving the idleness of the community at the expense of its struggling industry, fostering habits of dependence, destroying manliness and self-respect, and tending to render pauperism a permanent institution, a positive profession.

Coming to the attack from an opposite direction, we find a vast band, composed of organized societies and noble-hearted individuals, each advancing upon some definite and favorite point. . . .

[I]t might at first sight be thought that nothing more could possibly be needed to meet and hold in check the advance of pauperism. Indeed, to a superficial observer it would seem that with such mighty appliances as the State, the Church, and the philanthropist have devised and put into operation in every large city, pauperism must be doomed, and its utter extinction be only a question of time.

As a matter of fact, however, pauperism, far from decreasing in large cities, is found, as a rule, to be steadily on the increase, and in spite of all the money and labor and appliances which have been brought to bear upon it, it has hitherto baffled all attempts which have been made to lessen, much less repress it. . . .

The fact is, the trouble does not lie in the Church, still less in Christianity, but in *ourselves* — not in the teaching of the Church, for the Church has never taught her children, as a religious duty, or even as an act of grace, to *give, asking no questions* — the trouble lies in the natural tendency of man to shirk a plain and Scriptural, ay, and arduous duty, and to adopt easy, unchurchly and irrational methods. Now the basic axiom, the cardinal principle of the "Charity Organization Society" is diametrically opposed to all systems, all institutions, all charities, all forms of relief whatsoever, which avowedly or tacitly adopt the creed of Charles Lamb to "give and ask no questions," or which is worse, that system of injudicious questioning at the door, or on the street, which leads the beggar on to invent additional falsehoods.

The fundamental law of its operation is expressed in one word, "INVESTI-GATE." Its motto is: "No relief (except in the extreme cases of despair or imminent death) without previous and searching examination." It says virtually to the distributors of official relief, "Refrain from giving a single cent until the individual case of each applicant has been thoroughly examined. The money which will be saved to the community by this means (if official charity is honestly and judiciously administered) will pay all the additional expense involved, and leave a handsome surplus to the city. . . . "

But let us bring one or two of the leading axioms of this Society to the test of Scripture. In one of the publications of this Society, the Poormasters of England are advised, as a rule, to give no relief to able-bodied men, except in return for work done; and this plan, which has been widely adopted, has been found to work marvels. On the one hand it has forced many a lazy, shiftless man back to his own field of labor, when he found that he could no longer be maintained in idleness at the public expense; while, on the other hand, the work performed by those willing to labor, has proved a vast saving to the public treasury, being employed, as it has been, on a variety of public works. This work-test is one of the most perfect touchstones for discriminating between the deserving and the undeserving that has ever been devised. When the managers of a Boston charity attached thereto a wood-yard, and announced that relief would be given to no able-bodied man, unless willing to do a certain amount of work, the daily number of applicants fell off at once from one hundred and sixty to forty-nine. In every city, in which the test has been applied, it has been eminently successful.

Is it, we ask, a very hard-hearted thing for the public to require an equivalent of labor, from those who are able to give it, in return for the relief which they receive? Is it unchristian? Is it not in the sweat of his brow that man is to eat his bread? Is not the Commandment, "Six days *shalt* thou labor?" And does not the apostle lay it down as a law, that "if any will not work, neither shall he eat?"

. . . But let us advance a step; let us leave behind us the floating pauperism of a great city, and look for a moment at the *resident* poor. What, it may be asked, does this Society propose to do in their behalf? Suppose, for example, that upon investigation the applicant is found to be a hard-working man, but reduced to the very verge of poverty by no fault of his own. Now, here we are confronted by what may be called a test case. It is *par excellence* a deserving case. It is a fair sample of that large class which, under ever-varying circumstances, form the chief care of a true, charitable organization. Here is the modern type of the man whom the Samaritan succored; a case of "helplessness," but arising from no personal fault. What, it may be asked, would be the action of the Society in this and similar cases?

It must be borne in mind, that by far the larger percentage of all the confirmed paupers in the country have hung for a time on this very border-line of involuntary poverty, and only by the sheer neglect, or still oftener through the misdirected charity of benevolent people, have they been dragged down to the lowest depths of confirmed pauperism. If, therefore, pauperism as an institution, a profession, is ever to be broken up, it can only be done by restoring the involuntary poor to a position of self-support, self-respect, and honorable ambition. If left to themselves and no kind hand is held out to assist, they will inevitably sink lower and lower, till perchance they end their course in suicide or felony.

If, therefore, pauperism as an institution, a profession, is ever to be broken up, it can only be done by restoring the involuntary poor to a position of self-support, self-respect, and honorable ambition.

If, on the other hand, our charity is not tempered by judgment, they will as inevitably learn to be *dependent,* till at last, though by degrees, every vestige of manliness and ambition will have been destroyed, and they will come back as skilled beggars, to torment and curse the very people whose so-called charity has made them what they are.

To avoid these two extremes, both of which are fatal, is the grand object of the Charity Organization Society. It views man as God has made him, with capabilities of manliness and self-respect and holy ambition. It views him as a moral being with capabilities for good that may be excited and elevated; or marred and destroyed. Its axiom, accordingly, is, "HELP THE POOR TO HELP THEMSELVES." Do not attempt simply to heal over the wound, but cure it internally.

. . . Now, what the Charity Organization Society is putting forth its utmost powers to effect, is the instilling into the minds of the poor, sounder and more ennobling views of what the word "home," in the highest sense of that term, really implies, *and to help them to reach this ideal.*

But how is so great a result to be attained?

The answer which the Society gives to this question is full of sound, practical wisdom. It says in effect: "Bridge the chasm between the rich and the poor. Instead of allowing it to widen year by year, close it gradually up." But how? By giving a handsome subscription from a full purse to this or that charity? By small doles of money or clothing to some favored individual? By doing our charity by proxy? No! "The proposal," says this Society, "is to bring back the rich into such close relations with the poor as cannot fail to have a civilizing and healing influence; a sympathetic pressure of the hand; kind words of encouragement and advice; the very knowledge that an influential, kind friend

"The proposal," says this Society, "is to bring back the rich into such close relations with the poor as cannot fail to have a civilizing and healing influence; a sympathetic pressure of the hand; kind words of encouragement and advice; the very knowledge that an influential, kind friend is watching the case to do any service in his power; this would, ere long, knit all classes together in the bonds of mutual help and good-will; everything else would follow."

is watching the case to do any service in his power; this would, ere long, knit all classes together in the bonds of mutual help and good-will; everything else would follow."

But how, again, is this brilliant dream to be realized *practically?* How is it to be practically carried out? It was Dr. Chalmers, of Glasgow, who, in his heroic efforts to deal with the poor of his own parish in that city, hit upon the plan which has since been adopted wherever the task of bringing city pauperism under control has been attempted. That plan was to subdivide the parish into manageable sections under responsible visitors. The idea, thus struck out, has been adopted with endless modifications by both religious and philanthropic organizations. In New York, in Boston, in Edinburgh, in Elberfeld, wherever the poor are massed, it has been tried and approved. The Hebrew community in London, some years ago issued a report which showed that Dr. Chalmers' idea had solved for them one of the most difficult problems with which they had had to grapple.

The Charity Organization Society, adopting this germ-thought, insists as a *sine qua non* upon the necessity of a thorough and organized system of house-to-house visitation; the thorough investigation of the home-life, the relationships, the surroundings, one and all, of the home; and this it has applied not only to single parishes, not only to isolated communities, but to large cities—to a city like London, containing as many inhabitants as are to be found in the eight largest cities of the United States.

. . . Our space will not permit a full account of the vast variety of agencies and noble schemes which these Committees have put in operation, with the full approval of the Council, for the purpose of bettering the home-life of the poor. There is the establishment of Penny banks; the system of Loans with security, but without interest; the Provident Dispensaries; the Schools for teaching the elements of cooking and various details of domestic life; there is the establishment of Creches for the reception and care of infants while the mothers are absent at work; there are the Soup-kitchens and Dinner-kitchens—not the demoralizing charities which usually pass under this name, but places where the industrious poor, who have not time to market and prepare a meal, can purchase what they require of wholesome and well-cooked food to be taken to the home on their way from work. These are a fair sample of the agencies which the Society is putting into operation for the elevation of the poor. . . .

And when the time shall come when the care of the poor becomes a subject which every citizen (not only every Christian) feels it his duty to attend to—when the business habits of our merchants and bankers, the trained intelligence of our lawyers, the habits of command and administration of our military and civil officers, and the high qualities of our noblest citizens are all joined in the interests of the poor, in the grand aim of bettering and elevating their fellows—then, and not till then, can we hope to see the final repression of pauperism and the last trace of mendicity in our streets.

From *A Handbook of Charity Organization*, by Rev. S. Humphreys Gurteen (1882).

PHILANTHROPIC REALISM

"There is no country in the world in which the poor are more idle, dissolute, drunken, and insolent. The day you passed that act you took away from before their eyes the greatest of all inducements to industry, frugality, and sobriety, by giving them a dependence on somewhat else than a careful accumulation during youth and health for support in age and sickness. . . . Repeal that law and you will soon see a change in their manners. St. Monday and St. Tuesday will cease to be holidays."

—Benjamin Franklin, 1766,
commenting on British welfare

"Nothing should be done under the guise of charity, which tends to break down character. It is the greatest wrong that can be done to him to undermine the character of a poor man."

—Josephine Shaw Lowell,
founder of the New York Charity Organization Society, 1884

"To cast a contribution into a box brought to the hand, or to attend committees and anniversaries, are very trifling exercises of Christian self-denial and devotion, compared with what is demanded in the wary perambulations through the street, the contact with filth, and often with rude and repulsive people, the facing of disease, and distress, and all manner of heart-rending and heart-frightening scenes, and all the trials of faith, patience, and hope, which are incident to the duty we urge."

—William Rufner, *Charity and the Clergy,* 1853

"Those who have much to do with alms-giving and plans of human improvement soon see how superficial and comparatively useless all assistance or organization is, which does not touch habits of life and the inner forces which form character. The poor helped each year become poorer in force and independence.

"Christianity is the highest education of character. Give the poor that, and only seldom will either alms or punishment be necessary."

—Charles Loring Brace, *The Children's Aid Society,* New York, 1872

GETTING TO KNOW YOU

"And to do it most effectually you must be absolutely incognito, you must ferret the people out of their hovels as I have done, look into their kettles, eat their bread, loll on their beds under pretence of resting yourself, but in fact to find if they are soft. You will feel a sublime pleasure in the course of this investigation, and a sublimer one hereafter when you shall be able to apply your knolege to the softening of their beds, or the throwing a morsel of meat into the kettle of vegetables."

—Thomas Jefferson

"Ours was a strict, though in every case a friendly investigation—the object of which was to ascertain all the previous means and resources of which we should avail ourselves, ere we drew on the public charity at all. All who were conscious of possessing such means simply ceased to apply; and the number of applications fell in a month or two to about one-fifth of the number made under the old system. . . .

"The truth is, that our system, parsimonious as it was in the distribution of parish money, was exceeding popular; and to those who have any understanding of human nature this fact will not be inexplicable. We have only to think of the charm which lies in personal attention, and in the intercourse that we hold with the too often neglected poor, who after all stand much oftener in need of advice than they do of alms; and who, though they received less from us than in other parishes, received a great deal more, and especially if we include their own better management of their own affairs, from the other sources that we had opened up for them. We had no doubt greatly fewer applicants; but though less money was given, more trouble was taken with each of them; and we either ascertained their circumstances to be such, or placed them in such circumstances—that had they been anywhere else in Glasgow, and as well known as we knew them, no further care or cognizance of their state would have been deemed necessary."

—Dr. Thomas Chalmers, pastor of St. John's, Glasgow, 1819–1823,
then professor of theology in the University of Edinburgh

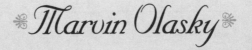

Marvin N. Olasky (born 1950) is professor of journalism at the University of Texas at Austin and a senior fellow at the Progress and Freedom Foundation and its Center for Effective Compassion in Washington, D.C. Author of more than ten books and coauthor of six others, he is best known for The Tragedy of American

Compassion, *which has been widely cited in recent American debates about welfare. But he does not just write about compassion. He and his wife are deeply involved in various practical initiatives in their community.*

How to Practice Effective Compassion ❧

During the nineteenth century, a successful war on poverty was waged by tens of thousands of local, private charitable agencies and religious groups around the country. The platoons of the greatest charity army in American history often were small. They were made up of volunteers led by poorly paid but deeply dedicated professional managers. And they were highly effective.

Thousands of eyewitness accounts and journalistic assessments show that poverty fighters of the nineteenth century did not abolish poverty, but they enabled millions of people to escape it. . . . What was their secret? It was not neglect. It was their understanding of the literal and biblical meaning of compassion . . .

SEVEN BASIC PRINCIPLES OF EFFECTIVE COMPASSION

Affiliation. A century ago, when individuals applied for material assistance, charity volunteers tried first to "restore family ties that have been sundered" and "reabsorb in social life those who for some reason have snapped the threads that bound them to other members of the community."

Bonding. A century ago, when applicants for help were truly alone, volunteers worked one-to-one to become, in essence, new family members. Charity volunteers a century ago usually were not assigned to massive food-dispensing tasks. They were given the narrow but deep responsibility of making a difference in one life over several years.

Categorization. A century ago, charities realized that two persons in exactly the same material circumstances but with different values need different treatment: . . . "Work tests" helped both in sorting and in providing relief with dignity.

Discernment. "Intelligent giving and intelligent withholding are alike true charity," . . . It was important to "reform those mild, well-meaning, tender-hearted, sweet-voiced criminals who insist upon indulging in indiscriminate charity."

Employment. Nineteenth-century New York charity leader Josephine Lowell wrote that "the problem before those who would be charitable is not how to deal with a given number of the poor; it is how to help those who are poor without adding to their numbers and constantly increasing the evils they seek to cure." If people were paid for not working, the number of non-workers would increase, and children would grow up without seeing work as a natural and essential part of life.

Freedom. Charity workers a century ago did not press for governmental programs, but instead showed poor people how to move up while resisting enslavement to governmental masters. . . . Life was hard, but static, multi-generational poverty of the kind we now have was rare; those who persevered could star in a motion picture of upward mobility.

God. "True philanthropy must take into account spiritual as well as physical needs," poverty-fighters a century ago noted.

From Marvin Olasky, "The New Welfare Debate: How to Practice Effective Compassion," *Imprimis*, Volume 24, No. 9, September 1996, pp. 2–5. Excerpted by permission of the author.

QUESTIONS FOR THOUGHT AND DISCUSSION

1. In the Gurteen selection, read the 1868 report on the Edinburgh Poor-law. What is its assessment of the government systems targeting poverty? How much have things changed since then?
2. The first principle of the Charity Organization Society was "Coordinate" ("banding together"). What concern lay behind Gurteen's proposal? What is his stated objective?
3. How does he compare the focus of "official charity" to that of "voluntary organization"—what he calls the "fourth stage" in the war on poverty? What does he cite as the key problem of existing systems?
4. The COS's second principle was "Investigate." What are his arguments for using work-tests? What do you think of his reasoning?

5. How does he differentiate between "paupers" and "the poor"? What are the goals in helping resident poor? What does the COS seek to avoid in helping the resident poor?

6. The third COS principle was "Recollect" (bringing the rich back in contact with the poor). What are the strategies for getting to know the poor? What part are the rich to play? What is his argument for these methods?

7. Of Olasky's seven principles of effective compassion—effectively Gurteen's principles—which do you find most striking? Overall, how do you find this system of dealing with poverty? What would be the strengths and weaknesses of this approach if relied on exclusively today?

8. Given the size of cities and the extent of poverty today, do you think it is possible for associations to be as effective without government assistance?

❊ SOCIAL UNIVERSALISM ❊

Social Universalism was a new school of philanthropic thought that combined theological liberalism with political socialism, representing a decisive break with the traditional, largely Christian, consensus on philanthropy. This school appealed especially to the intellectual and literary elite. Sometimes its defining features are emphasized as secular rather than sectarian or as stressing social, rather than individual, change. The movement did include both "social gospellers," such as Walter Rauschenbusch and Washington Gladden, who were motivated by Christian faith, as well as such secularists as Jane Addams.

They believed that human beings were naturally good, not evil, so the problem in society was the fault of the system, not sin.

But the Social Universalists had several common features. They believed that human beings were naturally good, not evil, so the problem in society was the fault of the system, not sin. Work-tests were therefore cruel, not tests for discernment. And the task of philanthropy should involve government, not just individuals. Above all, they believed—fatefully—that help should be universal and unconditional because human need was a "title" (or entitlement) to help.

Above all, they believed—fatefully—that help should be universal and unconditional because human need was a "title" (or entitlement) to help.

Although there are great differences in the ideas of the various strains of Social Universalism, the continuities are striking—especially the utopian and universalist notes. This school, of course, grew to even greater prominence in the twentieth century, peaking in the thirties in the New Deal era and then again in the sixties with the National Right to Welfare movement. Some of these efforts are now associated with bureaucratic, policy-oriented government, which until recently was assumed to be a product of Franklin Roosevelt's New Deal. Historians, however, have made it clear that Big Government impulses go back before World War I, flowering first under Herbert Hoover.

Today Social Universalism is championed by those, mainly liberal, activists and policy makers who acknowledge that the private-public partnership may have swung too far in favor of the public, but who contend there will be no decent solution to the problems without considerable government involvement. A decisive question faces this position: Given the havoc that government welfare programs have created or enabled, can there be hope of solutions relying largely on government initiatives?

❧ *Horace Greeley* ❧

Horace Greeley (1811–1872) was the influential editor of the New York Tribune, *which he founded in 1841 and commanded until his death. His opinions, exhortations, and actions greatly influenced American history. Many see a connection between the publication of his anti-slavery piece "Prayer for Twenty Millions" and the Emancipation Proclamation that Lincoln issued one month afterward. When Confederate General Robert E. Lee surrendered, Greeley promoted universal amnesty, and he created a furor by traveling to Richmond to pay the bail bond of Confederate President Jefferson Davis. The cry of "Go west, young man!" is attributed to him. He ran unsuccessfully for the presidency in 1872.*

Editorials ❧

"In the beginning GOD created the heaven and the earth."

The earth, the air, the waters, the sunshine, with their natural products, were Divinely intended and appointed for the use and sustenance of Man — not for a part only, but for the whole Human Family.

Civilized Society, as it exists in our day, has divested the larger portion of mankind of the unimpeded, unpurchased enjoyment of those natural rights. That larger portion may be perishing with cold, yet have no legally recognized rights to a stick of decaying fuel in the most unfrequented morass, or may be famishing, yet have no legal right to pluck and eat the bitterest acorn in the depths of the remotest wilderness. The defeasance or confiscation of Man's natural right to use any portion of the Earth's surface not actually in use by another, is an important fact, to be kept in view in every consideration of the duty of the affluent and comfortable to the poor and unfortunate.

. . . I set forth very plainly the Principles on which I proposed to demonstrate the expediency, justice, and duty of effecting the Social Organization I advocate. From the premises there laid down I deduced the duty of every Christian, every Philanthropist, every one who admits the essential Brotherhood of the Human Family, to labor earnestly and devotedly for a Social Order which shall secure to every human being within its sphere the full and true development of the nature wherewith God has endowed him, Physical, Intellectual and Moral. The absolute, indefeasible Right of every Child to proper nourishment and culture, of every Man to sample Opportunity to Labor and to the fair recompense of his Labor—the Right, in short, truly to Live, to cultivate the Soil and enjoy the product of his industry—these are the premises on which I now advocate, as I for six years have done, the Organization of Society on the basis of Associated interests and efforts in contradistinction to that hitherto prevailing. . . .

That there is beneficent and inspiriting truth in the theory that Man may be so trained and directed, so circumstanced and incited, that he will be inclined to Good as generally and as thoroughly as he now appears to be to Evil, I do joyfully believe.

. . . [Human desires are] good in themselves. Evil flows only from their repression or subversion.

. . . [Human desires are] good in themselves. Evil flows only from their repression or subversion. Give them full scope, free play, a perfect and complete development, and universal happiness must be the result. . . . Create a new form of Society in which this shall be possible . . . then you will have a perfect Society; then will you have "the Kingdom of Heaven." . . . [T]he heart of man is not depraved: that his passions do not prompt to wrong doing, and do not therefore by their action, produce evil.

From Horace Greeley, "Of Rights and Obligations," *New York Tribune*, 1847.

REDISTRIBUTION RESURGENT

"In this sense, the theory of the Communists may be summed up in the single sentence: Abolition of private property. . . . In short, the Communists everywhere support every revolutionary movement against the existing social and political order of things. . . . Let the ruling classes tremble at a Communist revolution. The proletarians have nothing to lose but their chains. They have a world to win. . . . Workingmen of all countries, unite!"

—Karl Marx and Friedrich Engels, *The Communist Manifesto*

"When I give food to the poor, they call me a saint. When I ask why the poor have no food, they call me a communist."

—Dom Helder Camara, Brazilian archbishop

"'I ain't got no choice in the matter.'" He stopped on the ungracious sound of his words. 'That ain't like I mean it. That ain't. I mean'—he stumbled—'what I mean, if a fella's got somepin to eat an' another fella's hungry—why, the first fella ain't got no choice.'"

—John Steinbeck, *The Grapes of Wrath*

Edward Bellamy

Edward Bellamy (1850–1898) is best known for his novel Looking Backward, *which sold over a million copies and was greatly revered in his day. He was born in Chicopee Falls, Massachusetts, and spent most of his life there. A trip to Europe when he was eighteen influenced him forever: "[A]mong the hovels of the peasantry my eyes were first opened to the extent and consequences of 'man's inhumanity to man.'" Bellamy returned to the United States, studied law, was admitted to the bar, and began to write fiction.*

Looking Backward's publication in 1888 brought him immediate, international fame. He writes the story of a man who fell asleep in 1887 and awoke in 2000. In "The Parable of the Stagecoach" below, the man is looking backward from the vantage point of 2000 to the conditions of the nineteenth century. In the following section, "The Golden Future of the Corporate State," his host, Dr. Leete, explains the economic system of the late nineteenth century.

Surpassed only by Uncle Tom's Cabin *and* Ben-Hur *in nineteenth-century sales, the novel was powerfully influential among writers and intellectuals. More than one-hundred-fifty "Bellamy Clubs" immediately sprouted up across the nation to discuss how to implement the book's social implications. Much of the book's success came because its mild utopian-socialist vision expressed itself as no more than "enlightened self-interest or wholesale common sense," not as a call to violent revolution. The success changed Bellamy from a reticent man to a vigorous enthusiast who believed that the change from capitalism to his collectivist utopia could occur in his lifetime. His exhausting traveling and campaigning ended prematurely when he contracted tuberculosis.*

Looking Backward ☙

THE PARABLE OF THE STAGECOACH

By way of attempting to give the reader some general impression of the way people lived together in those days, and especially of the relations of the rich and poor to one another, perhaps I cannot do better than to compare society as it then was to a prodigious coach which the masses of humanity were harnessed to and dragged toilsomely along a very hilly and sandy road. The driver was hunger, and permitted no lagging, though the pace was necessarily very slow. Despite the difficulty of drawing the coach at all along so hard a road, the top was covered with passengers who never got down, even at the steepest ascents. These seats on top were very breezy and comfortable. Well up out of the dust, their occupants could enjoy the scenery at their leisure, or critically discuss the merits of the straining team. Naturally such places were in great demand and the competition for them was keen, every one seeking as the first end in life to secure a seat on the coach for himself and to leave it to his child after him. By the rule of the coach a man could leave his seat to whom he wished, but on the other hand there were so many accidents by which it might at any time be wholly lost. For all that they were so easy, the seats were very insecure, and at every sudden jolt of the coach persons were slipping out of them and falling to the ground, where they were instantly compelled to take hold of the rope and help to drag the coach on which they had before ridden so pleasantly. It was naturally regarded as a terrible misfortune to lose one's seat, and the apprehension that this might happen to them or their friends was a constant cloud upon the happiness of those who rode.

Naturally such places were in great demand and the competition for them was keen, every one seeking as the first end in life to secure a seat on the coach for himself and to leave it to his child after him.

But did they think only of themselves? you ask. Was not their very luxury rendered intolerable to them by comparison with the lot of their brothers and sisters in the harness, and the knowledge that their own weight added to their toil? Had they no compassion for fellow beings from whom fortune only distinguished them? Oh, yes, commiseration was frequently expressed by those who rode for those who had to pull the coach, especially when the vehicle came to a bad place in the road, as it was constantly doing, or to a particularly steep hill. At such times, the desperate straining of the team, their agonized leaping and plunging under the pitiless lashing of hunger, the many who fainted at the rope and were trampled in the mire, made a very distressing spectacle, which often called forth highly creditable displays of feeling on the top of the coach. At such times the passengers would call down encouragingly to the toilers of the rope, exhorting them to patience, and holding out hopes of possible compensation in another world for the hardness of their lot, while others contributed to buy salves and liniments for the crippled and injured. It was agreed that it was a great pity that the coach should be so hard to pull, and there was a sense of general relief when the specially bad piece of road was gotten over. This relief was not, indeed, wholly on account of the team, for there was always some danger at these bad places of a general overturn in which all would lose their seats.

It must in truth be admitted that the main effect of the spectacle of the misery of the toilers at the rope was to enhance the passengers' sense of the value of their seats upon the coach, and to cause them to hold on to them more desperately than before. If the passengers could only have felt assured that neither they nor their friends would ever fall from the top, it is probable that, beyond contributing to the funds for liniments and bandages, they would have troubled themselves extremely little about those who dragged the coach.

I am well aware that this will appear to the men and women of the twentieth century an incredible inhumanity, but there are two facts, both very curious, which partly explain it. In the first place, it was firmly and sincerely believed that there was no other way in which Society could get along, except when the many pulled at the rope and the few rode, and not only this, but that no very radical improvement even was possible, either in the harness, the coach, the roadway, or the distribution of the toil. It had always been as it was, and it always would be so. It was a pity, but it could not be helped, and philosophy forbade wasting compassion on what was beyond remedy.

The other fact is yet more curious, consisting in a singular hallucination which those on the top of the coach generally shared, that they were not exactly like their brothers and sisters who pulled at the rope, but of finer clay, in some way belonging to a higher order of beings who might justly expect to be drawn. This seems unaccountable, but, as I once rode on this very coach and shared that very hallucination, I ought to be believed. The strangest thing about the hallucination was that those who had but just climbed up from the ground, before they had outgrown the marks of the rope upon their hands, began to fall under its influence. As for those whose parents and grandparents before them had been so fortunate as to keep their seats on the top, the conviction they cherished of the essential difference between their sort of humanity and the common article was absolute. The effect of such a delusion in moderating fellow feeling for the sufferings of the mass of men into a distant and philosophical compassion is obvious. To it I refer as the only extenuation I can offer for the indifference which, at the period I write of, marked my own attitude toward the misery of my brothers.

THE GOLDEN FUTURE OF THE CORPORATE STATE

"The movement toward the conduct of business by larger and larger aggregations of capital, the tendency toward monopolies, which had been so desperately and vainly resisted, was recognized at last, in its true significance,

It must in truth be admitted that the main effect of the spectacle of the misery of the toilers at the rope was to enhance the passengers' sense of the value of their seats upon the coach, and to cause them to hold on to them more desperately than before.

It had always been as it was, and it always would be so. It was a pity, but it could not be helped, and philosophy forbade wasting compassion on what was beyond remedy.

as a process which only needed to complete its logical evolution to open a golden future to humanity.

"Early in the last century the evolution was completed by the final consolidation of the entire capital of the nation. The industry and commerce of the country, ceasing to be conducted by a set of irresponsible corporations and syndicates of private persons at their caprice and for their profit, were entrusted to a single syndicate representing the people, to be conducted in the common interest for the common profit. The nation, that is to say, organized as the one great business corporation in which all other corporations were absorbed; it became the one capitalist in the place of all other capitalists, the sole employer, the final monopoly in which all previous and lesser monopolies were swallowed up, a monopoly in the profits and economies of which all citizens shared. The epoch of trusts had ended in The Great Trust. In a word, the people of the United States concluded to assume the conduct of their own business, just as one hundred-odd years before they had assumed the conduct of their own government, organizing now for industrial purposes on precisely the same grounds that they had then organized for political purposes. At last, strangely late in the world's history, the obvious fact was perceived that no business is so essentially the public business as the industry and commerce on which the people's livelihood depends, and that to entrust it to private persons to be managed for private profit is a folly similar in kind, though vastly greater in magnitude, to that of surrendering the functions of political government to kings and nobles to be conducted for their personal glorification." . . .

"But you have not yet told me how you have settled the labor problem. It is the problem of capital which we have been discussing," I said. "After the nation had assumed conduct of the mills, machinery, railroads, farms, mines, and capital in general of the country, the labor question still remained. In assuming the responsibilities of capital the nation had assumed the difficulties of the capitalist's position."

"The moment the nation assumed the responsibilities of capital those difficulties vanished," replied Doctor Leete. "The national organization of labor under one direction was the complete solution of what was, in your day and under your system, justly regarded as the insoluble labor problem. When the nation became the sole employer, all the citizens, by virtue of their citizenship, became employees, to be distributed according to the needs of industry."

"That is," I suggested, "you have simply applied the principle of universal military service, as it was understood in our day, to the labor question."

"Yes," said Doctor Leete, "that was something which followed as a matter of course as soon as the nation had become the sole capitalist. The people were already accustomed to the idea that the obligation of every citizen, not physically disabled, to contribute his military services to the defense of the nation was equal and absolute. That it was equally the duty of every citizen to contribute his quota of industrial or intellectual services to the maintenance of the nation was equally evident, though it was not until the nation became the employer of labor that citizens were able to render this sort of service with any pretense either of universality or equity. No organization of labor was possible when the employing power was divided among hundreds or thousands of individuals and corporations, between which concert of any kind was neither desired, nor indeed feasible. It constantly happened then that vast numbers who desired to labor could find no opportunity, and on the other hand, those who desired to evade a part or all of their debt could easily do so."

No organization of labor was possible when the employing power was divided among hundreds or thousands of individuals and corporations, between which concert of any kind was neither desired, nor indeed feasible.

"Service, now, I suppose, is compulsory upon all," I suggested.

"It is rather a matter of course than of compulsion," replied Doctor Leete. "It is regarded as so absolutely natural and reasonable that the idea of its being compulsory has ceased to be thought of. He would be thought to be an incredibly contemptible person who should need compulsion in such a case. Nevertheless, to speak of service being compulsory would be a weak way to state its absolute inevitableness. Our entire social order is so wholly based upon and deduced from it that if it were conceivable that a man could escape it, he would be left with no possible way to provide for his existence. He would have excluded himself from the world, cut himself off from his kind, in a word, committed suicide." . . .

LIVING ON THE PLASTIC

"A credit corresponding to his share of the annual product of the nation is given to every citizen on the public books at the beginning of each year, and a credit card issued to him with which he procures at the public storehouses, found in every community, whatever he desires whenever he desires it."

—Edward Bellamy, *Looking Backward,* 1888

"How, then, do you regulate wages?" I once more asked.

Doctor Leete did not reply till after several moments of meditative silence. "I know, of course," he finally said, "enough of the old order of things to understand just what you mean by that question; and yet the present order is so utterly different at this point that I am a little at a loss how to answer you best. You ask me how we regulate wages; I can only reply that there is no idea in the modern social economy which at all corresponds with what was meant by wages in your day."

"I suppose you mean that you have no money to pay wages in," said I. "But the credit given the worker at the government storehouse answers to his wages with us. How is the amount of the credit given respectively to the workers in different lines determined? By what title does the individual claim his particular share? What is the basis of allotment?"

"His title," replied Doctor Leete, "is his humanity. The basis of his claim is the fact that he is a man."

"The fact that he is a man!" I repeated, incredulously. "Do you possibly mean that all have the same share?"

"Most assuredly."

From Edward Bellamy, *Looking Backward, 2000–1887* (Boston: Ticknor, 1888).

A WAR TO END ALL POVERTY?

"Our covenant with ourselves did not stop there. Instinctively we recognized a deep need—the need to find through government the instrument of our united purpose to solve for the individual the ever-rising problems of a complex civilization. Repeated attempts at their solution without the aid of government had left us baffled and bewildered."

—Franklin Delano Roosevelt,
Second Inaugural Address, January 20, 1937

"The world is very different now, for man holds in his mortal hands the power to abolish all forms of human poverty."

—John F. Kennedy, Inaugural Address, January 20, 1961

"This administration today, here and now, declares unconditional war on poverty in America. . . . It will not be a short or easy struggle, no single weapon or strategy will suffice, but we shall not rest until that war is won. The richest nation on earth can afford to win it. We cannot afford to lose it."

—Lyndon B. Johnson, State of the Union Address, January 8, 1964

"[T]he conquest of poverty is well within our power."

—1964 Economic Report of the President

"The way to eliminate poverty is to give the poor people enough money, so that they won't be poor anymore."

—Johnson administration official,
quoted in the *Saturday Evening Post*, December 17, 1966

"When I go to welfare, I don't wait around for the stall. If I don't get treated with respect, I start hollering for the supervisor, and then I threaten legal action."

—Stanton Street Center staff member, 1960s

"[T]he elimination of poverty is well within the means of federal, state, and local governments. . . . [Poverty can be abolished] simply by a stroke of the pen. To raise every individual and family in the nation now below a subsistence income to the subsistence level would cost but $10 billion a year. That is less than two percent of the gross national product. It is less than ten percent of tax revenues."

—Ford Foundation-sponsored study
by the University of Michigan Survey Research Center, 1972

"I told George [Wiley] he should press as hard as possible while there was a feeling of guilt in the land, because the guilt wouldn't last nor would the contributions."

—Bishop John T. Walker, National Cathedral, Washington, D.C.

❧ Time Magazine ❧

Welfare: Trying to End the Nightmare ❧

A major new cause for the increase in AFDC [Aid to Families with Dependent Children] applicants is the effective campaign to get more people on the rolls who have a right to be there. Chief organizer of that movement is George Wiley, 40, executive secretary of the National Welfare Rights Organization (NWRO). A former leader of the Congress of Racial Equality and a Ph.D. in chemistry who still publishes in scholarly journals, Wiley now wears dashikis more often than business suits. In the four years since NWRO has been in operation, it has organized an estimated 100,000 welfare clients, almost all of them women, into a national force to raise benefits. Normally they use peaceful tactics, but there have been acts of violence. An NWRO invasion party once took over the office of Health, Education, and Welfare Secretary Robert Finch. Says one HEW official: "I tell you, they've educated a lot of people. They've brought the problem right into this building, and believe me, it's had an impact."

Bizarro © 1996 by Dan Piraro. Reprinted with permission of Universal Press Syndicate. All rights reserved.

The NWRO has absorbed much of the seemingly dissipated energy of the civil rights movement and has adopted the movement's militancy and some of its tactics. NWRO has had a significant effect upon the attitudes of the poor. Many now consider welfare aid a proper and legal claim and demand that it be satisfied. Say Mrs. Tillmon, NWRO president and a Watts mother of six: "We would like to see everybody get what's coming to them. Everybody is entitled to live in this country, regardless of race, creed, religion or sex. Do you expect people who can't make a living to go out and get hit by a car? It would cost a lot just to bury them."

"We would like to see everybody get what's coming to them. Everybody is entitled to live in this country, regardless of race, creed, religion or sex."

That attitude is a far cry from the 1930s and Ben Isaacs in Studs Terkel's *Hard Times:* "Shame? You tellin' me? I would go stand on that relief line, I would look this way and that way and see if there's nobody around that knows me. I would bend my head low so nobody would recognize me. The only scar it left on me is my pride, my pride." . . .

Ellis Murphy, 53, soft-spoken but increasingly bitter, runs one of the biggest welfare departments in the country in Los Angeles County. He has the doubtful guidance of the county welfare regulations, which he dutifully keeps just outside his office. They make a pile exactly five feet, two inches high. "If something isn't done soon," he says, "the whole idiotic patchwork will fall of its own weight. It's a disaster. At all levels of state and Federal Government, it's disgraceful that we have no master plan to direct this monumental spending." . . .

In Alameda County, California, Dion Lerch, 25, caseworker No. E-1655, says, "Look, after a while you become immune to all the misery you see; you become an animal. I can tell someone I'm cutting off his check, you're damn straight I can. With 125 cases it's hard to remember that they're all human beings. Sometimes they're just a number."

"With 125 cases it's hard to remember that they're all human beings. Sometimes they're just a number."

Al Marlens, "Welfare: Trying to End the Nightmare," *Time,* February 8, 1971. Reprinted with permission from Time Life Syndication.

TALKING OF ENTITLEMENT

Monthly distributions of corn to all were so corrupting to the Roman republic that "less than 150 years was sufficient to pauperize and render dependent a fearfully large proportion of one of the most manly races which have ever lived."

—Nathaniel Ware, 1845,
predicting the harmful effects of growing American welfare

"I must say . . . that this class of criticism which I read in the newspapers when I arrived on Sunday morning reminds me of the simple tale about the sailor who jumped into a dock, I think it was at Plymouth, to rescue a small boy from drowning. About a week later this sailor was accosted by a woman, who asked, 'Are you the man who picked my son out of the dock the other night?' The sailor replied modestly, 'That is true, ma'am.' 'Ah,' said the woman, 'you are the man I am looking for. Where is his cap?'"

—Winston Churchill, *Closing the Ring*

"What we've been doing, at the level we've been doing it, is almost worse than nothing at all. . . . We've raised expectations, but we haven't been able to deliver all we should have."

—Mayor Jerome Cavanaugh of Detroit, 1967

QUESTIONS FOR THOUGHT AND DISCUSSION

1. What are the key ideas that drive the Social Universalist approach to philanthropy?
2. Where do you see "entitlement" language in Greeley's editorial? Universalism?
3. According to Greeley, who or what is to blame for the predicament of the poor? Who is responsible to change the circumstances?
4. What does he believe about the nature of man and the possibility of change? In contrast to Social Calvinism, how would these beliefs affect the way funds would be dispersed?
5. In Bellamy's "The Parable of the Stagecoach," what is the chief goal of the passengers? What is their motivation toward this goal? How is compassion expressed in the story? In what is the compassion rooted? What are the two reasons for the way things were on the stagecoach? Has this parable any relevance to society today?
6. Read the paragraphs in "The Golden Future of the Corporate State." What do you think of Bellamy's vision of the nation as "one great business corporation"? What factors in the nineteenth century made this so appealing?
7. Read the box "A War to End All Poverty?" on pages 172-173. Which of these quotations do you find the most fatuous? What made it apparently self-evident in its time?
8. What is the purpose of the NWRO campaign, noted in the *Time* article? How has the NWRO affected the attitudes of the poor? How has welfare

affected the attitudes of those serving the poor? What place do "compassion" and "need" have in this type of system?

9. Many people today attack the "excesses, follies, and viciousness" of the bloated welfare system. But what are the links between the ideas in these readings and later views of entitlement?

❧SOCIAL DARWINISM❧

The third but passing school was Social Darwinism. Growing in popularity in the 1870s as an unabashed self-interest that coincided with post-Civil War industrialism, this school was really a counter-philanthropy or "party of anti-compassion" that was based on Charles Darwin's notion of natural selection and the survival of the fittest. Darwin's disciple Herbert Spencer wrote, "The unfit must be eliminated as nature intended, for the principle of natural selection must not be violated by the artificial preservation of those least able to take care of themselves." If the weaker were devoured and the fittest survived, it was not traditional morality but the law of nature. The economic doctrine of laissez faire was as inexorable as Newton's law of gravity.

Social Darwinists were clear-eyed about the perils of pauperism but flinty-hearted. On the one hand, the implications for the poor were chilling. Sociologist William Graham Sumner, for example, wrote, "A drunkard in the gutter is just where he ought to be, according to the fitness and tendency of things." On the other hand, the eugenic logic was horrifying. Simon Newcomb, an astronomer and mathematician, wrote, "Love of mankind at large should prompt us to take such measures as shall discourage or prevent the bringing forth of children by the pauper class."

Social Darwinism was championed by such leading intellectuals as Spencer and such prominent business leaders as Andrew Carnegie, Spencer's "best American friend" who sponsored his visit to the United States in 1882. Carnegie commonly used such phrases as "survival of the fittest," "race improvement," and "struggle for existence." His sunny little slogan, "All is well since all grows better" was his summary of thirty volumes of Spencer's thought. Today these arguments survive not so much as a school of thought as in the hard-heartedness of certain individuals toward the poor.

> **CLEAR-EYED AND COLD**
>
> "Bestow your favors on the good; for a goodly treasury is a store of gratitude laid up in the heart of an honest man. If you benefit bad men, you will have the same reward as those who feed stray dogs; for these snarl alike at those who give them food and at the passing stranger; and just so base men wrong alike those who help and those who harm them."
>
> —Isocrates, "To Demonicus"

"A beggar asked alms of a Spartan, who said, 'If I should give to you, you will be the more a beggar; and for this unseemly conduct of yours he who first gave to you is responsible, for he thus made you lazy.'"

—Plutarch, "Sayings of Spartans"

"Then, again, do not tell me, as a good man did today, of my obligation to put all poor men in good situations. Are they *my* poor? I tell thee, thou foolish philanthropist, that I grudge the dollar, the dime, the cent I give to such men as do not belong to me and to whom I do not belong. There is a class of persons to whom by all spiritual affinity I am bought and sold; for them I will go to prison, if need be; but your miscellaneous popular charities; the education at college of fools; the building of meeting-houses to the vain end to which many now stand; alms to sots; and the thousandfold Relief Societies;—though I confess with shame I sometimes succumb and give the dollar, it is a wicked dollar which by-and-by I shall have the manhood to withhold."

—Ralph Waldo Emerson, "Self-Reliance"

"As many more individuals of each species are born than can possibly survive; and as, consequently, there is a frequently recurring struggle for existence, it follows that any being if it vary however slightly in any manner profitable to itself, under the complex and sometimes varying conditions of life, will have a better chance of surviving, and thus be naturally selected."

—Charles Darwin, *The Origin of Species* (1859)

ARE THERE NO PRISONS?

This lunatic, in letting Scrooge's nephew out, had let two other people in. They were portly gentlemen, pleasant to behold, and now stood, with their hats off, in Scrooge's office. They had books and papers in their hands, and bowed to him.

"Scrooge and Marley's, I believe," said one of the gentlemen, referring to his list. "Have I the pleasure of addressing Mr Scrooge or Mr Marley?"

"Mr Marley has been dead these seven years," Scrooge replied. "He died seven years ago this very night."

"We have no doubt his liberality is well represented by his surviving partner," said the gentleman, presenting his credentials.

It certainly was; for they had been two kindred spirits. At the ominous word "Liberality," Scrooge frowned, and shook his head, and handed the credentials back.

"At this festival season of the year, Mr Scrooge," said the gentleman, taking up a pen, "it is more than usually desirable that we should make some slight provision for the Poor and destitute, who suffer greatly at the present time. Many thousands are in want of common necessaries; hundreds of thousands are in want of common comforts, sir."

"Are there no prisons?" asked Scrooge.

"Plenty of prisons," said the gentleman, laying down the pen again.

"And the Union workhouses?" demanded Scrooge. "Are they still in operation?"

"They are. Still," returned the gentleman, "I wish I could say they were not."

"The Treadmill and the Poor Law are in full vigour, then?" said Scrooge.

"Both very busy, sir."

"Oh! I was afraid, from what you said at first, that something had occurred to stop them in their useful course," said Scrooge. "I'm very glad to hear it."

—Charles Dickens, *A Christmas Carol*

Simon Newcomb

Simon Newcomb (1835–1909) was an astronomer who served in the U.S. Navy as chief of the Naval Observatory and later became a professor at Johns Hopkins University. He was awarded numerous medals, prizes, and honorary degrees, such as the gold medal of the Royal Astronomical Society. Newcomb's tables of the motions of the stars, planets, and moon are still used today by astronomers and navigators.

But Newcomb also took an active interest in public affairs. With William Graham Sumner he was a chief proponent of the Social Darwinism that originated with England's Herbert Spencer (whose ideas, despite their label, actually preceded Darwin's Origin of Species). When Newcomb retired, the Carnegie Institute awarded him grants to continue his studies until the end of his life.

Principles of Political Economy

It is often said that imbecility and mendacity are a growth of civilization, being unknown in primitive communities. Hence men look upon them as they look upon the diseases of civilization, namely, as something inseparably associated with progress. But a very little consideration will show that there is no such

Why are there no beggars in comparatively poor and simple communities? We answer, for the same reason that there are no great actors, philosophers, or mathematicians in such communities. It is because the community cannot afford such luxuries.

necessary connection. Why are there no beggars in comparatively poor and simple communities? We answer, for the same reason that there are no great actors, philosophers, or mathematicians in such communities. It is because the community cannot afford such luxuries. Where it is perfectly certain that no one can get anything in alms by any method of begging, mendacity can never arise. If, as may sometimes be the case, a child grows up too imbecile to make a living or do any work, his parents, friends, relatives, or acquaintances take charge of him as best they can, and are careful that he is not allowed to wander away and starve. Mendacity can gain a foothold only when the community gets so wealthy and benevolent as to present an economic demand for beggars and paupers.

. . . Here is a little girl, born of poor and rather demoralized parents, who is being reared without any definite object in life. From early childhood she becomes aware that sums of money which seem to her fabulous in amount are raised by rich people for the benefit of the poor. If she lives in Europe, she is accustomed to seeing boxes in churches plainly marked "For the poor," and she finds out what it means before she can read. On getting a little older she becomes conscious that she has no chance to get any share of this money except by being even poorer than her parents. If she learns to cook for wealthier people, to do housework, to sew, to nurse; and if she uses the knowledge thus acquired in such a way as not to be a burden upon others, then she will have no right to any of this money. To get her share of it, she must remain poor, miserable, and worthless. To see what effect this may have upon her education and aspirations, let us look at human nature from another point of view.

We may say that, in a certain sense, men are by nature poor, miserable, and worthless. That is to say, if a child grows into a man without ever being taught or required to exercise his faculties, he will grow into this kind of a being.

We may say that, in a certain sense, men are by nature poor, miserable, and worthless. That is to say, if a child grows into a man without ever being taught or required to exercise his faculties, he will grow into this kind of a being. To make a decent living, even of the lowest sort, he must take pains, practice self-denial, seek for acquaintances, and make for himself a good character among his fellow-men. It is therefore not necessary, in order that the demand for objects of charity should be supplied, that any person should deliberately make up his mind to be a beggar. To become such all he needs to do is to do nothing. He can then with a greater or less approximation to truth say, "I have never tried to become a burden on society, and yet I can get no work; I have nothing to do; I am nearly starved; I shall soon be naked; I have no house in which to lay my head; I cannot get money for the barest necessities of existence."

The lesson is this: Although what the man says may be true, yet, if there had been no charity, he and his parents would have taken a different view of life, and he would have had a different training and a different history. . . .

The way we deal with the poor and miserable we see around us has a most important effect upon the poor and miserable we do not see. The next generation will be brought into the world by this generation, and it depends entirely upon the acts of this generation how many poor and miserable there shall be in the next. The law that like brings forth like is as true with the human race as with animals and plants. The greater the number of the degraded classes who are allowed to produce offspring which are allowed to grow to maturity, the more rapidly will these classes increase. What effect we wish our acts to have does not come into the question in considering the consequences of those acts. What we are concerned with is the natural consequences of our acts and not the motives which prompt them. We cannot evade the conclusion that the inevitable result of our current forms of charity is to enable the poor, miserable, and worthless elements of the community to bring forth children, to enable those children to escape the perils of infancy and grow to manhood, and to deprive them of the strongest incentive to become useful members of society, namely, the prospect that they will starve to death unless they learn to make a living. This result is what the reasonable philanthropist must deplore. . . .

Now, although at first sight it might seem almost hopeless to attempt doing anything for this coming generation, yet by looking more closely we find that its happiness depends almost entirely upon our own actions. To promote its happiness we should bequeath to it physical and moral health, a thorough training in correct principles of action, and such laws and institutions as shall best allow it to promote its welfare. We should avoid allowing it to be encumbered by criminals. Love of mankind at large should prompt us to take such measures as shall discourage or prevent the bringing forth of children by the pauper and criminal classes. No measure of repression would be too severe in the attainment of the latter object. The consideration due to a degraded man of any class is as nothing compared with that due to the society of the future. Many a good man has gone to his grave through the failure of society to hang one criminal. No higher or purer source of human happiness exists than the tender sentiments of man towards man. But these very sentiments are a source of enduring injury in the repugnance which they generate to a really effective system of dealing with the dangerous class in our population.

After promoting the birth of good stock, the next step would be its proper education. Here only careful experiment can show what society is able to

Love of mankind at large should prompt us to take such measures as shall discourage or prevent the bringing forth of children by the pauper and criminal classes. No measure of repression would be too severe in the attainment of the latter object.

do. . . . The danger which besets most charitable institutions devoted to the rearing of children is that of being conducted from a sentimental rather than a scientific point of view.

From "Of Charitable Effort" in *Principles of Political Economy*, by Simon Newcomb (New York: Harper & Brothers, 1886).

THE LAWS OF NATURE AND NATURE'S JUNGLE

"The unfit must be eliminated as nature intended, for the principle of natural selection must not be violated by the artificial preservation of those least able to take care of themselves. . . . If we do not like the survival of the fittest, we have only one possible alternative, and that is the survival of the unfittest. The former is the law of civilization, the latter is the law of anticivilization."

—Herbert Spencer, British leader of Social Darwinism

"[S]ociety is constantly excreting its unhealthy, imbecile, slow, vacillating, faithless members to leave room for the deserving. A maudlin impulse to prolong the lives of the unfit stands in the way of this beneficent purging of the social organism."

—Herbert Spencer

"The poverty of the incapable, the distresses that come upon the imprudent, the starvation of the idle, and those shoulderings aside of the weak by the strong, which have so many in 'shallows and miseries' are the decrees of a large, far-seeing benevolence"—the same dispensation that "brings to early graves the children of diseased parents, and singles out the low-spirited, the intemperate, and the debilitated as the victims of an epidemic."

—Herbert Spencer

"The sick man is the parasite of society."

—Friedrich Nietzsche

"It is better for all the world, if instead of waiting to execute degenerate offspring for crime, or to let them starve for their imbecility, society can prevent those who are manifestly unfit from continuing their kind. The principle that sustains compulsory vaccination is broad enough to cover cutting the Fallopian tubes. . . . Three generations of imbeciles is enough."

—Oliver Wendell Holmes

"Nature's remedies against vice are terrible. She removes the victims without pity. A drunkard in the gutter is just where he ought to be, according to the fitness and tendency of things. Nature has set up on him the process of decline and dissolution by which she removes things which have survived their usefulness."

—William Graham Sumner, *What Social Classes Owe to Each Other*

"Before Spencer, all for me had been darkness; after him all had become light—and right."

—Andrew Carnegie

"I remember that light came as in a flood and all was clear. Not only had I got rid of theology and the supernatural, but I had found the truth of evolution. 'All is well since all grows better,' became my motto, my true source of comfort. Man was not created with an instinct for his own degradation, but from the lower he had risen to the higher forms. Nor is there any conceivable end to his march to perfection. His face is turned to the light, he stands in the sun and looks upward."

—Andrew Carnegie

"The growth of a large business is merely a survival of the fittest. . . . The American Beauty rose can be produced in the splendor and fragrance which bring cheer to its beholder only by sacrificing the early buds which grow up around it. This is not an evil tendency in business. It is merely the working-out of a law of nature and a law of God."

—John D. Rockefeller

"Our social machinery is almost as blindly cruel as our steel machinery."

—Walter Rauschenbusch

QUESTIONS FOR THOUGHT AND DISCUSSION

1. What does Newcomb mean in saying there is "an economic demand for beggars and paupers" in wealthy, benevolent communities? Why does he say there are no beggars in simpler communities?

2. What is in the character of humans that they would pursue and propagate poverty and pauperism, according to Newcomb?

3. What are Newcomb's main tactics for ending poverty? What are his complaints about existing forms of charity? What is his focus in ending poverty?

4. Where do you agree, and where do you disagree with the politics of Social Darwinism? What are some of its roots, as seen in earlier readings?

5. Do you hear echoes of Social Darwinism today? Where? What would be its consequences in our present situation?

CHARITY ONCE HAD HEART

"Charity has various Senses, but is Excellent in all of them. It imports; first, the Commiseration of the Poor, and Unhappy of Mankind, and extends a Helping-Hand to mend their Condition. They that feel nothing of this, are at best not above half of Kin to Human Race; since they must have no Bowels, which makes such an Essential Part thereof, who have no more Nature. A Man, and yet not have a Feeling of the Wants or Needs of his own Flesh and Blood! A Monster rather! And may he never be suffer'd to propagate such an unnatural Stock in the World."

—Benjamin Franklin, "Of Charity," *More Fruits of Solitude*

❋THE RISE OF THE FOUNDATION❋

If the nineteenth century's first great innovation—the voluntary association—came at the beginning, its second came at the end: the foundation. The two greatest pioneers of the scientific or professional philanthropic foundations were Andrew Carnegie and John D. Rockefeller Sr. Andrew Carnegie was a Social Darwinist and John D. Rockefeller a Social Calvinist, but both took a scientific approach to philanthropy. Certainly it began with a fact, not a philosophy—the reality of the unimaginable new wealth amassed by the titans of the Industrial Revolution, such as Joseph Rowntree and George Cadbury in England and Carnegie and Rockefeller in the United States. As Carnegie wrote of this explosive stage of capitalism, "The problem of our age is the proper administration of wealth."

In Europe, such Christian industrialists as Rowntree, Cadbury, and Angela Burdett-Coutts (patron of Charles Dickens) had founded their own private trusts and taken them in two new directions in giving. The first was "eliminating the cause" of problems rather than "ameliorating the consequences"; the second, providing a new form of social advocacy that sought to inform and persuade public opinion and so move national policy makers.

In the United States, both unusual and methodical approaches were taken in commerce and welfare. Whereas Cornelius Vanderbilt had solicited help from spiritualists to commune with the spirits of dead railroad magnates to divine his next steps, Carnegie and Rockefeller placed great emphasis in business on knowledge, technical training, and management skills. It was therefore natural that the latter two would do the same with their new business—philanthropy.

The modern foundation was Carnegie's and Rockefeller's investment in innovation. Regarding "the business of benevolence," Rockefeller wrote, "If a combination to do business is effective in saving waste and in getting better results, why is not combination far more important in philanthropic work?" Thus the Carnegie and Rockefeller foundations developed as naturally in philanthropy as United States Steel and Standard Oil did in business.

Carnegie had two other primary motivations behind his foundation, which should be noted. One was that the task of disbursing his surplus was far harder than he had anticipated. He believed it was a disgrace to die rich, but he couldn't give it away fast enough. Such was the magnitude of his fortune that the fundamental

"If a combination to do business is effective in saving waste and in getting better results, why is not combination far more important in philanthropic work?"
—JOHN D. ROCKEFELLER

article in his new creed of administrating his wealth was not working, and even attempting it left him exhausted and harried.

The other was more philosophical. Carnegie believed that the Jewish-Christian tradition had made the mistake of glorifying the poor. The main lesson poverty taught the poor, he argued, was the need to search for ways out. It was therefore the task of philanthropy—scientific and professional—to provide those ways out. Thus, though rooted historically in the decisively Christian accomplishments of the Wilberforce generation, American Scientific Philanthropy took its place squarely in the traditions of Greece and Rome. As "philanthropy" distinct from "charity," its purpose is to enhance the community through civic projects rather than to relieve suffering.

The Carnegie Institutes and the various Rockefeller Foundations and Trusts are powerful and enduring monuments to their vision. Here was the morality and social responsibility that their respective business enterprises so signally lacked. Twentieth-century philanthropy was given its flagship institution: the foundation.

> *As "philanthropy" distinct from "charity," its purpose is to enhance the community through civic projects rather than to relieve suffering.*

ATHENS OVER JERUSALEM

"The best philanthropy, the help that does the most good and the least harm, the help that nourishes civilization at its very root, that most widely disseminates health, righteousness, and happiness, is not what is usually called charity."

—John D. Rockefeller Sr., *The Difficult Art of Giving*

"In the first place, 'philanthropy' is a sickening word. It is generally looked upon as helping a man who hasn't a cent in the world. That sort of thing hardly interests me. I do not like the 'sob stuff' philanthropy. What I want to do is to try to cure the things that seem to be wrong."

—Julius Rosenwald,
Founder of Sears, Roebuck & Co., "Principles of Public Giving," 1929

Andrew Carnegie

Andrew Carnegie (1835–1919) was the first, and, along with John D. Rockefeller Sr., the greatest of the scientific philanthropists. Born in Dunfermline, Scotland in 1835, he and his family emigrated to Allegheny, Pennsylvania when he was thirteen.

Andrew's first job was as a "bobbin boy" for $1.20 per week in the cotton factory that employed his father. He worked his way up through a variety of low-paying jobs, including working in the Pittsburgh telegraph office, where he was among the first in the world to decipher Morse code by ear. Carnegie then entered the railroad industry and made increasingly profitable investments of his own, especially in oil.

At the age of thirty-eight, he staked all his possessions on a new American industry—steel. Through a combination of enterprise, opportunism, and ruthless empire building, Carnegie became the epitome of American business in the Gilded Age, also known as the era of "robber barons." He was variously dubbed "the Star-Spangled Scotchman," "St. Andrew" (by Mark Twain), the "Industrial Napoleon," and "Homo Croesus Americanus." When he sold the Carnegie Corporation to J. P. Morgan in 1901, he built a special vault in Hoboken, New Jersey, to contain the nearly $300 million worth of bonds he had made in profit.

Carnegie was a man of great personal charm and better read than most businessmen. He also enjoyed writing and published several books. The celebrated essay below appeared in the North American Review *in June 1889. (A month earlier Rockefeller already had practiced what Carnegie preaches in his article by giving an initial $600,000 toward the founding of the University of Chicago.) Carnegie was already well known as one of the richest men alive, and the essay caused a great splash on both sides of the Atlantic. Here was a rich man critiquing the practices of the wealthy class and speaking frankly on what to many millionaires were sacred subjects—one's money and personal goals.*

This essay has been described as "the most famous document in the history of American philanthropy." It lays out the philosophy behind Carnegie's vision of professional philanthropy embodied in a foundation. As previously mentioned, he argues that "The problem of our age is the proper administration of wealth." Interestingly, he hated the term "philanthropy" and does not use it in this essay. Nevertheless, Carnegie largely lived up to the dictum below of "not dying disgraced." He gave away more than $350 million before he died, leaving only a tenth of his fortune to be distributed by his foundation and less than $10 million to be apportioned in annual pensions to his wife and other relatives, friends, associates, and former neighbors. When he died in 1919 the last bond in the New Jersey vault had been given away, and the twentieth century was on its way to foundation-centered philanthropy.

'DEATH TO PRIVILEGE'
[Motto on the Carnegie Family Coat of Arms]

"Poor boys reared thus directly by their parents, possess such advantages over those watched and taught by hired strangers, and exposed to the temptations of wealth and position, that it is not surprising they become the leaders in every branch of human action. . . . Such boys always have marched, and always will march, straight to the front and lead the world; they are the epoch-makers."

—Andrew Carnegie, "The Advantages of Poverty," 1891

The Du Ponts "might believe themselves perceptive in observing the debilitating effects of food stamps for the poor" but were themselves living off a "boundless" supply of "privately funded food stamps. . . . The idea that you get a lifetime supply of food stamps based on coming out of the right womb strikes at my idea of fairness."

—Warren Buffett, *Omaha World Herald*, 1980

The Gospel of Wealth 🖋

The problem of our age is the proper administration of wealth, that the ties of brotherhood may still bind together the rich and poor in harmonious relationship. The conditions of human life have not only been changed, but revolutionized, within the past few hundred years. . . .

Today the world obtains commodities of excellent quality at prices which even the preceding generation would have deemed incredible. In the commercial world similar causes have produced similar results, and the race is benefited thereby. The poor enjoy what the rich could not before afford. What were the luxuries have become the necessaries of life. The laborer has now more comforts than the farmer had a few generations ago. The farmer has more luxuries than the landlord had, and is more richly clad and better housed. The landlord has books and pictures rarer and appointments more artistic than the king could then obtain.

The price we pay for this salutary change is, no doubt, great. We assemble thousands of operatives in the factory, and in the mine, of whom the employer can know little or nothing, and to whom he is little better than a myth. All intercourse between them is at an end. Rigid castes are formed, and, as usual, mutual ignorance breeds mutual distrust. Each caste is without sympathy with the other, and ready to credit anything disparaging in regard to it. Under the law of competition, the employer of thousands is forced into the strictest economies, among which the rates paid to labor figure prominently, and often there is friction between the employer and the employed, between capital and labor, between rich and poor. Human society loses homogeneity.

The price which society pays for the law of competition, like the price it pays for cheap comforts and luxuries, is also great; but the advantages of this law are also greater still than its cost—for it is to this law that we owe our wonderful material development, which brings improved conditions in its train. . . . [W]hile the law may be sometimes hard for the individual, it is best for the race, because it ensures the survival of the fittest in every department. We accept and welcome, therefore, as conditions to which we must accommodate ourselves, great inequality of environment; the concentration of business, industrial and commercial, in the hands of a few; and the law of competition between these, as being not only beneficial, but essential to the future progress of the race.

Having accepted these, it follows that there must be great scope for the exercise of special ability in the merchant and in the manufacturer who has to conduct affairs upon a great scale. That this talent for organization and management is rare among men is proved by the fact that it invariably secures enormous rewards for its possessor, no matter where or under what laws or conditions. The experienced in affairs always rate the man whose services can be obtained as a partner as not only the first consideration, but such as render the question of his capital scarcely worth considering; for able men soon create capital; in the hands of those without the special talent required, capital soon takes wings. Such men become interested in firms or corporations using millions; and, estimating only simple interest to be made upon the capital invested, it is inevitable that their income must exceed their expenditure and that they must, therefore, accumulate wealth. Nor is there any middle ground which such men can occupy, because the great manufacturing or commercial concern which does not earn at least interest upon its capital soon becomes bankrupt. It must either go forward or fall behind; to stand still is impossible. It is a condition essential to its successful operation that it should be thus far profitable, and even that, in addition to interest on capital, it should make profit. It is a law . . . that men possessed of this peculiar talent for affairs, under the free play of economic forces must, of necessity, soon be in receipt of more revenue than can be judiciously expended upon themselves; and this law is as beneficial for the race as the others.

Objections to the foundations upon which society is based are not in order, because the condition of the race is better with these than it has been with any

Under the law of competition, the employer of thousands is forced into the strictest economies, among which the rates paid to labor figure prominently, and often there is friction between the employer and the employed, between capital and labor, between rich and poor.

[W]hile the law may be sometimes hard for the individual, it is best for the race, because it ensures the survival of the fittest in every department.

other which has been tried. . . . Unequally or unjustly, perhaps, as these laws
sometimes operate, and imperfect as they appear to the Idealist, they are, nevertheless, like the highest type of man, the best and most valuable of all that
humanity has yet accomplished.

We start, then, with a condition of affairs under which the best interests
of the race are promoted, but which inevitably gives wealth to the few. Thus
far, accepting conditions as they exist, the situation can be surveyed and pronounced good. The question then arises, . . . What is the proper mode of
administering wealth after the laws upon which civilization is founded have
thrown it into the hands of the few? And it is of this great question that I
believe I offer the true solution. . . .

There are but three modes in which surplus wealth can be disposed of. It
can be left to the families of the decedents; or it can be bequeathed for public purposes; or, finally, it can be administered by its possessor during their lives. Under
the first and second modes most of the wealth of the world that has reached the
few has hitherto been applied. Let us in turn consider each of these modes. The
first is the most injudicious. In monarchical countries, the estates and the greatest portion of the wealth are left to the first son, that the vanity of the parent may
be gratified by the thought that his name and title are to descend unimpaired to
succeeding generations. The condition of this class in Europe today teaches the
failure of such hopes or ambitions. The successors have become impoverished
through their follies, or from the fall in the value of land. . . . Under republican
institutions the division of property among the children is much fairer; but the
question which forces itself upon thoughtful men in all lands is, Why should
men leave great fortunes to their children? If this is done from affection, is it not
misguided affection? Observation teaches that, generally speaking, it is not well
for the children that they should be so burdened. Neither is it well for the State.
Beyond providing for the wife and daughters moderate sources of income, and
very moderate allowance indeed, if any, for the sons, men may well hesitate; for
it is no longer questionable that great sums bequeathed often work more for the
injury than for the good of the recipients. Wise men will soon conclude that, for
the best interests of the members of their families, and of the State, such bequests
are an improper use of their means.

It is not suggested that men who have failed to educate their sons to earn
a livelihood shall cast them adrift in poverty. If any man has seen fit to rear his
sons with a view to their living idle lives, or, what is highly commendable, has
instilled in them the sentiment that they are in a position to labor for public
ends without reference to pecuniary considerations, then, of course, the duty of

the parent is to see that such are provided for in moderation. There are instances of millionaires' sons unspoiled by wealth, who, being rich, still perform great services to the community. Such are the very salt of the earth, as valuable as, unfortunately, they are rare. It is not the exception, however, but the rule, that men must regard; and, looking at the usual result of enormous sums conferred upon legatees, the thoughtful man must shortly say, "I would as soon leave to my son a curse as the almighty dollar," and admit to himself that it is not the welfare of the children, but family pride, which inspires these legacies.

"Everything I have, son, I have because your grandfather left it to me. I see now that that was a bad thing."

As to the second mode, that of leaving wealth at death for public uses, it may be said that this is only a means for the disposal of wealth, provided a man is content to wait until he is dead before he becomes of much good in the world. Knowledge of the results of legacies bequeathed is not calculated to inspire the brightest hopes of much posthumous good being accomplished by them. The cases are not few in which the real object sought by the testator is not attained, nor are they few in which his real wishes are thwarted. In many cases the bequests are so used as to become only monuments of his folly. It is well to remember that it requires the exercise of not less ability than that which acquires it, to use wealth so as to be really beneficial to the community. Besides this, it may fairly be said that no man is to be extolled for doing what he cannot help doing, nor is he to be thanked by the community to which he only leaves wealth at death. Men who leave vast sums in this way may fairly be thought men who would not have left it at all had they been able to take it with them. The memories of such cannot be held in grateful remembrance, for there is no grace in their gifts. It is not to be wondered at that such bequests seem so generally to lack the blessing.

The growing disposition to tax more and more heavily large estates left at death is a cheering indication of the growth of a salutary change in public opinion. The State of Pennsylvania now takes—subject to some exceptions—one tenth of the property left by its citizens. The budget presented in the British

It is well to remember that it requires the exercise of not less ability than that which acquires it, to use wealth so as to be really beneficial to the community.

Parliament the other day proposes to increase the death duties; and, most significant of all the new tax is to be a graduated one. Of all forms of taxation; this seems the wisest. Men who continue hoarding great sums all their lives, the proper use of which for public ends would work good to the community from which it chiefly came, should be made to feel that the community, in the form of the State, cannot thus be deprived of its proper share. By taxing estates heavily at death the State marks its condemnation of the selfish millionaire's unworthy life. . . .

There remains, then, only one mode of using great fortunes; but in this we have the true antidote for the temporary unequal distribution of wealth, the reconciliation of the rich and the poor—a reign of harmony, another ideal, differing, indeed, from that of the Communist in requiring only the further evolution of existing conditions, not the total overthrow of our civilization.

There remains, then, only one mode of using great fortunes; but in this we have the true antidote for the temporary unequal distribution of wealth, the reconciliation of the rich and the poor—a reign of harmony, another ideal, differing, indeed, from that of the Communist in requiring only the further evolution of existing conditions, not the total overthrow of our civilization. It is founded upon the present most intense Individualism, and the race is prepared to put it in practice by degrees whenever it pleases. Under its sway we shall have an ideal State, in which the surplus wealth of the few will become, in the best sense, the property of the many, because administered for the common good; and this wealth, passing through the hands of the few, can be made a much more potent force for the elevation of our race than if distributed in small sums to the people themselves. . . .

Poor and restricted are our opportunities in this life, narrow our horizon, our best work most imperfect; but rich men should be thankful for one inestimable boon. They have it in their power during their lives to busy themselves in organizing benefactions from which the masses of their fellows will derive lasting advantage, and thus dignify their own lives. The highest life is probably to be reached, not by such imitation of the life of Christ as Count Tolstoi gives us, but, while animated by Christ's spirit, by recognizing the changed conditions of this age, and adopting modes of expressing this spirit suitable to the changed conditions under which we live, still laboring for the good of our fellows, which was the essence of his life and teaching, but laboring in a different manner.

This, then, is held to be the duty of the man of wealth: To set an example of modest, unostentatious living, shunning display or extravagance; to provide moderately for the legitimate wants of those dependent upon him; and, after doing so, to consider all surplus revenues which come to him simply as trust funds, which he is called upon to administer, and strictly bound as a matter of duty to administer in the manner which, in his judgment, is best calculated to produce the most beneficial results for the community—the man of wealth thus becoming the mere trustee and agent for his poorer brethren, bringing to their service his superior wisdom, experience, and ability to administer, doing for them better than they would or could do for themselves. . . .

The best uses to which surplus wealth can be put have already been indicated. Those who would administer wisely must, indeed, be wise; for one of the serious obstacles to the improvement of our race is indiscriminate charity. It were better for mankind that the millions of the rich were thrown into the sea than so spent as to encourage the slothful, the drunken, the unworthy. Of every thousand dollars spent in so-called charity today, it is probable that nine hundred and fifty dollars is unwisely spent—so spent, indeed, as to produce the very evils which it hopes to mitigate or cure. . . .

In bestowing charity, the main consideration should be to help those who will help themselves; to provide part of the means by which those who desire to improve may do so; to give those who desire to rise the aids by which they may rise; to assist, but rarely or never to do all. Neither the individual nor the race is improved by almsgiving. Those worthy of assistance, except in rare cases, seldom require assistance. The really valuable men of the race never do, except in case of accident or sudden change. Every one has, of course, cases of individuals brought to his own knowledge where temporary assistance can do genuine good, and these he will not overlook. But the amount which can be wisely given by the individual for individuals is necessarily limited by his lack of knowledge of the circumstances connected with each. He is the only true reformer who is as careful and as anxious not to aid the unworthy as he is to aid the worthy, and, perhaps, even more so, for in almsgiving more injury is probably done by rewarding vice than by relieving virtue.

The rich man is thus almost restricted to following the examples of [those] who know that the best means of benefiting the community is to place within its reach the ladders upon which the aspiring can rise—free

"What I'm doing, essentially, is robbing from the rich and setting up foundations."

© 1995 by Sidney Harris, The Chronicle of Philanthropy.

The man of wealth thus becoming the mere trustee and agent for his poorer brethren, bringing to their service his superior wisdom, experience, and ability to administer, doing for them better than they would or could do for themselves.

libraries, parks, and means of recreation, by which men are helped in body and mind; works of art, certain to give pleasure and improve the public taste; and public institutions of various kinds, which will improve the general condition of the people; in this manner returning their surplus wealth to the mass of their fellows in the forms best calculated to do them lasting good.

Thus is the problem of rich and poor to be solved. The laws of accumulation will be left free, the laws of distribution free. Individualism will continue, but the millionaire will be but a trustee for the poor, entrusted for a season with a great part of the increased wealth of the community, but administering it for the community far better than it could or would have done for itself. The best minds will thus have reached a stage in the development of the race in which it is clearly seen that there is no mode of disposing of surplus wealth creditable to thoughtful and earnest men into whose hands it flows, save by using it year by year for the general good. This day already dawns. Men may die without incurring the pity of their fellows, still sharers in great business enterprises from which their capital cannot be or has not been withdrawn, and which is left chiefly at death for public uses; yet the day is not far distant when the man who dies leaving behind him millions of available wealth, which was free to him to administer during life, will pass away "unwept, unhonored, and unsung," no matter to what uses he leaves the dross which he cannot take with him. Of such as these the public verdict will then be: "The man who dies thus rich dies disgraced."

Such, in my opinion is the true gospel concerning wealth, obedience to which is destined some day to solve the problem of the rich and the poor, and to bring "Peace on earth, among men good will."

THE MUNIFICENT MAN

"Munificence differs from liberality in the largeness of the sums in which it deals. Its general character is magnitude. There is a sort of scientific skill implied in munificence. The occasion must be worthy of the expenditure, and the expenditure worthy of the occasion. There must also be a desire after what is noble. There is a grandeur of manner which imparts a special luster to the acts of a munificent man. . . . The occasions which are fitting for the display of munificence [are] first, the service of religion, and next the great public and patriotic services."

—Aristotle, *Ethics*, Book IV

"The prototype of the great American philanthropist is to be found in ancient Rome," not in the Scriptures.

—Robert Payton

"Acting in accordance with this advice, it becomes the duty of the millionaire to increase his revenues. The struggle for more is completely freed from selfish or ambitious taint and becomes a noble pursuit. Then he labors not for self, but for others; not to hoard, but to spend. The more he makes, the more the public gets. His whole life is changed from the moment that he resolves to become a disciple of the gospel of wealth, and henceforth he labors to acquire that he may wisely administer for others' good. His daily labor is a daily virtue. Instead of destroying, impairing, or disposing of the tree which yields such golden fruit, it does not degrade his life nor even his old age to continue guarding the capital from which alone he can obtain the means to do good. He may die leaving a sound business in which his capital remains, but beyond this die poor, possessed of no fortune which was free for him to distribute, and therefore, I submit, not justly chargeable with belonging to the class which 'lay up their treasures upon earth.'"

—Andrew Carnegie, "The Advantages of Poverty"

"At the conclusion of the long day, when Carnegie was at last ready to board that quaint vehicle posing as a train to take Princeton visitors back to the main line to New York and Philadelphia, he turned to [University President Woodrow] Wilson and thanked him for a most instructive day. As the story would later be told by generations of delighted Princetonians, Carnegie then said, 'I know exactly what Princeton needs and I intend to give it to her.' His momentarily ecstatic host, who had visions of libraries, laboratories, and law schools dancing in his head, eagerly asked, 'What?'

"'It's a lake. Princeton should have a rowing crew to compete with Harvard, Yale, and Columbia. That will take young men's minds off football.'"

—Joseph Frazier Wall, *Andrew Carnegie*

The following reading, heavily abbreviated, sets out Carnegie's vision of the best areas in which to practice professional philanthropy. His list was unlikely to please traditional philanthropists—churches were last, just below swimming pools. All in all, Carnegie's list owes more to Greece and Rome than to Jerusalem and Galilee.

The Best Fields for Philanthropy ❧

First. Standing apart by itself there is the founding of a university by men enormously rich, such men as must necessarily be few in any country. . . .

Second. The result of my own study of the question, What is the best gift which can be gift to a community? is that a free library occupies the first place, provided the community will accept and maintain it as a public institution, as much a part of the city property as its public schools, and, indeed, an adjunct to these. . . .

Third. We have another most important department in which great sums can be worthily used—the founding or extension of hospitals, medical colleges, laboratories, and other institutions connected with the alleviation of human suffering, and especially with the prevention rather than with the cure of human ills. . . .

Fourth. In the very front rank of benefactions public parks should be placed, always provided that the community undertakes to maintain, beautify, and preserve them inviolate. No more useful or more beautiful monument can be left by any man than a park for the city in which he was born or in which he has long lived, nor can the community pay a more graceful tribute to the citizen who presents it than to give his name to the gift. . . .

"All I know is that it's been there since I set up that foundation, and now I'm getting these wings."

Fifth. We have another good use for surplus wealth in providing our cities with halls suitable for meetings of all kinds, and for concerts of elevating music. . . .

Sixth. In another respect we are still much behind Europe. A form of benevolence which is not uncommon there is providing swimming-baths for the people. . . .

Seventh. Churches as fields for the use of surplus wealth have purposely been reserved for the last, because, these being sectarian, every man will be governed in his action in regard to them by his own attachments; therefore gifts to churches, it may be said, is not, in one sense, gifts to the community at large, but to special classes. Nevertheless, every millionaire may know of a district where the little cheap, uncomfortable, and altogether unworthy wooden structure stands at the crossroads, to which the whole neighborhood gathers on Sunday, and which, independently of the form of the doctrines taught, is the center of social life and source of neighborly feeling. The administrator of wealth makes a good use of part of his surplus if he replaces that building with a permanent structure of brick, stone, or granite, up whose side the honeysuckle and columbine may climb, and from whose tower the sweet-tolling bell may sound. The millionaire should not figure how cheaply this structure can be built, but how perfect it can be made. . . .

Many other avenues for the wise expenditure of surplus wealth might be indicated. I enumerate but a few—a very few—of the many fields which are open, and only those in great or considerable sums can be judiciously used. . . . It is not expected, neither is it desirable, that there should be general concurrence as to the best possible use of surplus wealth. For different men and different localities there are different uses. What commends itself most highly to the judgment of the administrator is the best use for him, for his heart should be in the work. . . .

In Christ's day, it is evident, reformers were against the wealthy. It is none the less evident that we are fast recurring to that position today; and there will be nothing to surprise the student of sociological development if society should soon approve the text which has caused so much anxiety: "It is easier for a camel to enter the eye of a needle than for a rich man to enter the kingdom of heaven." Even if the needle were the small casement at the gates, the words betoken serious difficulty for the rich. It will be but a step for the theologian from the doctrine that he who dies rich dies disgraced, to that which brings upon the man punishment or deprivation hereafter.

The gospel of wealth but echoes Christ's words. It calls upon the millionaire to sell all that he hath and give it in the highest and best form to the poor by administering his estate himself for the good of his fellows, before he is called upon to lie down and rest upon the bosom of Mother Earth. So doing, he will approach his end no longer the ignoble hoarder of useless millions; poor, very poor indeed, in money, but rich, very rich, twenty times a millionaire still, in the affection, gratitude, and administration of his fellow-men, and—sweeter far—soothed and sustained by the still, small voice within, which, whispering, tells him that, because he has lived, perhaps one small part of the great world has been bettered just a little. This much is sure: against such riches as these no bar will be found at the gates of Paradise.

Excerpted from *The Gospel of Wealth*, by Andrew Carnegie (London, F. C. Hagen & Co., 1889).

THE ROCKEFELLER BURDEN

"Your fortune is rolling up, rolling up like an avalanche! You must distribute it faster than it grows! If you do not, it will crush you, and your children, and your children's children."

—Rev. Frederick T. Gates,
chief philanthropic advisor to John D. Rockefeller Sr.

"I trembled as I witnessed the unreasoning popular resentment at Mr. Rockefeller's riches, to the mass of people, a national menace. It was not, however, the unreasoning public prejudice of his vast fortune that chiefly troubled me. Was it to be handed on to posterity as other great fortunes have been handed down by their possessors, with scandalous results to their descendants and powerful tendencies to social demoralization? I saw no other course but for Mr. Rockefeller and his son to form a series of great corporate philanthropies for forwarding civilization in all its elements in this land and in all lands; philanthropies, if possible, limitless in time and amount, broad in scope, and self-perpetuating."

—Rev. Frederick T. Gates

"When the 73-year-old Gates stepped down from the leadership of the institution that was his *summa,* he realized that one day it might well be as powerful as Standard Oil itself. 'When you die and come to approach the judgment of the Almighty God, what do you think He will demand of you?' he asked his colleagues at his retirement dinner. 'Do you for an instant presume to believe that He will inquire into your petty failures or trivial virtues? No. He will ask just one question, *What did you do as a trustee of the Rockefeller Foundation?'* "

—Peter Collier and David Horowitz, *The Rockefellers: An American Dynasty*

"Neither in the privacy of his home, nor at the table, nor in the aisles of his church, nor during business hours, nor anywhere was he secure from insistent appeal. . . . He was constantly hunted, stalked, and hounded almost like a wild animal."

—Frederick T. Gates, of John D. Rockefeller Sr.

QUESTIONS FOR THOUGHT AND DISCUSSION

1. What are the enormous changes hinted at in the first paragraph that Carnegie views as the spur to his new philanthropy?
2. Carnegie reveals his own philosophy of life in the paragraph, "The price which society pays for the law of competition." How does his Social Darwinism shape his view of wealth-creation and philanthropy?
3. What are Carnegie's "three modes" of dispensing surplus wealth? What is his assessment of each and why? Which do you favor?
4. What is his reasoning for how wealth has ended up in the hands of the few? To what end? How does he see charity and the poor?
5. Carnegie claims that his gospel of wealth "but echoes Christ's words." In actuality, there are stark differences with what Jesus was saying. What points did he miss? In what ways does he draw on the Judeo-Christian view of ownership as stewardship?

6. He argues that his method for administering surplus wealth will "solve the problem of the rich and the poor." What seeds in his own argument might flower into fatal problems for his approach? See the following box, "The Critics."

THE CRITICS

"I am quite unable to let off Mr. Carnegie in the pleasant and approving way in which Mr. Gladstone dismisses him. When I contemplate him as the representative of a particular class of millionaires, I am forced to say, with all personal respect, and without holding him in the least responsible for his unfortunate circumstances, that he is an anti-Christian phenomenon, a social monstrosity, and a grave political peril."

—Rev. Hugh Price Hughes,
British Methodist minister, in the *Nineteenth Century* magazine

"Just as formerly it was contended that political power should be in the hands of the few, because it would be better administered, so now it is contended—I quote Mr. Carnegie's words . . . —that 'the millionaire is entrusted for the time being with a great part of the increased wealth of the community, because he can administer it for the community far better than it could or would have done for itself.' This, of course, if accepted and carried out in any complete way, becomes patronage . . . and in the long run, society cannot afford to be patronized. It is better for any community to advance more slowly than to gain altogether by gifts rather than, in large part, by earnings. Within proper limits, the public is advantaged by the gifts of the rich, but if the method becomes the accepted method, to be expected and relied upon, the decline of public self-respect has begun. There is a public public spirit to be cherished as well as a private public spirit."

—William Jewett Tucker,
Andover Seminary professor, 1891

"The effort to make voluntary charity solve the problems of a major social crisis . . . results only in monumental hypocrisies and tempts selfish people to regard themselves as unselfish."

—Reinhold Niebuhr

"Carnegie gave over $40 million to build 2,059 libraries. . . . But a steelworker, speaking for many, told an interviewer, 'We didn't want him to build a library for us, we would rather have had higher wages.' At that time steelworkers worked twelve-hour shifts on floors so hot they had to nail wooden platforms under their shoes. Every two weeks they toiled an inhuman twenty-four hour shift, and then they got their sole day off. The best housing they could afford was crowded and filthy. Most died in their forties or earlier, from accidents or disease. . . ."

"By the turn of the century, Pittsburgh had the highest death rate in the United States. That was the year before Carnegie sold his steel company. Typhoid fever epidemics recurred, because Pittsburgh's council members wouldn't filter the drinking water; they disliked public spending. Besides, a water system would mean a dam, and a dam would yield cheap hydroelectric power, so the power companies would buy less coal; coal-company owners and their bankers didn't want any dams. Pittsburgh epidemics were so bad that boatmen on the Ohio River wouldn't handle Pittsburgh money, for fear of contagion."

—Annie Dillard,
An American Childhood

FOUR

CONTEMPORARY CHALLENGES TO VOLUNTARISM AND PHILANTHROPY

As THE INTRODUCTION TO THIS BOOK STATED, THE WORLDS OF GIVING, CARING, AND *volunteering are in a time of significant transition, if not crisis. But we should understand this in the original, classical sense rather than the modern, popular sense. Philanthropy is in crisis because it is passing through a time of testing and transition that will reveal the present state of its character and health—for better or worse.*

In this fourth part, we examine five of the major challenges facing philanthropy today.

1. The "CNNing" of perceptions. *Thanks to the immediacy of global communications, the circumstances in faraway lands are made known as they happen. Although this instant information can prompt instant response, it can also distract us from needs in our own backyards and desensitize us to sustained giving and caring.*

2. The "PhDing" of expertise. *Much good has come from the scientific approach of the professional foundation—effective, efficient, and directed giving. But the growing professionalization of giving has undermined traditional giving in important ways.*

3. The "NIMBYing" of concerns. *Isolated by privilege, people often give generously to support their own communities, enriching their lives through theater, museums, libraries, and the like. But their "not in my backyard" stance makes responding to the poor quite a stretch.*

4. The reverse "Cy Presing" of foundations. *In the past, foundations adhered to the intent of the donor, a principle known as cy pres. Recently, however, the trend is in the other direction, with foundation trustees operating sometimes in direct opposition to a founder's wishes.*

5. The "ODing" of compassion. *Another effect of global communications and media is the constant bombardment of images of suffering and need. But rather than responding in compassion, people often become overwhelmed and desensitized.*

Needless to say, the examples chosen are simply that—examples. But they illustrate both the range and profundity of the issues that require resolution if a culture of giving and caring is to retain its vital role in democratic societies.

POINT TO PONDER:

The "CNNing" of Perceptions

"Who is my neighbor?" This celebrated question from a lawyer elicited the answer that has become the banner-story of Western charity—the parable of the Good Samaritan. The parable, like all acts of mercy and generosity, turns on perceptions. What priorities and prejudices blind the priest and the Levite from seeing the traveler in need? How is the hated Samaritan foreigner sufficiently free from these prejudices and priorities to respond simply as one human being to another?

Jesus not only stunningly subverts the attitudes of his hearers but squarely puts the focus of action on our helping our neighbors in need. He strips away the types of prejudice that blind us from seeing whom we must help and what we must do.

Regarding our fellow human as a neighbor in need is only one part of the act of love and giving, but it is a crucial part. It is therefore not surprising that perceptions of need have been critically affected by the modern communications revolution—beginning with the railway and telegraph and now gathering momentum in the era of satellites, television, cellular telephones, and e-mail. Charles Dickens was quick to see the implications in creating a new form of "telescopic philanthropy"—of which his Mrs. Jellyby in Bleak House is a humorously recognizable type. We react to the dire images of far-off places served up by the media, all the while overlooking needs right beneath our noses. But the problem becomes infinitely more accelerated with the rise of television, and hence the "CNNing" of perceptions.

We react to the dire images of far-off places served up by the media, all the while overlooking needs right beneath our noses.

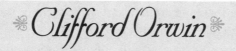

Clifford Orwin (born 1947) is Professor of Political Science at the University of Toronto and author of The Humanity of Thucydides. *This article is an abbreviated version of an address given in September 1995 in Seoul at the Global Convention on Tolerance and the Restoration of Morality and Humanity, sponsored by UNESCO and Kyung Hae University.*

TELESCOPIC PHILANTHROPY

"'Mrs. Jellyby,' said Mr. Kenge, . . . 'is a lady of very remarkable strength of character, who devotes herself entirely to the public. She has devoted herself to an extensive variety of public subjects, at various times, and is at present (until something else attracts her) devoted to the subject of Africa. . . .'

"We passed several more children on the way up, whom it was difficult to avoid treading on in the dark; and as we came into Mrs. Jellyby's presence, one of the poor little things fell downstairs—down a whole flight (as it sounded to me), with a great noise.

"Mrs. Jellyby, whose face reflected none of the uneasiness which we could not help showing in our own faces, as the dear child's head recorded its passage with a bump on every stair—Richard afterwards said he counted seven, besides one for the landing—received us with perfect equanimity. She was a pretty, very diminutive, plump woman, of from forty to fifty, with handsome eyes, though they had a curious habit of seeming to look a long way off. As if—I am quoting Richard again—they could see nothing nearer than Africa! . . .

"Peepy (so self-named) was the unfortunate child who had fallen downstairs, who now interrupted the correspondence by presenting himself with a strip of plaster on his forehead, to exhibit his wounded knees, in which Ada and I did not know which to pity most—the bruises or the dirt. Mrs. Jellyby merely added, with the serene composure with which she said everything, 'Go along, you naughty Peepy!' and fixed her fine eyes on Africa again."

—Charles Dickens, *Bleak House*

Distant Compassion

As human beings have always suffered, so have they responded to the suffering of others. Compassion is as old as the human race. What is new is our window on the distress of fellow human beings no matter how remote from us. Thanks to the impact of the information revolution, there is no instance of suffering anywhere that is out of range of the camera or that, once recorded, is not instantly available for display everywhere.

Often we view these reproductions "live" as the suffering actually occurs. Should we miss them the first time around, we can count on the most gripping ones being replayed again and again. Without leaving our living rooms we have the sorrows of the world at our fingertips. As the French commentator Pierre Hassner has noted, the power of televised horrors has vindicated (in a manner of speaking) Immanuel Kant's hope that a violation of right anywhere on earth would be felt everywhere on it.

Naturally this development has been widely noticed. People speak of the

"CNN factor." The theory is that thanks to the immediate and insistent diffusion of such images of suffering, democratic governments have come and will continue to come under pressure from their peoples to undertake humanitarian interventions. Thus may the gods of television pride themselves on furnishing their viewers with an education in humanity more universal, more vivid, more effective than any earlier one. This is a beautiful hope—but how plausible is it?

THE NEED FOR IMAGES

It is a fact that many viewers credit television with having awakened their concern for distant sufferings to which they would otherwise have remained indifferent. There is even a reason why television might seem particularly suited to such a role. Compassion depends on the imagination. Only insofar as we can imagine the sufferings that we ascribe to the other—and perhaps even only insofar as we can imagine those sufferings befalling ourselves—do these kindle our compassion for him. (It is for both these reasons that most children exhibit so little compassion.) Imagination, in turn, requires images, the more concrete the better. What will excite our sympathy for the people of Rwanda is not the grim tally of the dead or displaced, however horrific that may be. As the French sociologist Luc Boltanski has noted in his valuable study, *La Souffrance à distance* (Suffering at a Distance), a table of statistics on poverty, however grim, does not evoke compassion with the plight of the poor. What is needed are images of particular victims, pegs on which to hang our imagination. As Kant once remarked, "a suffering child fills our heart with sadness, while we learn with indifference the news of a terrible battle."

Only insofar as we can imagine the sufferings that we ascribe to the other—and perhaps even only insofar as we can imagine those sufferings befalling ourselves—do these kindle our compassion for him.

Of course, as we may as well admit at the outset, televised images of suffering trade at a substantial discount. The first point about such images on which to insist is also the most obvious. As with everything televised, we can always turn them off or tune them out, i.e., watch without seeing and listen without hearing. In the many households in which television serves as a permanent background din, the horrors that it displays remain in the background also. As for those viewers who do pay attention, they are always free to change the channel. The five hundred-channel universe will offer plenty of alternative fare. . . .

In the many households in which television serves as a permanent background din, the horrors that it displays remain in the background also.

Let's assume, however, that as good citizens we do watch the news each night. We then experience the rhythm of the typical newscast, which follows grave matters with trivial ones (e.g., weather, sports, "lifestyles," and enter-tainment news). Whatever sufferings may have assailed us at the top of the hour, our minds are eased back into the usual preoccupations of everyday life in a consumer society. Television producers tend to remember—they have con-fessed it to me—that their audience wishes to be entertained. And the right amount of suffering is entertaining—but only the right amount. . . . So while television doubtless renders distant sufferings more vivid, it does not thereby necessarily render them more real.

And the right amount of suffering is entertaining— but only the right amount.

The danger of blurring the line between real and fictive suffering is all the greater in the case of foreign affairs, our sense of the reality of which is none too solid to begin with. . . .

Can television, itself a "leisure-hour interest that [has] attained the rank of [a hobby]," bring home to us the reality of such faraway happenings? Yes and no. Recent writers have underscored the paradox that television at the same time brings distant matters closer to us and serves to distance us from these very mat-ters. The televiewer is not as such a teledoer (or even a doer of things close to home). As Curtis Gans puts it, "People say that television brings the interna-tional community into your living room, but what it really does is bring you into your living room" (and, he might have added, keep you there). . . .

I will not dwell on the vanity of looking to television to effect universal moral regeneration. The noteworthy fact is rather that, despite the ease of eva-sion, the CNN factor is real. Consider the terrible spectacles of starvation in Somalia, tribal slaughter in Rwanda, and ethnic cleansing in the former Yugoslavia. In the past, the first two of these would hardly have come to the attention of publics in the Western democracies, let alone have captured their imagination. Nor would Bosnia have assumed the role of the central foreign policy issue confronting those democracies. None of these cases is perceived by the relevant publics as crucial to their respective national interests. The widespread response to them has therefore indeed been "humanitarian," and has been stimulated largely by televised images. . . .

[Eighteenth-century philosopher] Jean-Jacques Rousseau [was] the first great modern proponent of a politics founded on compassion. . . . Rousseau was the first to seek to ground this concern in a direct emotional response to the sufferings of others. He was the first to interpret moral education as largely an education in compassion, relying precisely on exposure to images of the sort that we are discussing. . . .

Practically speaking, however, Rousseau placed no faith in a global or cos-mopolitan benevolence. . . .

> Distrust those cosmopolitans who go to great length in their books
> to discover duties they do not deign to fulfill around them. A
> philosopher loves the Tartars so as to be spared having to love his
> neighbor.

Rousseau's critique of what we would call "humanitarianism" follows from his analysis of the psychological basis of compassion. According to him the force of our commiseration varies with our capacity to relate to the specific sufferings and sufferer. Compassion tends to be most effective where spectator and victim have the most in common.

> It seems that the sentiment of humanity evaporates and weakens as
> it is extended over the whole world, and that we can't be moved by
> calamities in Tartary or Japan as we are by those of a European
> people. Interest and commiseration must in some way be com-
> pressed to be activated. Now since this inclination in us can only
> be useful to those with whom we have to live, it is good that the
> feeling of humanity, concentrated among fellow citizens, gains fresh
> force through the habit of seeing one another and the common
> interest that unites them.

Nearby sufferings foster compassion in those educated to respond to them; far-off ones provide the insensitive with an alibi for failing to act to relieve those nearby. Rousseau's critique of compassion at a distance anticipates Dickens's presentation of Mrs. Jellyby, so mindful of the plight of the natives of Borrioboola-Gha and so blind to the needs of her own children and the suffering of the London poor. . . .

Humanitarianism as so conceived may link human beings however dissimilar, but such links are liable to be fickle and highly unstable. To find, as the Good Samaritan did, a single victim by the roadside is one thing. To confront a succession of them on television, widely scattered around the globe, is something else entirely. Our humanitarian impulses may fire, but they will also tend to sputter. On the one hand, we wish that we could help; on the other, we are only too likely to feel ourselves absolved by the fact of this very wish. . . .

The CNN factor is real, but it remains to be seen whether its effectiveness will stand the test of time. The final pitfall of the new abundance of televised suffering is also the most ironic. It is the danger that constant exposure to such suffering will not sensitize but inure us to it. It has long been observed that those whose daily fare is the suffering of others tend toward indifference to it—"it is," as Rousseau remarks, "by dint of seeing death and suffering that priests and doctors become pitiless." Such is now our situation as spectators. As one victim recedes from view another always appears to replace it. Televised misery resembles the hydra: It persists (if sometimes with a new head) no matter how hard we attack it.

Will world reserves of beneficence expand to meet increased demand, or will there be an ever thinner spreading of the same naturally limited supply?

The globalization of the spectacle of suffering may broaden the horizons of our compassion, but will it do so without diluting its force? Will world reserves of beneficence expand to meet increased demand, or will there be an ever thinner spreading of the same naturally limited supply? The international flow of humanitarian concern may come to resemble that of capital. Both will migrate freely, and their allegiances will prove almost equally fickle. Last year the Tutsis attracted attention, six months ago the Chechens, today the Bosnian Muslims. Newer, fresher causes will siphon air time and humanitarian sentiment from older, tedious, and intractable ones. Like those residents of great cities who become hardened to the misery that lies always near to hand, we voyeurs of the global village will turn away from the distant sufferings that come daily within our purview.

Clifford Orwin, "Distant Compassion," *The National Interest*, No. 48 Spring 1996. Reprinted by permission of *The National Interest*.

WHO IS MY NEIGHBOR?

"Further, all men are to be loved equally. But since you cannot do good to all, you are to pay special regard to those who, by the accidents of time, or place, or circumstance, are brought into closer connection with you."

—St. Augustine, *On Christian Doctrine*

"To be attached to the subdivision, to love the little platoon we belong to in society, is the first principle (the germ as it were) of public affections. It is the first link in the series by which we proceed towards a love to our country, and to mankind. . . . Men are not tied to one another by papers and seals. They are led to associate by resemblances, by conformities, by sympathies."

—Edmund Burke

"Mr. Fantom: I despise a narrow field. O for the reign of universal benevolence! I want to make all mankind good and happy.

"Mr. Goodman: Dear me! Sure that must be a wholesale sort of a job: had you not better try your hand at a town or a neighborhood first?

"Mr. Fantom: Sir, I have a plan in my head for relieving the miseries of the whole world. . .

"Mr. Goodman: The utmost extent of my ambition at present is, to redress the wrongs of a poor apprentice, who has been cruelly used by his master. . . .

"Mr. Fantom: You must not apply to me for the redress of such petty grievances. . . . It is provinces, empires, continents, that the benevolence of the philosopher embraces; every one can do a little paltry good to his next neighbor.

"Mr. Goodman: Every one can but I do not see that every one does. . . . [You] have such a noble zeal for the millions, [yet] feel so little compassion for the units."

—*McGuffey's Reader*

"If an angry bigot assumes this bountiful cause of Abolition, and comes to me with his last news from Barbadoes, why should I not say to him, 'Go love thy infant; love thy wood-chopper: be good-natured and modest: have that grace; and never varnish your hard, uncharitable ambition with this incredible tenderness for black folk a thousand miles off. Thy love afar is spite at home.' Rough and graceless would be such greeting, but truth is handsomer than the affectation of love. Your goodness must have some edge to it—else it is none."

—Ralph Waldo Emerson, "Self-Reliance"

"You can't love humanity; you can only love people."

—Graham Greene

QUESTIONS FOR THOUGHT AND DISCUSSION

1. What is the theory of the "CNN factor"? What cases does Orwin mention for which television has been a significant factor? Can you think of others?

2. In what ways has television affected our perception of needs? How does it distort reality? Why does Orwin say that compassion requires images?

3. Can you think of cases where a reverse CNN factor has been in effect—where plights have been overlooked because there hasn't been substantial television coverage?

4. What are the pitfalls of having a steady diet of televised suffering? What does Orwin consider the paradox of television? Why?

5. Weigh the pros and cons of the implications of television for philanthropy. Where do you agree with Orwin and where do you disagree?

6. Think back on cases where television coverage has influenced your own giving. How do these cases differ from others where you have first-hand knowledge of the needs? Has your interest in these cases been sustained over time? Why or why not?

HUMANITY OR MY NEIGHBOR?

"Oh, how I love Humanity, With love so pure and pringlish,
And how I hate the horrid French, Who never will be English!
The International Idea, The largest and the clearest,
Is welding all the nations now, Except the one that's nearest.
This compromise has long been known, This scheme of partial pardons,
In ethical societies, And small suburban gardens—
The villas and the chapels Where I learned with little labour
The way to love my fellow-man And hate my next-door neighbour."

—G. K. Chesterton, "The World State"

"It is easier to love humanity . . . than to love one's neighbor."

—Eric Hoffer

POINT TO PONDER:

The "PhDing" of Expertise

The second challenge to contemporary philanthropy is far more contro-versial because it touches not the general public but those who are professionals in the field. As such this challenge flies in the face of orthodox opinion and even of common sense.

Professionalism, we would surely all agree, is better than its opposite—being unprofessional, amateurish, or mediocre. "Professional," in other words, has justifiably been equated with "excellence." An attack on one is viewed as an attack on the other, and is hotly resisted. The strong appeal of the Carnegie-Rockefeller innovation in philanthropic foundations is that they provide a "scientific" and "professional" approach to giving that delivers us from the well-meaning but bumbling amateurs of the past.

But now a school of social critics has risen who charge that professionals, specialists, and experts can actually disable rather than enable—especially in the service industries. And it turns out that their general criticisms of exces-sive professionalism are already prefigured in the history of giving—even among some of the most professional of philanthropists, such as Andrew Carnegie. In short, the idea that professionalization (the "PhDing") is a prob-lem would not be entertained for a second by some people. But if the "businessmen of philanthropy," such as Carnegie, themselves foresaw the prob-lem, it is worth deeper reflection.

John McKnight

John McKnight (born 1931) is director of the Community Studies Program at the Center for Urban Affairs and Policy Research of Northwestern University and the author of Community Building from the Inside Out. *He was mentored by Ivan Illich, author and editor of* Disabling Professions, *the first thinker to draw atten-tion to the negative effects of professionalization encroaching upon daily life.*

DISABLING PROFESSIONS

"Professions could not become dominant and disabling unless people were already experiencing as a lack that which the expert imputes to them as a need. . . . Need, used as a noun, became the fodder on which professions were fattened into dominance. . . .

"Our major institutions have acquired the uncanny power to subvert the very purposes for which they had been engineered and financed originally. Under the rule of our most prestigious professions, our institutional tools have as their principal product paradoxical counterproductivity—the systematic disabling of the citizenry. A city built around wheels becomes inappropriate for feet."

—Ivan Illich, *The Disabling Professions*

"One reason [for the current lack of care], no doubt, is that a lot of people are uncaring and irresponsible, but far more important is the attitude of the responsible private individuals who no longer see themselves as the seat of moral initiative. Good deeds have been given over to experts: the acts that constitute the social morality of our time are being performed by paid professionals in large public agencies. Helping the needy, the sick, and the aged has become an operation whose scale and character leave little room for the virtuous private person. Our ancestors in their idiosyncratic charitable endeavors look like moral amateurs."

—Christina Sommers, "Where Have All the Good Deeds Gone?"

The Careless Society 🐾

The story begins as the European pioneers crossed the Alleghenies and started to settle the Midwest. The land they found was covered with forests. With great effort they felled the trees, pulled up the stumps, and planted their crops in the rich, loamy soil.

When they finally reached the western edge of the place we now call Indiana, the forest stopped and ahead lay a thousand miles of the great grass prairie. The Europeans were puzzled by this new environment. Some even called it the Great Desert. It seemed untillable. The earth was often very wet and it was covered with centuries of tangled and matted grasses.

The settlers found that the prairie sod could not be cut with their cast-iron plows, and that the wet earth stuck to their plowshares. Even a team of the best oxen bogged down after a few yards of tugging. The iron plow was a useless tool to farm the prairie soil. The pioneers were stymied for nearly two decades. Their western march was halted and they filled in the eastern regions of the Midwest.

In 1837, a blacksmith in the town of Grand Detour, Illinois, invented a new tool. His name was John Deere, and the tool was a plow made of steel. It was sharp enough to cut through matted grasses and smooth enough to cast off the mud. It was a simple tool, the "sodbuster," that opened the great prairies to agricultural development.

Sauk County, Wisconsin, is the part of that prairie where I have a home. It is named after the Sauk Indians. In 1673, Father Marquette was the first European to lay his eyes upon their land. He found a village laid out in regular patterns on a plain beside the Wisconsin River. He called the place Prairie du Sac. The village was surrounded by fields that had provided maize, beans, and squash for the Sauk people for generations reaching back into unrecorded time.

When the European settlers arrived at the Sauk Prairie in 1837, the government forced the native Sauk people west of the Mississippi River. The settlers came with John Deere's new invention and used the tool to open the area to a new kind of agriculture. They ignored the traditional ways of the Sauk Indians and used their sodbusting tool for planting wheat.

Initially, the soil was generous and the farmers thrived. However, each year the soil lost more of its nurturing power. It was only thirty years after the Europeans arrived with their new technology that the land was depleted. Wheat farming became uneconomical and tens of thousands of farmers left Wisconsin seeking new land with sod to bust.

It took the Europeans and their new technology just one generation to make their homeland into a desert. The Sauk Indians, who knew how to sustain themselves on the Sauk Prairie, were banished to another kind of desert called a reservation. And even they forgot about the techniques and tools that had sustained them on the prairie for generations.

And that is how it was that three deserts were created: Wisconsin, the reservation, and the memories of a people.

A century and a half later, the land of the Sauks is now populated by the children of a second wave of European farmers who learned to replenish the soil through the regenerative powers of dairying, ground-cover crops, and animal manures. These third- and fourth-generation farmers and townspeople do not realize, however, that a new settler is coming soon with an invention as powerful as John Deere's plow.

The new technology is called "bereavement counseling." It is a tool forged at the great state university, an innovative technique to meet the needs of those experiencing the death of a loved one, a tool that can "process" the grief of the people who now live on the Prairie of the Sauk.

As one can imagine the final days of the village of the Sauk Indians before the arrival of the settlers with John Deere's plow, one can also imagine these final days before the arrival of the first bereavement counselor at Prairie du Sac. In these final days, the farmers and the townspeople mourn the death of a mother, brother, son, or friend. The bereaved are joined by neighbors and kin. They meet grief together in lamentation, prayer, and song. They call upon the words of the clergy and surround themselves with community.

It is in these ways that they grieve and then go on with life. Through their mourning they are assured of the bonds between them and renewed in the knowledge that this death is a part of the past and the future of the people on the Prairie of the Sauk. Their grief is common property, an anguish from which the community draws strength and which gives it the courage to move ahead.

Into this prairie community the bereavement counselor arrives with the new grief technology. The counselor calls the invention a service and assures the prairie folk of its effectiveness and superiority by invoking the name of the great university while displaying a diploma and license.

At first, we can imagine that the local people will be puzzled by the bereavement counselor's claims. However, the counselor will tell a few of them that the new technique is merely to assist the bereaved's community at the time of death. To some other prairie folk who are isolated or forgotten, the counselor will offer help in grief processing. These lonely souls will accept the intervention, mistaking the counselor for a friend.

For those who are penniless, the counselor will approach the County Board and advocate the "right to treatment" for these unfortunate souls. This right will be guaranteed by the Board's decision to reimburse those too poor to pay for counseling services.

There will be others, schooled to believe in the innovative new tools certified by universities and medical centers, who will seek out the bereavement counselor by force of habit. And one of these people will tell a bereaved neighbor who is unschooled that unless his grief is processed by a counselor, he will probably have major psychological problems in later life.

Several people will begin to contact the bereavement counselor because, since the County Board now taxes them to *ensure* access to the technology, they will feel that to fail to be counseled is to waste their money and to be denied a benefit, or even a right.

Finally, one day the aged father of a local woman will die. And the next-door neighbor will not drop by because he doesn't want to interrupt the bereavement counselor. The woman's kin will stay home because they will have learned that only the bereavement counselor knows how to process grief in the proper way. The local clergy will seek technical assistance from the bereavement counselor to learn the correct form of service to deal with guilt and grief. And the grieving daughter will know that it is the bereavement counselor who really cares for her, because only the bereavement counselor appears when death visits this family on the Prairie of the Sauk.

It will be only one generation between the time the bereavement counselor arrives and the disappearance of the community of mourners. The counselor's new tool will cut through the social fabric, throwing aside kinship, care, neighborly obligations, and community ways of coming together and going on. Like John Deere's plow, the tools of bereavement counseling will create a desert where a community once flourished.

And finally, even the bereavement counselor will see the impossibility of restoring hope in clients once they are genuinely alone, with nothing but a service for consolation. In the inevitable failure of the service, the bereavement counselor will find the desert even in herself.

There are those who would say that neither John Deere nor the bereavement counselor has created a desert. Rather, they would argue that these new tools have great benefits and that we have focused unduly upon a few negative side effects. Indeed, they might agree with Eli Lilly, founder of the famous drug company, whose motto was "A drug without side effects is no drug at all."

... E. F. Schumacher helped clarify for many of us the nature of those physical tools that are so counterproductive that they become impediments. There is an increasing recognition of the waste and devastation created by these new physical tools, from nuclear generators to supersonic transports. They are the sons and daughters of the sodbuster.

It is much less obvious that the bereavement counselor is also the sodbuster's heir. It is more difficult for us to see how service technology creates deserts. Indeed, there are even those who argue that a good society should scrap its nuclear generators in order to recast them into plowshares of service. They would replace the counterproductive *goods* technology with the *service* technology of modern medical centers, universities, correctional systems, and nursing homes. It is essential, therefore, that we have new measures of service technologies that will allow us to distinguish those that are impediments from those that are monuments.

We can assess the degree of impediment incorporated in modern service technologies by weighing four basic elements. The first is the monetary cost. At what point do the economics of a service technology consume enough of the commonwealth that all of society becomes eccentric and distorted?

At what point do the economics of a service technology consume enough of the commonwealth that all of society becomes eccentric and distorted?

. . . The second element to be weighed was identified by Ivan Illich as "specific counterproductivity." Beyond the negative side effect is the possibility that a service technology can produce the specific inverse of its stated purpose. Thus, one can imagine sickening medicine, stupidifying schools, and crime-making corrections systems.

The evidence grows that some service technologies are now so counterproductive that their abolition is the most productive means to achieve the goal for which they were initially established. Take, for example, the experiment in Massachusetts where, under the leadership of Dr. Jerome Miller, the juvenile correction institutions were closed. As the most recent evaluation studies indicate, the Massachusetts recidivism rate has declined while comparable states with increasing institutionalized populations see an increase in youthful criminality.

There is also the discomforting fact that during doctor strikes in Israel, Canada, and the United States, the death rate took an unprecedented plunge.

Perhaps the most telling example of specifically counterproductive service technologies is demonstrated by the Medicaid program, which provides "health care for the poor." In most states, the amount expended for medical care for the poor is now greater than the cash welfare income provided for that same poor population. Thus, a low-income mother is given $1.00 in income and $1.50 in medical care. It is perfectly clear that the single greatest cause of her ill health is her low income. Nonetheless, the response to her sickening poverty is an ever-growing investment in medical technology—an investment that now consumes her income.

The third element to be weighed is the loss of knowledge. Many of the settlers who came to Wisconsin with John Deere's sodbuster had been peasant farmers in Europe. There, they had tilled the land for centuries using methods that replenished its nourishing capacity. However, once the land seemed unlimited and John Deere's technology came to dominate, they forgot the tools and methods that had sustained them for centuries in the old land and created a new desert.

The same process is at work with the modern service technologies and the professions that use them. One of the most vivid examples involves the methods of a new breed of technologists called pediatricians and obstetricians. During the first half of the twentieth century, these technocrats came, quite naturally, to believe that the preferred method of feeding babies was with a manufactured formula rather than breast milk. Acting as agents for the new lactation technology, these professionals persuaded a generation of women to abjure breastfeeding in favor of their more "healthful" way.

In the fifties in a Chicago suburb, there was a woman named Marion Thompson who still remembered that babies could be fed by breast as well as by can. However, she could find no professional to advise her. She searched for someone who might still remember something about the process of breast-feeding. Fortunately, she found one woman whose memory included the information necessary to begin the flow of milk. From that faint memory, breastfeeding began its long struggle toward restoration in our society. She and six friends started a club that multiplied itself into thousands of small communities and became an international association of women dedicated to breastfeeding: La Leche League. This popular movement reversed the technological imperative in only one generation and has established breastfeeding as a norm in spite of the countervailing views of the service technologists.

Indeed, the American Academy of Pediatrics finally took the official position that breastfeeding is preferable to nurturing infants from canned products. It was as though the Sauk Indians had recovered the Wisconsin prairie and allowed it once again to nourish a people with popular tools.

The fourth element to be weighed is the "hidden curriculum" of the service technologies. As they are implemented through professional techniques, the invisible message of the interaction between professional and client is, "You will be better because I know better." As these professional techniques proliferate across the social landscape, they represent a new praxis, an ever-growing pedagogy that teaches this basic message of the service technologies. Through the propagation of belief in authoritative expertise, professionals cut through the social fabric of community and sow clienthood where citizenship once grew.

It is clear, therefore, that to assess the purported benefits of service technologies, they must be weighed against the sum of the socially distorting monetary costs to the commonwealth; the inverse effects of the interventions; the loss of knowledge, tools, and skills regarding other ways; and the anti-democratic consciousness created by a nation of clients. When the benefits are weighed in this balance, we can begin to recognize how often the tools of professionalized service make social deserts where communities once bloomed.

Unfortunately, the bereavement counselor is but one of many new professionalized servicers that plow over our communities like John Deere's sodbusting settlers.

. . . This chapter, imagining the advent of bereavement counselors in the Sauk Prairie, was written in October 1984. On September 18, 1986, the following article appeared in the *Sauk-Prairie Star,* the newspaper for the citizens of Sauk Prairie.

Through the propagation of belief in authoritative expertise, professionals cut through the social fabric of community and sow clienthood where citizenship once grew.

GRIEVING WILL BE SEMINAR TOPIC

Sauk Prairie High School guidance staff will present a seminar on grieving for freshmen and seniors at Sauk Prairie High School during the week of September 22–26. The seminar is being presented due to the recent losses of classmates for students in the classes of 1990 and 1987.

Freshmen will attend the seminar in conjunction with required health classes. Students who have no health classes first semester will be assigned a presentation during study halls.

Seniors will attend the seminar in conjunction with family living classes. Students who do not have a family living class will be assigned a presentation.

Parents are welcome to call the Guidance Center to discuss any concerns they may have. Parents must authorize students not attending the seminars.

John McKnight, *The Careless Society: Community and Its Counterfeits* (New York: Basic Books, 1995). © 1995 by John McKnight. Reprinted by permission of Basic Books, a member of Perseus Books LLC.

PLEASE, NO GO-BETWEENS

"Man is certainly a benevolent animal. A never sees B in distress without thinking C ought to relieve him directly."

—Sydney Smith

Charity is "a work requiring great tenderness and sympathy, and agents, who do their work for a price rather than for love, should not be trusted to execute the wishes of donors. The keepers of poor-houses (like undertakers) fall into a business, unfeeling way of doing their duties; which is wounding and often partial and cruel to the objects of their attention."

—Rev. William Ruffner, 1853

"Compassion has been outlawed by science."

—Fyodor Dostoyevsky, *Crime and Punishment*

"The promoter of organized charity protests against 'the wasteful and mischievous method of undirected relief.' He means, naturally, relief that is not directed by somebody else than the person giving it— undirected by him and his kind—professional almoners—philanthropists who deem it more blessed to allot than to bestow. . . . Organized charity is an insipid and savorless thing; its place among moral agencies is no higher than that of root beer.

"Christ did not say, 'Sell that thou hast and give to the church to give to the poor.' He did not mention the Associated Charities of the period. I do not find the words, 'The Little Sisters of the Poor ye have always with you,' nor, 'Inasmuch as ye have done it unto the least of these Dorcas societies ye have done it unto me.' Nowhere do I find myself commanded to enable others to comfort the afflicted and visit the sick and those in prison. Nowhere is recorded God's blessing upon him who makes himself a part of a charity machine—no, not even if he be the guiding lever of the whole mechanism.

"Organized charity is a delusion and a snare. It enables Munniglut to think himself a good man for paying annual dues and buying transferable meal tickets. Munniglut is not thereby a good man. On the Last Great Day, when he cowers in the Ineffable Presence and is asked for an accounting it will not profit him to say, 'Hearing that A was in want, I gave money for his need to B.' Nor will it advantage B to say, 'When A was in distress I asked C to relieve him, and myself allotted the relief according to a resolution of D, E, and F.'"

—Ambrose Bierce, "Charity"

"Let me say . . . that the last men I should appoint to manage a business are experts. The expert mind is too narrow. . . . I wish to trust my fund to a committee dominated by able men of affairs, who have within reach the expert element with which they can confer. Besides this, I wish a larger number of officials directly from the people in the committee, as I am satisfied that unless the institution be kept in touch with the masses, and therefore popular, it cannot be widely useful."

—Andrew Carnegie

"Mr. Rockefeller's method of giving away money impersonally on the basis of investigation by others is careful and conscientious; but it must have cut him off almost completely from the real happiness which good deeds ought to bring the doer, the happiness of giving personally not only one's money, but one's sympathy and labor. He has already done an enormous amount of good, and is going to do much more for many years to come. We all wish that he had got more joy out of it."

—Charles W. Eliot,
Harvard University president and Rockefeller Foundation trustee

"I was hungry and you formed a committee to investigate my hunger . . .
I was homeless and you filed a report on my plight . . .
I was sick and you held a seminar on the situation of the underprivileged . . .
You have investigated all aspects of my plight.
And yet I am still hungry, homeless, and sick."

—Anonymous

QUESTIONS FOR THOUGHT AND DISCUSSION

1. What is the parallel McKnight sees between the John Deere plow and bereavement counseling? What are the different types of desert that are being or have been created on the Sauk Prairie, according to him?

2. Although not "professional," what is the bedrock of popular mourning on the Prairie that makes it so strong? How does McKnight imagine professionalization destroying this bedrock? At what point does he anticipate the final abdication of mourning?

3. What about "service technologies" makes it difficult to see their potential counterproductivity? What assumptions do we often make when we see credentials?

4. In what ways do "expertise," "efficiency," and "specialization" become counterproductive in the world of giving, caring, and volunteering?

5. Most of us, understandably, associate "professionalism" with "excellence" and its opposite with "amateurishness" and "mediocrity." But what do you think of McKnight and Illich's argument?

6. Can you think of examples where service professionals have come to defeat the original purpose for which they were intended? Can you think of areas of your life where you've abdicated to a professional what you could do yourself or within your community?

POINT TO PONDER: _____

The "NIMBYing" of Concerns

The third challenge facing philanthropy today touches on a key group of people—major donors. And its error is precisely the opposite of the earlier "CNN" factor. Whereas the antidote to "telescopic philanthropy" is a due sense of who is my "neighbor" and what is my "little platoon," the "NIMBYing" of concerns takes this emphasis to an equal and opposite extreme. Charity not only "begins at home," as Sir Thomas Browne wrote famously in his Religio Medici (1635)—it begins and ends at home.

The reasons for this challenge lie in the modern trend away from traditional communities, where rich and poor were never too far apart, and toward "lifestyle enclaves," where people of similar incomes pursue ways of life that never impinge on the realities of the poor. The problem, then, is not lack of generosity, but the restriction of generosity to their own (or, more accurately, to "people like us") kinds of projects. The "NIMBY," or "Not in my backyard" response then becomes a natural defense of privilege to the unwanted challenge of caring for the needy.

Needless to say, the "NIMBY" factor heavily reinforces the modern split between "philanthropy" and "charity." Those who view life from within their lifestyle enclave are natural "symphonyites" who give effortlessly to enrich their own communities. To be a "soup-kitchener" and cross the social lines to care for the poor and needy is a costly decision that requires moral initiative.

❦ *Robert B. Reich* ❦

Robert B. Reich (born 1946) served as Secretary of Labor in the Clinton administration. Previously a member of the faculty of Harvard's John F. Kennedy School of Government, Reich is a contributing editor of The New Republic, the national editor of The American Prospect, and a regular commentator for National Public Radio. His books include The Work of Nations and The Next American Frontier. The following reading is an abbreviated version of an article in The New York Times Magazine.

THE REVOLT OF THE ELITES

"There has always been a privileged class, even in America, but it has never been so dangerously isolated from its surroundings. . . . Since their work depends so heavily on 'networking,' they settle in 'specialized geographical pockets' populated by people like them. These privileged communities—Cambridge, the Silicon Valley, Hollywood—become 'wondrously resilient' centers of artistic, technical, and promotional enterprise. . . . To an alarming extent the privileged classes have made themselves independent not only of crumbling industrial cities but of public services in general. . . . In effect, they have removed themselves from the common life."

—Christopher Lasch,
The Revolt of the Elites and the Betrayal of Democracy

"We're getting to be like Mexico and Brazil, with the rich living behind fences like they do in Hollywood."
—Ted Turner, *New York Times*, August 1996

The Secession of the Successful ∜

The idea of "community" has always held a special attraction for Americans. In a 1984 speech, President Ronald Reagan celebrated America's "bedrock"—"its communities where neighbors help one another, where families bring up kids together, where American values are born." Gov. Mario M. Cuomo of New York, with a very different political leaning, has been almost as lyrical. "Community . . . is the reality on which our national life has been founded," he said in 1987.

There is only one problem with this picture. Most Americans no longer live in traditional communities. They live in suburban subdivisions bordered by highways and sprinkled with shopping malls, or in tony condominiums and residential clusters, or in ramshackle apartment buildings and housing projects. Most of them commute to work and socialize on some basis other than geographic proximity. And most people pick up and move to a different neighborhood every five years or so.

But Americans generally have one thing in common with their neighbors: they have similar incomes. And that simple fact lies at the heart of the new community. This means that their educational backgrounds are likely to be similar, that they pay roughly the same in taxes, and that they indulge in the same consumer impulses. "Tell me someone's ZIP code," the founder of a direct-mail company once bragged, "and I can predict what they eat, drink, drive—even think."

Americans who own their homes usually share one political cause with their neighbors: a near obsessive concern with maintaining or upgrading property values. And this common interest is responsible for much of what has brought neighbors together in recent years. Complete strangers, although they may live on the same street or in the same condominium complex, suddenly feel intense solidarity when it is rumored that low-income housing will be constructed in their midst or that a poorer school district will be consolidated with their own.

The renewed emphasis on "community" in American life has justified and legitimized these economic enclaves. If generosity and solidarity end at the border of similarly valued properties, then the most fortunate can be virtuous citizens at little cost. Since most people in one neighborhood or town are equally well off, there is no cause for a guilty conscience. If inhabitants of another area are poorer, let them look to one another. Why should *we* pay for *their* schools?

So the argument goes, without acknowledging that the critical assumption has already been made: "we" and "they" belong to fundamentally different communities. Through such reasoning, it has become possible to maintain a self-image of generosity toward, and solidarity with, one's "community" without bearing any responsibility to "them"—the other "community."

America's high earners—the fortunate top fifth—thus feel increasingly justified in paying only what is necessary to ensure that everyone in their community is sufficiently well educated and has access to the public services they need to succeed. . . . But the continuing debate over whether the wealthy are paying their fair share of taxes obscures a larger issue, with more profound implications for America: the fortunate fifth is quietly seceding from the rest of the nation. . . .

The secession is taking several forms. In many cities and towns, the wealthy have in effect withdrawn their dollars from the support of public spaces and institutions shared by all and dedicated the savings to their own private services. As public parks and playgrounds deteriorate, there is a proliferation of private health clubs, golf clubs, tennis clubs, skating clubs, and every other type of recreational association in which costs are shared among members. Condominiums and the omnipresent residential communities dun their members to undertake work that financially strapped local governments can no longer afford to do well—maintaining roads, mending sidewalks, pruning trees, repairing street lights, cleaning swimming pools, paying for lifeguards and, notably, hiring security guards to protect life and property. (The number of private security guards in the United States now exceeds the number of public police officers.)

Americans who own their homes usually share one political cause with their neighbors: a near obsessive concern with maintaining or upgrading property values.

Of course, wealthier Americans have been withdrawing into their own neighborhoods and clubs for generations. But the new secession is more dramatic because the highest earners now inhabit a different economy from other Americans. The new elite is linked by jet, modem, fax, satellite, and fiber optic cable to the great commercial and recreational centers of the world, but it is not particularly connected to the rest of the nation.

That is because the work this group does is becoming less tied to the activities of other Americans. Most of their jobs consist of analyzing and manipulating symbols—words, numbers, or visual images. Among the most prominent of these "symbolic analysts" are management consultants, lawyers, software and design engineers, research scientists, corporate executives, financial advisers, strategic planners, advertising executives, television and movie producers, and other workers whose job titles include terms like "strategy," "planning," "consultant," "policy," "resources," or "engineer."

These workers typically spend long hours in meetings or on the telephone and even longer hours in planes or hotels—advising, making presentations, giving briefings, and making deals. Periodically, they issue reports, plans, designs, drafts, briefs, blueprints, analyses, memorandums, layouts, renderings, scripts, or projections. In contrast with people whose jobs tend to be tedious and repetitive, symbolic analysts find their work varied and intellectually challenging. In fact, the work is often enjoyable.

These symbolic analysts are in ever greater demand in a world market that places an increasing value on identifying and solving problems. Requests for their software designs, financial advice, or engineering blueprints come from all parts of the globe. This largely explains why most (but by no means all) symbolic analysts have become wealthier, even as the ever-growing worldwide supply of unskilled labor continues to depress the wages of other Americans.

"Generosity is a reflection of what one does with his or her resources—and not what he or she advocates the government do with everyone's money," Ronald Reagan said in 1984.

Successful Americans have not completely disengaged themselves from the lives of their less fortunate compatriots. Some devote substantial resources and energies to helping the rest of society, not through their tax payments, but through voluntary efforts. "Generosity is a reflection of what one does with his or her resources—and not what he or she advocates the government do with everyone's money," Ronald Reagan said in 1984.

The argument is fair enough: Government is not the only device for redistributing wealth. In his speech accepting the presidential nomination at the Republican National Convention in 1988, George Bush said that the real magnanimity of America was to be found in a "brilliant diversity" of private charities, "spread like stars, like a thousand points of light in a broad and peaceful sky."

No nation congratulates itself more enthusiastically on its charitable acts than America; none engages in a greater number of charity balls, bake sales, benefit auctions, and border-to-border hand holdings for good causes. Much of this is sincerely motivated and admirable.

But close examination reveals that many of these acts of benevolence do not help the needy. Particularly suspect is the private giving of those in the top income-tax bracket. Studies have revealed that their largess does not flow mainly to social services for the poor—to better schools, health clinics, or recreational centers. Instead, most voluntary contributions of wealthy Americans go to the places and institutions that entertain, inspire, cure, or educate wealthy Americans—art museums, opera houses, theaters, orchestras, ballet companies, private hospitals, and elite universities.

Most voluntary contributions of wealthy Americans go to the places and institutions that entertain, inspire, cure, or educate wealthy Americans—art museums, opera houses, theaters, orchestras, ballet companies, private hospitals, and elite universities.

And even these charitable contributions are relatively skimpy. Last year, American households with incomes of less than $10,000 gave an average of 5.5 percent of their earnings to charity or to a religious organization; those making more than $100,000 a year gave only 2.9 percent. After the 1988 tax-code overhaul reduced the benefits of charitable giving, the very rich became even stingier. According to Internal Revenue Service data, taxpayers earning $500,000 or more slashed their average donations to $16,062 in 1988 from $47,432 in 1980.

Corporate philanthropy is following the same general pattern. In recent years, the largest American corporations have been sounding the alarm about the nation's fast-deteriorating primary and secondary schools. Few are more eloquent and impassioned about the need for better schools than American executives. "How well we educate all of our children will determine our competitiveness globally, and our economic health domestically, and our communities' character and vitality," said a report of The Business Roundtable, a New York-based association of top executives.

Accordingly, there are numerous "partnerships" between corporations and public schools: scholarships for poor children qualified to attend college, and programs in which businesses adopt individual schools by making conspicuous donations of computers, books, and, on occasion, even money. That such activities are loudly touted by corporate public relations staffs should not detract from the good they do.

Despite the hoopla, business donations to education and charitable causes actually tapered off markedly in the 1980s, even as the economy boomed.

Despite the hoopla, business donations to education and charitable causes actually tapered off markedly in the 1980s, even as the economy boomed. In the 1970s, corporate giving to education jumped an average of 15 percent a year. In 1990, however, giving was only 5 percent over that in 1989;

in 1989 it was 3 percent over 1988. Moreover, most of this money goes to colleges and universities—in particular, to alma maters of symbolic analysts, who expect their children and grandchildren to follow in their footsteps. Only 1.5 percent of corporate giving in the late 1980s was to public primary and secondary schools.

Notably, these contributions have been smaller than amounts corporations are receiving from states and communities in the form of subsidies or tax breaks. Companies are quietly procuring such deals by threatening to move their operations—and jobs—to places around the world with a more congenial tax climate. The paradoxical result has been even less corporate revenue to spend on schools and other community services than before. The executives of General Motors, for example, who have been among the loudest to proclaim the need for better schools, have also been among the most relentless in pursuing local tax abatements and in challenging their tax assessments. GM's successful efforts to reduce its taxes in North Tarrytown, N.Y., where the company has had a factory since 1914, cut local revenues by $1 million in 1990, part of a larger shortfall that forced the town to lay off scores of teachers. . . .

In all these ways, the gap between America's symbolic analysts and everyone else is widening into a chasm. Their secession from the rest of the population raises fundamental questions about the future of American society. In the new global economy—in which money, technologies, and corporations cross borders effortlessly—a citizen's standard of living depends more and more on skills and insights, and on the infrastructure needed to link these abilities to the rest of the world. But the most skilled and insightful Americans, who are already positioned to thrive in the world market, are now able to slip the bonds of national allegiance, and by so doing disengage themselves from their less favored fellows. The stark political challenge in the decades ahead will be to reaffirm that, even though America is no longer a separate and distinct economy, it is still a society whose members have abiding obligations to one another.

The executives of General Motors, for example, who have been among the loudest to proclaim the need for better schools, have also been among the most relentless in pursuing local tax abatements and in challenging their tax assessments.

The stark political challenge in the decades ahead will be to reaffirm that, even though America is no longer a separate and distinct economy, it is still a society whose members have abiding obligations to one another.

Robert B. Reich, "The Secession of the Successful," *The New York Times Magazine,* January 20, 1991, p. 17. Copyright © 1991 by The New York Times Co. Reprinted by permission.

I DON'T WANT TO KNOW ABOUT IT

"Mr. Podsnap was well to do, and stood very high in Mr. Podsnap's opinion. Beginning with a good inheritance, he had married a good inheritance, and had thriven exceedingly in the Marine Insurance way, and was quite satisfied. He could never make out why everybody was not quite satisfied. . . .

"There was a dignified conclusiveness—not to add a grand convenience—in this way of getting rid of disagreeables which had done much towards establishing Mr. Podsnap in his lofty place in Mr. Podsnap's satisfaction. 'I don't want to know about it; I don't choose to discuss it; I don't admit it!' Mr. Podsnap had even acquired a peculiar flourish of his right arm in often clearing the world of its most difficult problems, by sweeping them behind him (and consequently sheer away) with those words and a flushed face. For they affronted him."

—Charles Dickens, *Our Mutual Friend*

"Poverty is an anomaly to rich people. It is very difficult to make out why people who want dinner do not ring the bell."

—Walter Bagehot

"I believe it is wrong for people who have made it up the ladder to pull the ladder up behind them."
—Thomas P. "Tip" O'Neill Jr., former Speaker of the House

"The millions who are poor in the United States tend to become increasingly invisible. . . . It takes an effort of the intellect and will even to see them. . . . That the poor are invisible is one of the most important things about them. They are not simply neglected, . . . they are not seen."
—Michael Harrington, *The Other America*

QUESTIONS FOR THOUGHT AND DISCUSSION

1. What is the contrast between the traditional community in the American's mind's eye to what is depicted here by Reich? What does he see as the basis of commonality within the average modern community? How does this affect what is valued in the community and how the community is defined?
2. What does Reich mean when he says, "it has become possible to maintain a self-image of generosity toward, and solidarity with, one's 'community' without bearing any responsibility to" the poor? What is happening here? How are the needs of the poor being addressed?
3. For the wealthiest Americans, there has been a "secession of the successful," Reich charges. In what ways has this "fortunate fifth" withdrawn from the rest of the nation? In what ways have you witnessed or participated in this secession?
4. What does the "lifestyle enclave" mean for giving? Which of the earlier styles of giving (from Athens or Jerusalem-Galilee) does this reinforce?
5. How far does this analysis fit your city and neighborhood? How do effective and caring givers break out of the "NIMBY" factor?

POINT TO PONDER: _____

The Reverse "Cy Presing" of Foundations

The fourth challenge contemporary philanthropy faces concerns the faithfulness of philanthropic institutions to their author's intentions. Authors and their intentions have taken a beating in Western cultural life recently. Some radical literary critics have pronounced that "the author is dead"; it is for readers, not authors, to interpret a text. For example, liberal constitutional interpreters have claimed that the intention of the framers of a document is irrelevant; a constitution is what each generation says it means.

But a third area of author's intentions is now also becoming controversial— philanthropy, as foundations are being praised or attacked for conforming to or contravening their founders' intentions.

Cy pres is the name of a legal principle affecting foundations, which was developed by the Romans before the Christian era. The expression is an abbreviation of the Norman French for "as near as possible." It requires executors to adhere to the original intent of the donor but recognizes that donors sometimes lay down conditions that later become impossible or highly inappropriate. The goal is to approach the original purpose as closely as possible.

Originally, the principle was invoked mostly when the donor's intent was rendered nearly impossible because of changed situations. Among well-known examples overtaken by history: In the fifteenth century a fund was established to provide "faggots for the burning of heretics" and "endowments for the purpose of redeeming Christians held in slavery by Mohammedan powers." In our own century a sum of money was left to provide Christmas dinners for horses in Kansas City and another fund to provide "a baked potato at each meal for each young woman" at Bryn Mawr College in Pennsylvania.

Today, however, the movement is in the opposite direction. Some modern trustees of foundations are pursuing a course that might be described as "reverse cy pres-ing." They are freely disbursing foundation funds in ways that would make the founder spin in his or her grave.

Doubtless the significance of certain changes in the course of foundations may be disputed. One person's betrayal is another's loyalty. But some course changes are indisputably a contradiction of the founder's intentions—and in this sense a "reverse cy pres-ing." Naturally the issue of "reverse cy pres-ing" raises questions for existing foundations. But it also raises questions for major donors considering what to do with their wealth. Carnegie's three options—

wealth can be left to one's heirs, bequeathed for public purposes, or disbursed by the possessors during their lives—now have serious question marks over each of the possible choices.

REVERSAL OF FORTUNE

"Inherited wealth is as certain death to ambition as cocaine is to morality."

—Cornelius Vanderbilt

"The history of charities abounds in illustrations of the paradoxical axiom that, while charity tends to do good, perpetual charities tend to do evil."

—Julius Rosenwald

"I am certain that those who seek by perpetuities to create for themselves a kind of immortality on earth will fail, if only because no institution and no foundation can live forever."

—Julius Rosenwald

"Fortunes tend to self destruction by destroying those who inherit them."

—Henry Ford

One obvious response is to limit the lifetime of the foundation. For example, chemical magnate John M. Olin told his trustees to wind down his foundation before its funds could be diverted to unwanted causes. So in the early 1990s, the $120 million John M. Olin Foundation began the process of spending itself out of existence, which could take fifteen to twenty years.

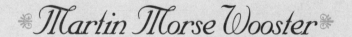

Martin Morse Wooster

Martin Morse Wooster (born 1957) is a visiting fellow at Capital Research Center, an editor of The American Enterprise and Reason, and a columnist for The Washington Times. The following reading is an abbreviation of a chapter from his book on the way foundations drift or shift from their founders' purpose.

ITCHING PALMS

"But there is often no external discipline for either courts or foundations. Foundation officials, like judges, may well serve for life or as long as they care to. Foundation officers and judges share three other characteristics: both sets of people are unelected; both are unrepresentative of the public; and, where a donor has not been specific, both are essentially unaccountable. In one way, foundation officials are more independent and powerful than judges. Unlike judges, those officials may get to choose their successors. . . .

"But, as has been the case with judges who make the Constitution mean what the judges want, there are few effective ways of enforcing the stated intentions against foundation officers who ignore the donor's desires. . . . "

—Robert H. Bork, "Interpreting the Founder's Vision"

The "Ford Foundation could create more human happiness than it does with its grant programs by buying a drink for every man, woman, and child in the world and going out of business."

—observer cited by Robert H. Bork, "Interpreting the Founder's Vision"

"How firm a Foundation, we saints of the Lord.
We've built on the faith of our excellent Ford.
We've laundered and lightened the Trustees' Report.
And left for California,
And left for California,
And left for California,
The place to resort.
"How firm the Foundation has been for E.C.A.
And for Hutchins, for Davis, what those boys get ain't hay.
What more can we do than for them we have done?
Way out in Pasadena,
Way out in Pasadena,
Way out in Pasadena,
We bask in the sun.
"How firm a Foundation, we've Funds by the score.
Have you an idea? We'll establish one more.
We smile through the smog; (some say that we smirk);
Out here in Pasadena,
Out here in Pasadena,
Out here in Pasadena,
The Funds do the work."

—Robert Maynard Hutchins,
president, Ford Foundation's "Fund for the Republic" (1952)
whose motto was "Feel free" and whose deliberate attacks
on conservative positions particularly galled Henry Ford II

REVERSE ALCHEMY

"A recent study of U.S. philanthropy reported that foundations giving mostly to liberal causes held more assets than foundations giving mostly to conservative causes by a ratio of 17-to-1. . . . I would be willing to bet that out of every 18 entrepreneurs in this country, there are fewer than 17 dedicated left-wingers. . . .

"Ford. Pew. MacArthur. Packard. The stories are as familiar as the names. The great fortunes of modern capitalism turned to the service of anti-market initiatives. The great names of the American Century now fronting for the centrifugal forces of multiculturalism. The fruits of technological genius now funding the corrosive campaigns of junk science. What's happening in the foundation world today is a kind of reverse alchemy with free market gold being turned into philanthropic dross."

—Foundation Management Institute Chairman Neal Freeman

"For years, the Pew oil family awarded thousands of grants anonymously, erected splendid buildings without a single bronze plaque carrying the Pew name. Now Pew's [Pew Charitable Trusts] light is out from under the bushel. The agenda? Activist, strategic, a far cry from its Presbyterian beginnings. Michael Joyce, head of the conservative Lynde and Harry Bradley Foundation in Milwaukee, says that for conservatives, Pew 'has become the flagrant example of our times of twisting and distorting donor intent in order to serve a liberal agenda.'"

—Philadelphia *Inquirer Magazine*, March 1998

The Great Philanthropists and the Problem of "Donor Intent": The Ford Foundation

In judging whether the Ford Foundation violates donor intent, one must assess the intentions of two men: Henry Ford (1863–1947) and his grandson, Henry Ford II (1917–1987) . . .

The evidence suggests that the Ford Foundation routinely violates every charitable principle of Henry Ford, and in a lesser way, those of Henry Ford II. In his last years, even Henry Ford II, who was certainly not conservative, railed against "the liberals" who had seized control of the foundation.

The conventional history of the Ford Foundation is that Henry Ford left no instructions on how his money should be used, thus leaving the trustees free to do whatever they pleased with his fortune. According to foundation historian

Waldemar Nielsen, who worked for the Ford Foundation for many years, when Henry Ford died in 1947, four lawyers, supervised by Tex Moore (brother-in-law of Henry Luce), combed Ford's personal and corporate papers and "were unable to find a single sentence or a single note from old Henry expressing any interest in, or ideas about, his philanthropy."

It is true that Ford left no explicit instructions on how his money should be spent. But his philosophy of charity was very clear, and was consistently expressed throughout his life. His views were simply ignored by those who staffed and led the Ford Foundation. . . .

HENRY FORD'S PHILOSOPHY OF GIVING

Henry Ford . . . created philanthropies that outlived him and still honor his wishes. As early as 1911, he created a home for underprivileged boys. But his major works were the Henry Ford Hospital in Detroit and two related efforts in Dearborn, Michigan—Greenfield Village and the Edison Institute (now the Henry Ford Museum). The Henry Ford Hospital is still one of Detroit's leading hospitals, and millions of visitors flock to Greenfield Village each year to see the historic houses that Ford collected and reassembled.

Throughout his life, Ford was besieged by requests for aid. As early as 1914, after introducing one of the nation's first profit-sharing plans, swarms of people lined up outside his house. By 1915, he received two hundred letters a day for aid; by 1924, the number had climbed to 10,000 a week, and a team of private secretaries sent out over fifty form letters in response.

Ford often gave money spontaneously to poor people he met during his travels. But he always refused to give to organizations he could not directly control. He would not give to community chests, the predecessors of the United Way, and he consistently opposed any form of charity that might reward idleness. . . . In a 1924 interview, he said,

"I believe in living wages—I do not believe in charity. I believe we should all be producers."
—HENRY FORD

I believe in living wages—I do not believe in charity. I believe we should all be producers. Organized charity and schools of philanthropy and the whole idea of "giving" to the poor are on the wrong track. They don't produce anything. If a railroad had a bad piece of track that wrecked cars every day and piled them in the ditch it would cure nothing to merely build a fine repair shop. The track itself should be fixed. Charity and philanthropy are the repair shops and the efficiency, however high, does not remove the cause of the human wrecks.

For those who had experienced misfortune and were willing to work, Ford had plenty of jobs at good wages at his plants. He prided himself on taking people that others might have considered hopeless and turning them into productive workers. He routinely hired the disabled. In 1919, nearly twenty percent of his workers had some sort of disability, including one employee who had lost both hands, four whose legs or feet were gone, four who were totally blind, 123 who only had one hand or arm, and 1,560 with hernias. . . .

"A CHANCE AND NOT CHARITY"

Given his belief in self-reliance, Ford always told reporters that he planned to use his wealth to create jobs and cars, not a foundation. "Mr. Ford," William L. Stidger asked in 1923, "the people want to know what you are going to do with your huge fortune when you die?"

"Why do they want to know?" Ford replied.

"I presume because it is getting to be a habit with wealthy men to do some useful and social thing with the vast sums of money that they accumulate. Take Mr. Rockefeller, he has established the Rockefeller Foundation," Stidger said.

"So they want to know what I'm going to do with my money. Well, you can tell them there is no 'going to do' about it. I am doing it now! I am investing my money in men, every cent of it, and will continue to do so. When people ask me what I am going to do with my money they usually mean what bunch of secretaries or societies I am going to select to dole out my 'charity.' My money is going to keep on going where it is going now—into men," Ford said.

"Then the business itself is to be the Ford Foundation?" Stidger asked.

"That's right. The organization is to be the Ford Foundation. I want that Foundation to be the life-saving opportunity of millions of men and women to be self-supporting and self-sustaining. My old motto, 'A chance and not charity,' will be the spirit of the Ford Foundation. I do not believe in giving folks things. I do believe in giving them a chance to make things for themselves!" . . .

"When people ask me what I am going to do with my money they usually mean what bunch of secretaries or societies I am going to select to dole out my 'charity.' My money is going to keep on going where it is going now—into men."
—HENRY FORD

"I want that Foundation to be the life-saving opportunity of millions of men and women to be self-supporting and self-sustaining."
—HENRY FORD

CREATION OF THE FORD FOUNDATION

On January 15, 1936, Henry Ford took the only option he could to preserve family control of the Ford Motor Company. He created the Ford Foundation. The existing Ford Motor Company stock was converted into two types: non-voting Class A common stock, which comprised ninety-five percent of the total stock, and voting Class B common stock. Ford drafted a will leaving the Class A shares to the Ford Foundation and the Class B shares to his son and grandchildren. Edsel Ford drafted a similar will. The Ford estate was thus divided into two parts, leaving the wealth Ford created to philanthropy and the Ford Motor Company to the family.

Ford did *not* create the Ford Foundation out of altruism or to restore his reputation. Unlike the great fortunes created before the Income Tax Act of 1913, no one called Ford a "robber baron" or wicked capitalist. Nor was he seen as a paragon of conspicuous consumption. He lived simply and reinvested most of the profits he made back into his business. . . .

In 1948, as the wills of Edsel and Henry Ford were being probated, Henry Ford II signed a statement that he would later regret. He declared that the Ford family would make no effort to use the inheritance of his father and grandfather to control the Ford Foundation. Henry Ford II would be chairman of the board of the foundation and his brother Benson would be a trustee, but their influence would be no greater than any other Ford Foundation employee. . . . By signing this document, Henry Ford II ensured that the intentions of his family would be steadily undermined. . . .

THE FUND FOR THE REPUBLIC

[Foundation Associate Director] Robert Maynard Hutchins chafed while in Pasadena. He wrote satirical poetry about the Ford Foundation, calling it "Itching Palms." But in 1952 the foundation reorganized. Among the changes were the creation of several specialized funds. To study civil liberties, the foundation created the Fund for the Republic with $15 million. Hutchins became its first and only president.

Hutchins was eager to head the organization. "I've got a new job," he wrote to his friend Thornton Wilder. "It's spending $15 million stolen from the Ford Foundation on civil liberties & racial & religious discrimination, if you know what I mean. It's not bad. It's better than the Ford Foundation." As early as August 1951, Hutchins wrote a memo saying he would deal in "unpalatable causes," and offered ways for the Ford Foundation to distance itself from possible controversy.

. . . Hutchins condensed this into a decoration in his office, which consisted of a sampler embroidered with the words, "FEEL FREE." During its short life, the Fund for the Republic acted like a bullfighter waving a red cape at conservatives and daring them to attack. Among its activities were spending hundreds of thousands of dollars for a report on Hollywood blacklisting, having *Washington Post* cartoonist Herbert Block prepare a television documentary on civil liberties, and hiring Clinton Rossiter to write a report on American communism. (Rossiter in turn hired Earl Browder, former head of the Communist Party USA, as a consultant. Browder was at the time under indictment for perjury.)

THE FOUNDATION IN THE 1960s

. . . By 1957, all Henry Ford II could do about the Ford Foundation was complain. In 1956, the nightmare the elder Henry Ford had sought to avoid came true. The Ford Foundation, in the largest stock offering of its time, began selling its Ford Motor shares. Because of New York Stock Exchange prohibitions against selling non-voting corporate stock, the shares were converted into voting-class stock. Although the Ford family was able to retain control of forty percent of the voting shares, the Ford Motor Company was now a public enterprise.

At the same time, Henry Ford II resigned as chairman of the Ford Foundation board of trustees, preferring to concentrate on Ford Motor affairs. With every share of Ford Motor stock sold, his influence on the foundation declined. As president of the Ford Motor Company, he commanded one of the world's largest companies. But as a Ford Foundation trustee, he cast only one of sixteen votes.

During the 1960s, the Ford Foundation continued to grow. In a 1969 report, *The Law and the Lore of Endowment Funds,* the foundation addressed the issue of how colleges and universities could ensure that their endowments would grow relatively free of restrictions, thus touching on the problems of donor intent. "The courts in all jurisdictions pay at least lip service to the necessity of observing the donor's intent," authors William L. Cary and Craig B. Bright wrote. "In practice the attempt to ascertain that intent is often an exercise in futility, which ultimately ends with the predilections of the court masquerading as the wishes of a deceased donor who is no longer able to speak for himself."

. . . In the late 1960s, the divorce between the Ford family and the Ford

"The foundation's trustees referred your grant proposal to their 'when pigs fly' subcommittee."

© 1994 by Mark Litzler, The Chronicle of Philanthropy.

Foundation was completed. In 1967, Detroit suffered a severe riot, and Henry Ford II resolved to rebuild the city. He led an effort to construct the Renaissance Center, a major office building, and hired thousands of unemployed blacks to work in Ford Motor plants. According to Peter Collier and David Horowitz, Cristina Ford (Henry Ford II's wife) urged him to help the Henry Ford Hospital, which was still serving Detroit as it had since the elder Henry Ford created it. However, it was now in a bad neighborhood and needed funds. Henry Ford II's brother, Benson, asked the Ford Foundation three times for money for the hospital, and was rejected each time. Henry Ford II also asked Ford Foundation president McGeorge Bundy for a grant, but was told that "giving to hospitals is not part of our program."

Cristina Ford, Collier and Horowitz say, was outraged. "How can you do this?" she told Bundy. "Do you forget that the old man left three billion dollars to the foundation? He gave it to you instead of to his own children!" Bundy was unpersuaded, so Cristina Ford went to Ford Foundation trustee Robert McNamara and told him how bothered she was that the foundation would spend $45 million on a new headquarters building but nothing on one of Henry Ford's favorite charities. McNamara said he would do what he could. Henry Ford II also conducted an intensive lobbying effort. In 1973, the Ford Foundation gave $100,000,000 to the Henry Ford Hospital, but McGeorge Bundy announced that this was a "terminal" grant.

HENRY FORD II'S RESIGNATION

. . . During Bundy's tenure, the Ford Foundation lost a billion dollars of its endowment—a third of its assets—due to a combination of bad investments and massive grant programs. As Waldemar Nielsen notes, the effects of inflation made the loss even greater: "by dint of bad financial and investment management [the foundation] has dissipated almost three fourths of the real value of its assets [since 1970], a loss of something in the order of $6 billion of philanthropic resources measured in current dollars. No disaster of comparable magnitude has ever been recorded."

By late 1976, Henry Ford II had lost patience with the Ford Foundation. "I don't think I can stand this much longer," he told long-time associate Walter Hayes. "This place is a madhouse." Unable to stop the abuses he saw, he could only call attention to them by resigning. In a letter to the trustees, he said, "after thirty-three years I have come to the point where I have pretty much done all there is to do as a trustee and have said all there is to say." He urged the trustees to have more respect for the free-enterprise system that had created the fortune they were spending. "In effect, the foundation is a creature of capitalism," he wrote, "a statement that, I'm sure, would be shocking to many professional staff people in the field of philanthropy. It is hard to discern recognition of this fact in anything the foundation does. It is even more difficult to find an understanding of this in many of the institutions, particularly the universities, that are the beneficiaries of the foundation's grant programs." He added, "I'm not playing the role of the hard-headed tycoon who thinks all philanthropoids are Socialists and all university professors are Communists. I'm just suggesting to the trustees and the staff that the system that makes the foundation possible very probably is worth preserving."

Accompanying his letter was a cartoon from a 1964 issue of the *New Yorker* which showed a prim man in a tight suit confronting a subordinate who was throwing currency out an open window. "Just a minute, young man," read the caption. "That's not the way we do things at the Ford Foundation." Henry Ford II personally inscribed the cartoon in a firm, unwavering hand. "To my fellow trustees with warm and high regard. Maybe this fellow has a better idea." For a while, the cartoon hung in the Ford Foundation's lobby. In 1987, a *USA Today* reporter searched the foundation offices for some trace of the Ford family. He found one grainy portrait of Henry Ford in a development officer's suite — the only evidence that the Ford Foundation respected the memory of Henry Ford, Edsel Ford, and Henry Ford II.

After his resignation, Henry Ford II regretted his 1948 decision to abandon control of the Ford Foundation. In a late 1977 interview, he said that if he could live again, he would have divided his grandfather's estate into three parts — one-third for Greenfield Village and the Henry Ford Museum, one-third for the

"I'm not playing the role of the hard-headed tycoon who thinks all philanthropoids are Socialists and all university professors are Communists. I'm just suggesting to the trustees and the staff that the system that makes the foundation possible very probably is worth preserving."
—HENRY FORD

Henry Ford Hospital, and one-third for the Ford Foundation. The foundation would have been only "one-third as big, and therefore it wouldn't have gotten into so many different kinds of things, but nevertheless might have been able to do a substantial job in the meantime."

In a 1990 biography of Henry Ford II, Walter Hayes, a long-time friend and former Ford Motor vice-president, recalled a 1979 conversation with Henry Ford II. Ford said that if he had not abandoned family control of the Ford Foundation, it would have remained in Detroit and have had the primary purpose of serving the local area. There would have been national programs, Hayes recalled, but the main goal would have been to aid the needy in Detroit.

Could Detroit's institutions have absorbed all the Ford Foundation's wealth? Would a Detroit-based foundation have done as much good as a global philanthropy? "They couldn't have done a worse job than the one that has been done," Henry Ford II replied, "no matter what they did."

From Martin Morse Wooster, *The Great Philanthropists and the Problem of "Donor Intent"* (Washington, D.C.: Capital Research Center, 1994). © 1994 by Capital Research Center. Reprinted with permission from the author.

DEAD HAND

"It is not so kindly charity, for men to give what they can keep no longer; besides, such donations are most subject to abuse."

—Thomas Fuller

"He who governed the world before I was born shall take care of it likewise when I am dead. My part is to improve the present moment."

—John Wesley

"A miser, being dead, and fairly interred, came to the banks of the Styx, desiring to be ferried over along with the other ghosts. Charon demands his fare, and is surprised to see the miser, rather than pay it, throw himself into the river, and swim over to the other side, notwithstanding all the clamor and opposition that could be made of him. All hell was in a uproar; and each of the judges was meditating some punishment suitable to a crime of such dangerous consequence to the infernal revenues. Shall he be chained to the rock with Prometheus? or tremble below the precipice in company with the Danaides? or assist Sisyphus in rolling his stone? No, says Minos, none of these. We must invent some severer punishment. Let him be sent back to the earth, to see the use his heirs are making of his riches."

—David Hume, "Of Avarice"

"My desire is that the work which I have been carrying on, or similar beneficial work, shall continue during this and future generations. Conditions upon the earth inevitably change; hence, no wise man will bind Trustees forever to certain paths, causes, or institutions. I disclaim any intention of doing so. On the contrary, I give my Trustees full authority to change policy or causes hitherto aided, from time to time, when this, in their opinion, has become necessary or desirable. They shall best conform to my wishes by using their own judgment."

—Andrew Carnegie

"It is eminently desirable . . . that the dead hand should be removed from charitable bequests and that the power to determine to what specific objects that should be applied should be left in the hands of living men who can judge of the necessities and the needs in the light of the knowledge which they have as contemporaries, and not that they shall find their hands tied by the will of the man who is long years dead. The wisdom of living men will always exceed the wisdom of any man, however wise, who has been long since dead."

—Starr Murphy, lawyer of John D. Rockefeller Sr.

QUESTIONS FOR THOUGHT AND DISCUSSION

1. What patterns of wealth creation and giving did Henry Ford show in his life and business? What types of philanthropy did he not support?

2. What did Ford mean by "I believe in living wages—I do not support charity"? How did this philosophy affect his business, how he lived, and what he planned to do with his fortune? Why was the Ford Foundation created?

3. What did Robert Hutchins mean when he wrote Thorton Wilder that he had a new job "spending $15 million stolen from the Ford Foundation on civil liberties & racial & religious discrimination, if you know what I mean"? How would you describe his attitude toward the foundation and Ford's patterns of giving?

4. What is the significance of McGeorge Bundy telling Henry Ford II, "giving to hospitals is not part of our program," when he asked for a grant? To whose program is he referring?

5. Do you support or regret the Ford Foundation's freedom to depart from Henry Ford's philosophy of business and charity? Why?

6. What do you think of Starr Murphy's statement, "The wisdom of living men will always exceed the wisdom of any man, however wise, who has long since been dead" (see box, "Dead Hand")? What is the implication of this way of thinking for *cy pres*?

7. What responsibility does a major donor have to posterity's use of his or her wealth? How should this use be affected by changes in values and the society?

8. What lessons do you take away from this reading?

THE APPLICANT

In Ambrose Bierce's story, the founder and namesake of the Abersush Home for the Aged disappeared from town, leaving a large endowment but no formal directions for the operation of the home. In his absence and thanks to the trustees' apathy, the home's superintendent, Mr. Tilbody, has reconstructed the Home into "a kind of castle in Spain," hosting only "prosperous middle-aged gentlemen, consummately good-humored and civilly willing to pay for their board and lodging." On this snowy Christmas Eve, Mr. Tilbody is just leaving the Home for some last-minute shopping when an applicant for the Home rings the doorbell: a stooped old man dressed like a scarecrow, brushing the snow from his shoulders.

"Hello! just in time; a moment later and you would have missed me. Come, I have no time to waste; we'll walk a little way together."

"Thank you," said the old man, upon whose thin and white but not ignoble face the light from the open door showed an expression that was perhaps disappointment; "but if the trustees—if my application—"

"The trustees," Mr. Tilbody said, closing more doors than one, and cutting off two kinds of light, "have agreed that your application disagrees with them."

Certain sentiments are inappropriate to Christmastide, but Humor, like Death, has all seasons for his own.

"Oh, my God!" cried the old man, in so thin and husky a tone that the invocation was anything but impressive, and to at least one of his two auditors sounded, indeed, somewhat ludicrous. To the Other—but that is a matter which laymen are devoid of the light to expound.

"Yes," continued Mr. Tilbody, accommodating his gait to that of his companion, who was mechanically, and not very successfully, retracing the track that he had made through the snow; "they have decided that, under the circumstances—under the very peculiar circumstances, you understand—it would be inexpedient to admit you. As superintendent and *ex officio* secretary of the honorable board"— as Mr. Tilbody "read his title clear" the magnitude of the big building, seen through its veil of falling snow, appeared to suffer somewhat in comparison—"it is my duty to inform you that, in the words of Deacon Byram, the chairman, your presence in the Home would—under the circumstances—be peculiarly embarrassing. I felt it my duty to submit to the honorable board the statement that you made to me yesterday of your needs, your physical condition, and the trials which it has pleased Providence to send upon you in your very proper effort to present your claims in person; but, after careful, and I may say prayerful, consideration of your case—with something too, I trust, of the large charitableness appropriate to the season—it was decided that we would not be justified in doing anything likely to impair the usefulness of the institution intrusted (under Providence) to our care."

They had now passed out of the grounds; the street lamp opposite the gate was dimly visible through the snow. Already the old man's former track was obliterated, and he seemed uncertain as to which way he should go. Mr. Tilbody had drawn a little away from him, but paused and turned half toward him, apparently reluctant to forego the continuing opportunity.

"Under the circumstances," he resumed, "the decision—"

But the old man was inaccessible to the suasion of his verbosity; he had crossed the street into a vacant lot and was going forward, rather deviously toward nowhere in particular—which, he having nowhere in particular to go to, was not so reasonless a proceeding as it looked.

And that is how it happened that the next morning, when the church bells of all Grayville were ringing with an added unction appropriate to the day, the sturdy little son of Deacon Byram, breaking a way through the snow to the place of worship, struck his foot against the body of Amasa Abersush, philanthropist.

—Ambrose Bierce, "The Applicant" in *The Collected Writings of Ambrose Bierce*

(New York: The Citadel Press, 1989). Copyright © 1946, 1974 by The Citadel Press.
Reprinted by permission of Citadel Press/Kensington Publishing Corp.

POINT TO PONDER: _____

The "ODing" of Compassion

Over the Christmas season of 1995, Washington, D.C.'s Combined Federal Campaign placed large, handsome posters all over town, including the capital city's post offices. "Children, Homeless, The Environment, Health Care, Education, Hunger, AIDS, Substance Abuse, Domestic Violence . . . " Thirty global problems screamed from the poster—each massive, emotionally charged, and overwhelming—and the concluding slogan said starkly, "It's up to you!"

Children • Homeless • The Environment
International Relief and Development
Conservation • Health Care • Education
Hunger • Emergency Services • Housing
The Arts • Human and Civil Rights •
Neighborhoods • AIDS • Rehabilitation
Advocacy • Medical Research • Elderly
Substance Abuse • Illiteracy • Animals
Domestic Violence • Recreation • Justice
Families • Persons with Disabilities • Safety

It's up to you!

1995 COMBINED FEDERAL CAMPAIGN OF THE NATIONAL CAPITAL AREA

Few people seemed to glance at the poster for long, certainly not like they did at the cheery Post Office posters next to it. "Thanks, but no thanks," they seemed to say. "If it's up to me, it just won't happen. The world's need is too big. It comes too fast. There's little that I can do that will make a difference on that scale."

The poster's burdensome appeal highlights the fifth major challenge confronting philanthropy—"compassion fatigue" or the "overdosing" on concern that is the burden of world need in the global village. A host of issues and dilemmas are raised, but none more urgent than the challenge of sustaining compassion, or in the words of the reading here, the task of "seeing things through."

❧ Robert Payton ❧

Robert Payton (born 1926) was the founder and first director of the Center on Philanthropy at Indiana University, where he continues as a professor and senior fellow. He received his master's degree in history from the University of Chicago and has received several honorary doctorates. He served as a United States ambassador to the Republic of Cameroon in West Africa from 1967–1969 and as *president of C.W. Post College and Hofstra University in New York. From 1977–1987 he presided over the Exxon Education Foundation before becoming a scholar-in-residence at the University of Virginia. Payton spends a significant amount of time lecturing on philanthropy for foundations, community groups, scholars, and students. He has traveled extensively to Eastern Europe, the former Yugoslavia, and Northern Ireland to explore the role of philanthropy in resolving ethnic conflict and in building civil society.*

In the shortened article, "Helping the Underserved Abroad," Payton discusses the unprecedented humanitarian campaign ignited by rock performer Bob Geldof in response to the massive famine in Ethiopia in 1984.

COMPASSION FATIGUE

"A sympathetic person is placed in the dilemma of a swimmer among drowning men, who all catch at him, and if he gives so much as a leg or a finger, they will drown him."

—Ralph Waldo Emerson

"My young friend looks at the evening news program. There is footage from Ethiopia. The famine has recurred and there are babies crying again, children looking dully at the camera again. She glances from the screen to me and says in surprise, 'I thought that it was over.'

"I look up sharply and then I think: Of course. The girl is used to problems that can be resolved in a half-hour, before the last commercial. At 13, she is a member of the restless audience whose attention is grabbed by the changing problems and datelines of our traveling news show. To her, Ethiopia is an old story. . . .

"We are great at performing the one-night stands for causes. Christmas dinner for the poor, collections for victims of fire or flood or famine.

"But if the emergency turns chronic, if we give the problem our best shot and it doesn't shatter, it's hard for many of us to sustain the same level of concern and caring. Wasn't Ethiopia an old story? Didn't we wage a war on poverty? Didn't we *do* homelessness last year. . . .

"But any crisis may become as routine as mealtime. Feed people on Monday, and they are hungry again on Tuesday. Help someone find a roof over his head one night, and he has the nerve to need one the next night. Dig a bullet out of one body, chase a delusion out of someone's mind, and they may return full of fresh bullets and replenished delusions. Help people, and they may come back for second helpings.

"For many of us, there is a slow process by which a gift can begin to feel like an obligation, generosity can turn into resentment, and sympathy can turn hard. How many have turned angry at problems that wouldn't stay solved, at people who wouldn't be cured.

"They call it compassion fatigue. They say that it is endemic now in urban centers such as New York City, where people are just 'tired' of seeing the homeless, the street people. . . .

> "I wonder what personal price we pay for disillusionment. I wonder what moral costs are tallied up by people who learn to turn away from pain. . . . How hard it is to learn to be tough-minded without becoming hard-hearted."
>
> —Ellen Goodman, "Compassion Fatigue,"
> *The Washington Post*, February 3, 1990

Helping the Underserved Abroad: The Case of Famine Relief 🐾

The news report was of famine in Ethiopia. From the first seconds it was clear this was a horror on a monumental scale. The pictures were of people who were so shrunken by starvation that they looked like beings from another planet. . . . The camera wandered amidst them like a mesmerized observer, occasionally dwelling on one person so that he looked directly at me, sitting in my comfortable living room surrounded by the fripperies of modern living which we were pleased to regard as necessities. . . .

Right from the first few seconds it was clear that this was a tragedy which the world had somehow contrived not to notice until it had reached a scale which constituted an international scandal. . . .

The images played and replayed in my mind. What could I do? I could send some money. Of course I could send some money. But that did not seem enough. . . . To expiate yourself truly of any complicity in this evil meant you had to give something of yourself.

This [essay] is a commentary on that passage from the autobiography of British rock musician Bob Geldof. Stripped to its essentials, Geldof's experience offers a model of the modern philanthropic mind at work (in my words now, not his):

- This news affects me, personally.
- These images are unbearable.
- This terrible thing has been going on, and I've been so preoccupied with myself that I didn't even know it was happening. I am comfortable and secure while these people are in agony and near death.
- I can do something about it. I can give money—but giving money isn't enough. I have to become involved.

. . . The same images that Bob Geldof watched on BBC in October 1984 were later carried by NBC television in the nightly news from New York. The film had been taken by an African, Muhammad Amin, working with narrator Michael Buerk, both employed by VisNews on assignment from BBC. Amin had been the catalyst and had managed to win permission from the Ethiopian government to take pictures at the refugee camp at Korem. The report had the same stunning impact in the United States that it had in England earlier. The NBC news telephone lines were jammed with calls. By the next morning there were people lined up outside the offices of international relief agencies waiting to make contributions. Geldof's personal reaction was replicated literally millions of times in the United States and Europe. . . .

Why were these pictures different? Why did so many people respond with gifts and other offers of help? No one seems to know. There had been other films of famine in Africa carried by NBC earlier. The photographic subjects at that time were the victims of famine and civil war in Chad. These news reports generated not a single telephone call to NBC News. Is there a lower level of human interest in suffering in Chad than in Ethiopia? Or is the difference in response explicable only on esthetic grounds?

. . . Whatever the cause, tens of thousands of contributions flowed into the offices of private voluntary organizations all across the United States (and Canada and Western Europe). The initial wave of response caught the organizations off-guard. Only four American organizations had relief programs in Ethiopia; within a few months, there were two dozen. News coverage blossomed. . . . Bob Geldof organized Band Aid, which recorded a song that became an instant success and inspired the American recording of "We Are the World," which met with similar success here.

Between October 1984 and midsummer 1985, America and Europe were engaged with public and private efforts on a vast scale to relieve the suffering of the estimated fourteen million people at risk in Ethiopia alone. Public enthusiasm overwhelmed the political obstacles. . . .

The high point of public consciousness was reached with the Live Aid concert simultaneously staged at Wembley Stadium in London and at John F. Kennedy Stadium in Philadelphia on July 13, 1985. The consensus is that the all-day telecast reached the largest audience in history. Estimates of the money raised reached $80 million. (Ireland made the highest per capita contribution.) The U.S. effort added a domestic need to its agenda: USA for Africa would devote part of the funds raised to the needs of the poor in the United States as well as the famine victims in Africa. The European versions remained focused on the African famine. By the time that Hands Across America occurred, the divided agenda was further complicated by competition among the performers. The

By the time that Hands Across America occurred, the divided agenda was further complicated by competition among the performers.

Hands Across America event was scheduled on the same day as the international run for famine relief, organized by Geldof, that was held in Europe and elsewhere. Several observations may be in order:

Coalitions brought together by an emergency do not seem to hold together well over time. Other priorities divide attention and cause conflict.

- Coalitions brought together by an emergency do not seem to hold together well over time. Other priorities divide attention and cause conflict.

- A rock promoter in California commented that with an array of performers like that assembled for the Live Aid concert, he could produce an audience of that size without a famine. The cause did not generate the audience; the entertainers did.

Those who made the Ethiopian famine their first priority overlooked the people in need at home.

- Those who made the Ethiopian famine their first priority overlooked the people in need at home. The domestic claims for help are closer and more persistent as well as better organized. The distant problem seemed fated to lose place to the more immediate one.

- No one seems to know whether spectacular benefits recruit new contributors, especially among the young. The young lady who said, at the Live Aid concert, that "It's fun to have fun and do good at the same time" may not make another gift unless she is entertained royally for doing so.

- The most common question among professional fund raisers is whether Live Aid and its long list of imitators have introduced a lasting change in the way funds are raised. The history of Farm Aid, now ended, may indicate that a life span of three or four years is the most that one should expect. (Others did not even succeed the first time.)

Those who were there before the world discovered the Ethiopian famine and who will remain there through the next one are the private voluntary organizations (PVOs). More than a hundred of them belong to the coordinating organization InterAction. From InterAction's self-study, it appears that most PVOs want to be *development* rather than *relief* organizations. They are in the relief business because they have to be—because their contributors want them to be. Only a few PVOs resolutely stay out of the relief field for policy reasons. . . .

The relief mandate forces PVOs to be where the action is. Some rushed with unseemly haste into Ethiopia. PVOs were often forced to transfer staff from other crisis areas to be able to staff programs in the more visible and better-publicized crisis in Africa. As one PVO administrator said, "Our whole concept of where need is depends on where the cameras are aimed" (Personal correspondence, 1985a). In summary:

- The sense of crisis and emergency and acute suffering seem to be the incentives for philanthropic response that work best. Appeals to pity tend to focus almost exclusively on children or on children and their mothers. (There is almost an implication that men should be able to do something.)

- There is a low threshold of audience willingness to stay with such images. Audience fatigue comes quickly, and it is followed by donor fatigue.

- The PVO dependence on relief crises to raise money may not work in the long run: "We can't expect to attract donors through guilt and then expect them to get excited about development."

- There is a shortage of experienced relief workers who are trained in handling emergency situations. Few people make their career in relief work.

- On the other side of the desk, too few grant makers, private or public, have a personal knowledge of what goes on in a refugee relief camp or in a village struggling to recover from a famine.

The response to the Ethiopian famine in 1984–85 was a success. Millions of lives were saved. The response to the famine was also a failure; the famine has recurred. As pessimists argued during the first famine, relief efforts only postpone the change that must take place. Bad governments remain in power, their policies continue. Those who pursue military objectives look upon the sufferings of the innocent as part of the consequences of the war—and the war is the other party's fault. The war goes on. People shift their attention to other things: by midsummer 1985, the famine had lost place to the struggle against apartheid in South Africa. People find themselves able to think of other things, including more pressing problems. There is a sense that the intensity of the response to the Ethiopian famine was misplaced—why did we think that it was so important?

As pessimists argued during the first famine, relief efforts only postpone the change that must take place.

The famine is back. By late summer 1987, newspapers carried regular reports and even features about the approach of famine in Mozambique, Angola, Sudan, and Ethiopia. Government action to make food supplies available was taken early, but without the intense public pressure brought to bear in 1984. The public assessment of Ethiopia is mixed with its opinion of affairs in Africa generally: probably beyond help, possibly beyond hope.

The first response, that of Bob Geldof and so many of the rest of us, set records. The relief agencies were pushed to the limit. Many of them became overcommitted and suffered badly when contributions faltered and declined by late 1985. None of the appeals since then has approached the high levels of those inspired in the eight months between October 1984 and July 1985.

In a seminar on the Ethiopian famine, one of the participants had grown weary of the issue after eighteen months. "I've come to this decision with regret because I always enjoy being with you for discussion of any subject. The fact is, however, that I am very busy and I am really not very interested in Ethiopia, or I should say, I think I've had enough of Ethiopia" (Personal correspondence, 1985b). Weighed against my friend's fatigue is the determination of all those people who continue to work for agencies that bring aid to the suffering wherever they are. They call on us for help. Sometimes we respond with great enthusiasm, even generosity. But we cannot be depended on.

If there is a lesson here, it is that one. The weakness of philanthropy is that it cannot see things through. The challenge to philanthropy is to find a way to convert the irregular energy of relief into the sustained dynamic of development.

The challenge to philanthropy is to find a way to convert the irregular energy of relief into the sustained dynamic of development.

Robert L. Payton, "Helping the Underserved Abroad: The Case of Famine Relief," in *The Future of the Nonprofit Sector* by Virginia A. Hodgkinson, Richard W. Lyman, and Associates (San Francisco: Jossey-Bass Inc., 1989). Reprinted by permission of John Wiley & Sons Inc..

SAMARITROPHOBIA

"He coined a new word for Sylvia's disease, 'Samaritrophobia,' which he said meant, 'hysterical indifference to the troubles of those less fortunate than oneself.'"

—Kurt Vonnegut Jr., *God Bless You, Mr. Rosewater*

"I used to live in a country supposed to be peculiarly infested by beggars; but I believe I was not so much asked for charity in Venice as I am in New York. There are as many beggars on our streets as in Venice, and as for the organized efforts to get at one's compassion, there is no parallel for New York anywhere. The letters asking aid for air funds, salt and fresh, for homes and shelters, for reading-rooms and eating-rooms, for hospitals and refuges, for the lame, halt, and blind, for the old, for the young, for the enhungered and ashamed, of all imaginable descriptions, storm in with every mail, so that one hates to open one's letters nowadays; for instead of finding a pleasant line from a friend, one finds an appeal, in print imitating typewriting, from several of the millionaires in the city for aid of some good object to which they have lent the influence of their signatures, and inclosing an envelope, directed but not stamped, for your subscription. You do not escape from the proof of poverty even by keeping indoors amidst your own luxurious environment; besides, your digestion becomes impaired, and you have to go out, if you are to have any appetite for your dinner; and then the trouble begins on other terms."

—William Dean Howells, "Tribulations of a Cheerful Giver"

"The final dispensation of one's wealth preparing for the final exit is I found a heavy task—all sad— . . . You have no idea the strain I have been under. . . . Millionaires who laugh are rare, very rare, indeed."

—Andrew Carnegie

"Pity the poor millionaire, for the way of the philanthropist is hard."
—Andrew Carnegie, Letter to the Editor, *The Independent*, 26 July 1913

"Open no letter except such as your secretary lays before you as from your family."
—Andrew Carnegie's advice to Mrs. Russell Sage on how to be a philanthropist

"You see my business is trying to arouse human pity. There are a few things that'll move people to pity, a few, but the trouble is, when they've been used several times, they no longer work. Human beings have the horrid capacity of being able to make themselves heartless at will. So it happens, for instance, that a man who sees another man on the street corner with only a stump for an arm will be so shocked the first time that he'll give him sixpence. But the second time it'll be only a threepenny bit. And if he sees him a third time, he'll hand him over coldbloodedly to the police . . . the rich of the earth indeed create misery, but they cannot bear to see it."

—Jeremiah Peachum,
in Bertolt Brecht's *The Threepenny Opera*

"People are concerned about the plight in Africa, but if there was no famine we'd have sold as many tickets."

—Bill Graham, promoter of Live Aid

QUESTIONS FOR THOUGHT AND DISCUSSION

1. Why did the news report of the famine have such a powerful effect on Bob Geldof? How did the camera influence his perception of the famine?
2. Based on Geldof's essay, Payton lays out a "model of the modern philanthropic mind." What is the incentive for responding to need? Who or what is the focus of his points? What is the significance for sustained giving?
3. Payton mentions that "public enthusiasm overwhelmed the political obstacles." Why is enthusiasm never enough to "see things through"?
4. What are the pros and cons of using forms of entertainment to entice people to give?
5. With the benefit of hindsight, how might responses to such a famine have been handled better? What were the pluses and minuses of the outpouring of interest for the PVOs in Ethiopia?
6. Do you feel the force of "compassion fatigue" in your own life? What antidotes do you use to counter it and continue to care for the world's need in a way that "sees things through"?

I CAN DO SOMETHING

"I am only one,
But still I am one.
I cannot do everything,
But still I can do something;
And because I cannot do everything
I will not refuse to do the something that I can do."

—Edward Everett Hale

"I don't do any great thing; I do small things with great love."

—Mother Teresa

"A young man was walking on the beach one morning and saw in the distance something that looked like someone dancing on the sand. As he got closer, he saw an old man picking up something on the beach and running toward the water and throwing it out beyond the breaking waves. This puzzled the young man, and he approached the old man to ask, 'What are you doing?' The old man replied, 'The surf has washed these starfish onto the beach and they will die when the sun rises. So I'm throwing them back into the sea, so they'll live.' The young man said, 'There must be thousands of starfish on this long beach. You can't possibly make a difference.' The old man ignored the young man, stooped down to pick up another starfish, and gently tossed it back into the sea. Then he looked at the young man and said, 'I made a difference to that one.'"

—Cristina Harter of General Electric,
quoted in *Heroes After Hours*

FIVE
FOUR CONCLUDING REFLECTIONS

POINT TO PONDER:

Generosity Is More than Giving Money

The story is told of a wealthy church member who went to his minister and complained, "As far as I can see, this Christian business is just one continuous 'Give, give, give.'"

"Congratulations!" the minister responded, "That's the best definition of the Christian life I've heard for a long time."

"Jewish" and "Muslim" might well be substituted for "Christian" in the story, for all three biblical faiths stress the spiritual obligations of giving. But the particular faith is not the point. That one person's ground for complaint is another's ground for congratulation illustrates once again the surprising elusiveness of the wonder of giving.

As we have seen, giving is far more than a straightforward transfer of resources from one person to another. Even when many of the deeper issues have been brought to light about the meaning of money, the motives for giving, and so on, giving remains an art that can never be reduced to formulae and mechanical procedures. In this concluding section, therefore, we examine four reflections that help sharpen and sustain the wise art of giving.

First is the fact that generosity is much more than giving money.

Edwin Samuel

Edwin Herbert, second Viscount Samuel (1898–1978), was a Jewish civil servant, professor, and writer. Born in London and raised in England, he served in the British Army from 1917–1919 before earning his degree from Balliol College, Oxford. In 1920 he moved to British Palestine where he entered the Palestine Civil Service as a district officer, eventually rising to director of broadcasting in 1945. After 1948 he entered the academic world, serving as visiting professor in public administration at universities in the United States and Germany, and as lecturer at Hebrew University in Jerusalem for over a decade. A writer on issues of public administration and government, he was also a popular author of short stories, with six collections published, including The Man Who Liked Cats *(1974). The following passage, from a story in his collection,* A Cottage in Galilee *(1957), is a modern counterpoint to Jesus' famous comments on "the widow's mite."*

THE ONLY SAFE RULE OF GIVING

"Jesus sat down opposite the place where the offerings were put and watched the crowd putting their money into the temple treasury. Many rich people threw in large amounts. But a poor widow came and put in two very small copper coins, worth only a fraction of a penny. Calling his disciples to him, Jesus said, 'I tell you the truth, this poor widow has put more into the treasury than all the others. They all gave out of their wealth; but she, out of her poverty, put in everything—all she had to live on.'"

—Mark 12:41-44

"I do not believe one can settle how much we ought to give. I am afraid the only safe rule is to give more than we can spare. In other words, if our expenditure on comforts, luxuries, amusements, etc., is up to the standard common among those with the same income as our own, we are probably giving away too little. If our charities do not at all pinch or hamper us, I should say they are too small. There ought to be things we should like to do and cannot do because our charitable expenditure excludes them."

—C. S. Lewis, *Mere Christianity*

Big Givers

Two thousand years of *Galut* have left us with a low standard of office accommodation. Poky holes in the ghettoes of Eastern Europe have given way to poky rooms in modern office buildings in Israel. The office staff are packed into these rooms like rabbits into a hutch—two and three and four to each. In many poky rooms, the desks are placed so close together that there is hardly any place for visitors to sit down. And if a visitor does arrive and starts his argument (no-one ever has a *conversation* with an official) he disturbs not one person but all the other officials in the room.

The Jewish Agency is no exception to this system of cheese-paring economy in staff accommodation. It is one more of the burdens their staff must bear, together with low salaries and public contumely. For no-one *loves* a public official in Israel, be he a civil servant or a Jewish Agency man.

The other day, I found myself sitting in one of the Jewish Agency rabbit hutches, trying to discuss with one of its four occupants the contents of a pamphlet I was commissioned to write. We made but slow headway. First, the telephone rang and one of the other rabbits in the room had a long wrangle with someone in Haifa. When that was over and *we* got down to business again, a rabbit from the adjacent hutch burst in and had a long discussion with my rabbit about a missing letter. It is one of the conventions of Israel that inter-office conversations *always* take precedence over interviews with the public.

I am well hardened to these difficulties; but even I was beginning to feel somewhat frustrated when in marched a portly American, with a panama hat on the back of his head. His wife, Mrs. Portly American, wore lots of frills, unsuitable even for a woman half her age. She sweated, I mean perspired, I mean glowed—profusely. It was August, when wealthy Americans come to take a look at their poor relations in Israel. If they haven't any poor relations of their own, they just look at poor Israel, which they support through the U.J.A. campaign.

There was a time when the national leaders of each of the Jewish communities throughout the world were the rabbi and the teacher. Now they are the fund-raisers, who decide how much each member of the community must contribute. If you are wealthy, you are admitted to the aristocracy of the Big Givers for whom an expensive lunch is arranged at the beginning of the campaign. A high-pressure national salesman is put on to speak; and the five or ten percent increase in donations extorted at that meeting sets the tone for the whole campaign among the lesser fry. A Big Giver is a Very Important Person Indeed. And when Big Givers come to Israel, their arrival is suitably announced in the Social and Personal column of the *Jerusalem Post* and we are all suitably impressed.

If you are wealthy, you are admitted to the aristocracy of the Big Givers for whom an expensive lunch is arranged at the beginning of the campaign.

Well, Mr. and Mrs. Portly American turned out to be Mr. and Mrs. Mortimer Richmond, of Miami. I had duly read about their arrival a few days before; and here he was giving the once-over to the Jewish Agency. But someone had blundered. Instead of being taken at once into the Presence, where he would be received in a large room with a carpet, he had been ushered by some uncomprehending valet into our rabbit hutch. Oh, the shame of it! Mr. and Mrs. Mortimer Richmond came to rest against the table of the rabbit nearest the door — a poor, round-shouldered, inoffensive man, with white hair, a straggly mustache, and watery blue eyes. Mr. Richmond glared and said: "I want the Boss."

The inoffensive rabbit bowed. Realizing the awful solecism that had been committed, he apologized profusely: "*Selicha, Selicha!*" he murmured. He slid round the edge of his desk and out of the door like a wraith, beckoning the Big Givers to follow him. He took them to the Presence and returned to his hutch, mopping his brow.

I, meanwhile, was getting nowhere with my own business, thanks to the constant commotion in the hutch. I turned to my rabbit and said: "For God's sake! Let's get out of here and continue our conversation where it's quieter. What about the cafe round the corner?" My rabbit agreed, and we sat in the shade of a big awning and discussed my business over our lemonades. We could see from our vantage point all the coming and going at the Jewish Agency across the street. Just when we were finishing our talk, a big, black, empty limousine drew up. Mr. and Mrs. Mortimer Richmond came out of the Agency building, accompanied by the Boss, who saw them off with many smiles and bows. Today's Big Giver had been suitably welcomed.

My rabbit had a broad grin on his face as he watched the scene. "What's so funny?" I asked. "These Big Givers make me sick."

"There's a rich joke in all this," said my rabbit, "which you'd only understand if you worked in the Agency. Did you notice the man who got up and took those unfortunate Americans out of our room?"

"You mean the man with the white hair and the stoop?"

"Yes: that's Aharon — Aharon Malinovsky. He's our prize specimen. If only our American friends knew about Aharon, they'd throw their weight around less."

"What do you mean?"

"You'll see when I tell you Aharon's history. He came here like so many of us — from Poland in the 1920s. His son, Benjamin, had come here first. Worked as a laborer — a Public Works roadman, I think. Then, as soon as he could show that he was established, he brought in his parents. That's Aharon: his wife died many years ago. But when they came, they lived with Benjamin, of course. He had a room near the Abyssinian Church. In Poland, Aharon had been a Hebrew teacher; but he was too decrepit even then to face a class of tough sabras. So his son helped to set him up in a little stationery shop. His wife kept the books. When she died—some time in the thirties—Aharon got into a fearful muddle with his accounts and had to shut down. He soon got a new job, however, as a peddler of Hebrew encyclopedias and even made a little money.

"This was fortunate, as Benjamin had just got married and had moved into a new flat. It wasn't big enough for all three of them; so Aharon stayed at the old room (he still lives there). Benjamin had by now been promoted. He was a Public Works foreman—quite a well-paid job in those days. But he couldn't look after Aharon any longer; he had a wife to support; and, later, came the children.

"Well, Aharon got on all right, living in the old room near the Abyssinian Church; feeding in restaurants in the Jaffa Road and peddling his encyclopedias, until the war broke out. No more paper: no more encyclopedias. For a time he almost starved. Then an influential school friend of his daughter-in-law managed to get Aharon a job in the Jewish Agency. He thought it was wonderful: a corner of an office all of his own and a regular salary. The salary was lucky, as his son Benjamin had once more been promoted, this time to be Chief P.W.D. Storekeeper. As such, he had a lot to do with the Army Stores. This was war-time and Public Works were doing an enormous amount of defense work on Army account. So Benjamin had to meet a lot of Army officers and invite them home and stand them drinks. This was an expensive business, with whisky at war-time prices, even if wangled out of the N.A.A.F.I. Benjamin had a very good salary by now, as Chief Storekeeper. But his entertaining kept him constantly in debt, and his poor old father—Aharon—used to help him out regularly at the end of the month."

"What a shame!" I said.

"But Benjamin wasn't the tenth of his liabilities. Aharon helps *everyone*. You should just see what our office is like on *Rosh Chodesh!* Every beggar in town knows Aharon—*Adon* Aharon, they all call him. As he's hardly ever at home, they all call at our office, one after the other. But he's much too courteous—and too retiring—to give them anything in *our* presence. So he and they conspire to pretend they've come about business. Up gets Aharon and goes out 'to look for the file.' They follow him into the corridor where he gives each a few piastres and they wander out again, showering blessings on his name. If there's ever a man who deserved them, it's Aharon: he's pure, unadulterated goodness, all through."

"But how does he manage all this on his Agency salary?" I asked. "He can't be very highly paid," and I just checked myself from adding "or he wouldn't be sitting in such an over-crowded rabbit hutch."

Aharon helps everyone. You should just see what our office is like on Rosh Chodesh! Every beggar in town knows Aharon—Adon Aharon, they all call him.

"God knows. After they deduct his income tax, his *Histadrut* dues, and *Kupat Cholim,* and the pension fund, the J.N.F. and the *Keren Hayesod,* there's precious little left, as I know all too well. But Aharon then starts his monthly subscriptions to half the societies in town—the *Magen David Adom,* the Anti-Tuberculosis League, the Blind School, the Crippled Children, the Mental Home, the *Moshav Zekenim* and heaven knows what else besides. They all put up their stickers on his door jambs—to keep off the evil eye of the collectors. But he modestly removes them at night with hot water; so he has to see the collectors as well and show them his receipts, which seems to embarrass him very much. He's always grumbling about them."

"But the man's a modern-day saint!" I said.

"And that's only the half of it. If any of us in the office is in trouble, you'll be sure old Aharon will hear of it first. He's got a nose for distress. I don't know how he ever finds out. No one tells him; but it seems he can guess by people's faces. He'll sidle up to someone—one of his colleagues, I mean—and start an innocent conversation until he finds out what the trouble is. Then he quietly goes about putting it right, and out of his own pocket, too. He'd never think of telling us about it. We'd all chip in, of course. But, oh no, that's Aharon's private affair. No wonder he walks around with that stoop of his: he certainly has half the trouble of the world on his own shoulders."

He'll sidle up to someone—one of his colleagues, I mean—and start an innocent conversation until he finds out what the trouble is. Then he quietly goes about putting it right, and out of his own pocket, too.

"But he looks so ill and shabby himself," I said. " Does he keep *nothing* for his own use?"

"Hardly a thing. When there was that appeal for clothing for the *ma'abarot* a few winters ago, of course, it was Aharon who turned up among the first, with his bundle. And as he's worn his second-best suit ever since, I suspect that it was his Sabbath clothes that he disposed of."

"He doesn't look to me as if he's long for this world," I added.

"I'm afraid you're right. He's used up all his savings. He's hardly got enough now for a square meal. And yet, would you believe it? Almost every afternoon, after a hard day's work in that office of ours, off he goes to the Talpiot *ma'abara* to teach Hebrew to old Kurdish women. They adore him and cluck over him like old hens. At least they make him eat a little now and again. It's rather pathetic—isn't it?—the way that some of those who have so little are often the most generous."

🌺   🌺   🌺

A few months later, I happened to see in the *Jerusalem Post* the familiar mourning announcements: "Aharon Malinovsky is no more! To the veteran Zionist, from his Jewish Agency colleagues." And several other notices, in the same vein, from some of the charities that he had helped.

As I passed along the Jaffa Road later in the morning, I saw a crowd outside the *Bikkur Cholim* Hospital. Hundreds of people, many in black. An extraordinary medley, even for Jerusalem—old rabbis and schoolchildren, Yemenis and soldiers on leave; housewives and office-workers: lots of people from the *ma'abara*. All strangely aimless and still. No noise except for an occasional sniffle. Everyone was withdrawn and intent on his own recollections of Aharon. It might have been some national hero, except for the absence of the Cabinet. They never hear of such important occasions as Aharon's death until the ceremony is all over.

But the single eulogy outside the mortuary, delivered by one of the Teachers' Association who had known Aharon in Poland, was deeply moving. For once, there were no exaggerations. By the end of it, most of us were in tears: and I'm not ashamed to admit it. I only hope that Mr. Mortimer Richmond (may he live to be a hundred and twenty!) will have as impressive a funeral. We in Jerusalem have our own standards: *we* know who are the Big Givers.

We in Jerusalem have our own standards: we know who are the Big Givers.

Edwin Samuel, "Big Givers," *A Cottage in Galilee* (New York: Abelard-Schuman, 1958), pp. 152–160. © 1958 by Edwin Samuel. All attempts have been made to locate the copyright holder.

'MARS AND VENUS' ON GIVING STYLES

- Traditionally, men have exercised the gift of giving mainly through giving money and women through volunteering.
- Men are often motivated to give because of peer pressure, but women are more likely to be inspired to join others to make a difference.
- For men giving money is often the end of the process; for women it is only the beginning.
- Men tend to think in terms of "big deals," "big organizations," and "big buildings" whereas women generally think about people.
- Women generally take longer than men to make up their minds, but once committed they often stay with a project longer than men.
- Many men think in terms of statistics; women want to hear stories.
- Men generally give money in a strategic way, but women tend to give money more spontaneously when moved by an issue.

—Karol Emmerich, from a speech on "Women and Philanthropy"

QUESTIONS FOR THOUGHT AND DISCUSSION

1. What factors does Samuel see as creating the phenomenon of the "Big Givers" in both Israel and the Jewish community? What does the shift of leadership from "the rabbi and the teacher" to "the fund-raisers" signify?

2. How would you describe Mr. and Mrs. Portly American? What is the narrator's attitude toward them? What does he say is their reason for coming to Israel? What is his attitude toward other people like them— the "Big Givers"? Do you think his assessment is fair or harsh and ungrateful?

3. How did the narrator know that "someone had blundered" when the Richmonds walked into the office?

4. What is the "rich joke" that the narrator's "rabbit" knows?

5. What were the marks of generosity in Aharon Malinovsky's life? To whom, how, and what did he give? In what ways does his giving speak of the Jewish *tzedakah* and dignity of the recipient discussed in part 2? How is this contrasted with the generosity of the "Big Givers"?

6. How do you have to live so as to have a funeral with "no exaggerations" in the tributes?

7. In the Mark passage in the box at the beginning, "The Only Safe Rule of Giving," why does Jesus say the widow was more generous? Why is it that poor people are generally more generous (proportionately) than rich people?

8. In a world that not only values but needs "Big Givers," how do we keep a healthy assessment of what is true generosity?

NEW POWER, NEW PERKS

"JERRY: 'You're going to start your own charity?'"

"GEORGE: 'I think I could be a philanthropist. A kick-ass philanthropist! I would have all this money, and people would love me. Then they would come to me . . . and beg! And if I felt like it, I would help them out. And then they would owe me big time! (Thinking to himself) . . . First thing I'm gonna need is a driver . . .'"

—From a "Seinfeld" episode in which George's boss gives him a check of $20,000 for the "Human Fund," a charity George has made up

POINT TO PONDER:

Always Be Aware of the Role of Need

Probably nothing distorts or ruins the straightforward good intentions of giving more than the unacknowledged presence of need, whether in those who give or those who receive. Even more elusive is defining what constitutes a "need." Conservatives in many Western countries are now challenging the equation of "need" and "entitlement" in recent welfare thinking. But this is only a small part of the bigger problem of the way that need distorts giving.

La Rochefoucauld, the seventeenth-century French philosopher, wrote, "There are few things we should keenly desire if we really knew what we wanted." But by definition needs and desires are different, because we must know that we desire something, whereas we can be in deep need of something yet not know it. As political theorist Michael Ignatieff says, "Just as we often desire what we do not need, so we often need what we do not consciously desire."

Similarly, if we can deceive ourselves about what we need, we can be even more wrong when prescribing what others need—and the presumption can become a doorway for arrogance when we presume that we know better than they do.

Or again needs change when we shift from the level of "basic goods" that we need to survive as human beings, such as food, shelter, and protection, to the higher level of "human goods" that we need to thrive, such as dignity, respect, love, community, and freedom. Again by definition the higher class of needs cannot all be made a matter of political rights—it is logically possible to claim freedom as a political right but not love. But when we make the lower class into political rights, we often think it absolves us from considering the higher class at all, without which human life is stunted. Ignatieff says, "The test of responsible political argument is to know which needs can be satisfied through politics and which cannot."

We explore the role of need in giving through William Shakespeare's King Lear. Often acclaimed as his greatest play, King Lear is a tragedy of human need. In particular it examines the relationship of need to human obligation, and the difference between what is owed us because of social obligation and what is owed us as naked human beings. Love, Lear learns, is a need but not a right, even for a king. But the play is a tragedy because he only learns what he truly needs by suffering. Only in madness does he achieve clarity of sight.

> "The test of responsible political argument is to know which needs can be satisfied through politics and which cannot."
> —MICHAEL IGNATIEFF

❧ *William Shakespeare* ❧

William Shakespeare (1564–1616) is the greatest playwright in the English language and arguably the greatest in any language. He was born in Stratford-on-Avon, and little is known of his younger days. But by 1597 he had written a dozen plays, and by 1600 he had begun to create the great tragedies for which he is most famous—Hamlet, Macbeth, and King Lear. Sometime after 1612 he retired from the stage and returned to Stratford.

      Only the King James Bible exceeds Shakespeare's influence on the English language. And the number of Shakespearean phrases, characters, and concepts that have become part of our cultural vocabulary would be too many to count. His graceful sonnets are also masterpieces of poetry.

      King Lear is the most devastating and complex of all his tragedies. The aged king seeks to retire from authority and announces he will apportion his land among his three daughters according to how well each publicly states her love for him. Cordelia, the youngest, alone loves him too well to play his game, and he punishes her with banishment.

      Lear soon regrets his decision. He attempts to continue the life of a king, accompanied by a band of a hundred knights, being hosted and attended by his two remaining daughters in their castles. But Goneril and Regan have little love or patience with their father, especially now that he has made himself subject to their mercy. Deprived of his retinue and dishonored by his daughters, he exiles himself onto the heath during a raging storm. In the lightning, rain, and howling winds the king experiences what it is like to be at the mercy of the merciless, and he begins to lose his mind. He experiences how wretched life is for the poor and outcast when he is forced to shelter with an insane vagrant, a blind man, and his own court jester.

      Three scenes from the play follow. The first, from Act 1, includes the infamous "love auction" in which Lear uses his royal benefaction to mask his need to be needed. The second, from Act 2, portrays his clash with his two cold-hearted daughters over what he thinks he "needs" and what they think they "owe" him as king and father—"O, reason not the need!" he cries out in protest at their callous assessments. The third scene, from Act 3, shows the terrible clarity Lear gains through suffering and his realization that man is only "a poor, bare, fork'd animal" who cannot claim what he once sought as a right, and cannot get what he once gave so royally but falsely to obtain.

In the lightning, rain, and howling winds the king experiences what it is like to be at the mercy of the merciless, and he begins to lose his mind. He experiences how wretched life is for the poor and outcast when he is forced to shelter with an insane vagrant, a blind man, and his own court jester.

It should be stressed that some of the deepest points do not lie on the surface of the text (as they do with other articles). But they will come out as we discuss the deep drama of Shakespeare's portrayal.

King Lear ❧

ACT 1, SCENE 1

Lear. . . . Give me the map there. Know that we have divided
    In three our kingdom; and 'tis our fast intent
    To shake all cares and business from our age,
    Conferring them on younger strengths, while we
    Unburthen'd crawl toward death. Our son of Cornwall,
    And you, our no less loving son of Albany,
    We have this hour a constant will to publish
    Our daughters' several dowers, that future strife
    May be prevented now. The princes, France and Burgundy,
    Great rivals in our youngest daughter's love,
    Long in our court have made their amorous sojourn,
    And here are to be answer'd. Tell me, my daughters
    (Since now we will divest us both of rule
    Interest of territory, cares of state),
    Which of you shall we say doth love us most,
    That we our largest bounty may extend
    Where nature doth with merit challenge?
    Goneril, Our eldest-born, speak first.

Goneril. Sir, I love you more than [words] can wield the matter,
    Dearer than eyesight, space, and liberty,
    Beyond what can be valued, rich or rare,
    No less than life, with grace, health, beauty, honor;
    As much as child e'er lov'd, or father found;
    A love that makes breath poor, and speech unable:
    Beyond all manner of so much I love you.

Cordelia. *[Aside.]* What shall Cordelia speak? Love, and be silent.

Lear. Of all these bounds, even from this line to this,
    With shadowy forests and with champains rich'd,

With plenteous rivers and wide-skirted meads,
We make thee lady. To thine and Albany's [issue]
Be this perpetual. What says our second daughter,
Our dearest Regan, wife of Cornwall? [Speak.]

Regan. I am made of that self metal as my sister,
And prize me at her worth. In my true heart
I find she names my very deed of love;
Only she comes too short, that I profess
Myself an enemy to all other joys
Which the most precious square of sense [possesses],
And find I am alone felicitate
In your dear Highness' love.

Cordelia. [Aside.] Then poor Cordelia!
And yet not so, since I am sure my love's
More ponderous than my tongue.

Lear. To thee and thine hereditary ever
Remain this ample third of our fair kingdom,
No less in space, validity, and pleasure,
Than that conferr'd on Goneril.—Now, our joy,
Although our last and least, to whose young love
The vines of France and milk of Burgundy
Strive to be interess'd, what can you say to draw
A third more opulent than your sisters'? Speak.

Cordelia. Nothing, my lord.

Lear. Nothing?

Cordelia. Nothing.

Lear. Nothing will come of nothing, speak again.

Cordelia. Unhappy that I am, I cannot heave
My heart into my mouth. I love your Majesty
According to my bond, no more nor less.

Lear. How, how, Cordelia? Mend your speech a little,
Lest you may mar your fortunes.

Cordelia. Good my lord,
    You have begot me, bred me, lov'd me: I
    Return those duties back as are right fit,
    Obey you, love you, and most honor you.
    Why have my sisters husbands, if they say
    They love you all? Happily, when I shall wed
    That lord whose hand must take my plight shall carry
    Half my love with him, half my care and duty.
    Sure I shall never marry like my sisters,
    [To love my father all].

Lear. But goes thy heart with this?

Cordelia. Ay, my good lord.

Lear. So young, and so untender?

Cordelia. So young, my lord, and true.

Lear. Let it be so: thy truth then be thy dow'r!
    For by the sacred radiance of the sun,
    The [mysteries] of Hecat and the night;
    By all the operation of the orbs,
    From whom we do exist and cease to be;
    Here I disclaim all my paternal care,
    Propinquity and property of blood,
    And as a stranger to my heart and me
    Hold thee from this for ever. The barbarous Scythian,
    Or he that makes his generation messes
    To gorge his appetite, shall to my bosom
    Be as well neighbor'd, pitied, and reliev'd,
    As thou my sometime daughter.

Kent. Good my liege—

Lear. Peace, Kent!
    Come not between the dragon and his wrath;
    I lov'd her most, and thought to set my rest
    On her kind nursery. *[To Cordelia.]* Hence, and avoid
    my sight!—
    So be my grave my peace, as here I give

Her father's heart from her. Call France. Who stirs?
Call Burgundy. Cornwall and Albany,
With my two daughters' dow'rs digest the third;
Let pride, which she calls plainness, marry her.

ACT 2, SCENE 4

> *Angry and wounded by Goneril's treatment of him,*
> *Lear has left her castle and brought his retinue to Regan's castle.*
> *Enter Cornwall, Regan, Gloucester, Servants.*

Lear. Good morrow to you both.

Cornwall. Hail to your Grace!

> *Kent here set at liberty.*

Regan. I am glad to see your Highness.

Lear. Regan, I think [you] are; I know what reason
    I have to think so. If thou shouldst not be glad,
    I would divorce me from thy [mother's] tomb,
    Sepulchring an adult'ress. *[To Kent.]* O, are you free?
    Some other time for that. *[Exit Kent.]* Beloved Regan,
    Thy sister's naught. O Regan, she hath tied
    Sharp-tooth'd unkindness, like a vulture, here.

> *Points to his heart.*

    I can scarce speak to thee; thou'lt not believe
    With how deprav'd a quality—O Regan!

Regan. I pray you, sir, take patience. I have hope
    You less know how to value her desert
    Than she to scant her duty.

Lear. Say? How is that?

Regan. I cannot think my sister in the least
    Would fail her obligation. If, sir, perchance
    She have restrain'd the riots of your followers,
    'Tis on such ground and to such wholesome end
    As clears her from all blame.

Lear. My curses on her!

Regan. O sir, you arc old,
　　Nature in you stands on the very verge
　　Of his confine. You should be rul'd and led
　　By some discretion that discerns your state
　　Better than you yourself. Therefore I pray you
　　That to our sister you do make return.
　　Say you have wrong'd her.

Lear. Ask her forgiveness?
　　Do you but mark how this becomes the house!
　　"Dear daughter, I confess that I am old; [Kneeling.]
　　Age is unnecessary. On my knees I beg
　　That you'll vouchsafe me raiment, bed, and food."

Regan. Good sir, no more; these are unsightly tricks.
　　Return you to my sister.

Lear. [Rising.] Never, Regan:
　　She hath abated me of half my train;
　　Look'd black upon me, strook me with her tongue,
　　Most serpent-like, upon the very heart.
　　All the stor'd vengeances of heaven fall
　　On her ingrateful top! Strike her young bones,
　　You taking airs, with lameness! . . .

　　　　　　　　Soon Goneril enters and holds hands with Regan.
　　　　　　　　They side together against Lear, arguing to reduce the
　　　　　　　　number of knights in his loyal and boisterous retinue.

Goneril. Why might not you, my lord, receive attendance
　　From those that she calls servants or from mine?

Regan. Why not, my lord? If then they chanc'd to slack ye,
　　We could control them. If you will come to me
　　(For now I spy a danger), I entreat you
　　To bring but five and twenty; to no more
　　Will I give place or notice.

Lear. I gave you all—

Regan. And in good time you gave it.

Lear. Made you my guardians, my depositaries,
　　But kept a reservation to be followed
　　With such a number. What, must I come to you
　　With five and twenty? Regan, said you so?

Regan. And speak't again, my lord, no more with me.

Lear. Those wicked creatures yet do look well-favor'd
　　When others are more wicked; not being the worst
　　Stands in some rank of praise. *[To Goneril.]* I'll go with thee,
　　Thy fifty yet cloth double five and twenty,
　　And thou art twice her love.

Goneril. Hear me, my lord:
　　What need you five and twenty? ten? or five?
　　To follow in a house where twice so many
　　Have a command to tend you?

Regan. What need one?

O, reason not the need!
our basest beggars
Are in the poorest thing
superfluous.

Lear. O, reason not the need! our basest beggars
　　Are in the poorest thing superfluous.
　　Allow not nature more than nature needs,
　　Man's life is cheap as beast's. Thou art a lady;
　　If only to go warm were gorgeous,
　　Why, nature needs not what thou gorgeous wear'st,
　　Which scarcely keeps thee warm. But for true need—
　　You heavens, give me that patience, patience I need!
　　You see me here, you gods, a poor old man,
　　As full of grief as age, wretched in both.
　　If it be you that stirs these daughters' hearts
　　Against their father, fool me not so much
　　To bear it tamely; touch me with noble anger,
　　And let not women's weapons, water-drops,
　　Stain my man's cheeks! No, you unnatural hags,
　　I will have such revenges on you both
　　That all the world shall—I will do such things—
　　What they are yet I know not, but they shall be
　　The terrors of the earth! You think I'll weep:
　　No, I'll not weep.

I have full cause of weeping, but this heart

Storm and tempest.

Shall break into a hundred thousand flaws
Or ere I'll weep. O Fool, I shall go mad!

Exeunt [Lear, Gloucester, Gentleman, and Fool].

ACT 3, SCENE 4

*The "heath," to which Lear flees, is not just a place but
a state of mind—beyond rational, civilized, human society.
Here Lear achieves his greatest clarity.*

Kent. Good my lord, enter here.

Lear. Wilt break my heart?

Kent. I had rather break mine own. Good my lord, enter.

Lear. Thou think'st 'tis much that this contentious storm
Invades us to the skin; so 'tis to thee;
But where the greater malady is fix'd,
The lesser is scarce felt. Thou'dst shun a bear,
But if [thy] flight lay toward the roaring sea,
Thou'dst meet the bear i' th' mouth. When the mind's free,
The body's delicate; [this] tempest in my mind
Doth from my senses take all feeling else,
Save what beats there—filial ingratitude!
Is it not as this mouth should tear this hand
For lifting food to't? But I will punish home.
No, I will weep no more. In such a night
To shut me out? Pour on, I will endure.
In such a night as this? O Regan, Goneril!
Your old kind father, whose frank heart gave all—
O, that way madness lies, let me shun that!
No more of that.

Kent. Good my lord, enter here.

Lear. Prithee go in thyself, seek thine own ease.

This tempest will not give me leave to ponder
On things would hurt me more. But I'll go in.
[To the Fool.] In, boy, go first.—You houseless poverty—
Nay, get thee in; I'll pray, and then I'll sleep.

                                               Exit [Fool].

Poor naked wretches, wheresoe'er you are,
That bide the pelting of this pitiless storm,
How shall your houseless heads and unfed sides,
Your [loop'd] and window'd raggedness, defend you
From seasons such as these? O, I have ta'en
Too little care of this! Take physic, pomp,
Expose thyself to feel what wretches feel,
That thou mayst shake the superflux to them,
And show the heavens more just.

Edgar. [Within.] Fathom and half, fathom and half!
     Poor Tom!

                                   [Enter Fool from the hovel].

Fool. Come not in here, nuncle, here's a spirit.
     Help me, help me!

Kent. Give me thy hand. Who's there?

Fool. A spirit, a spirit! he says his name's poor Tom.

Kent. What art thou that dost grumble there i' th'
     straw? Come forth.

                             Enter Edgar [disguised as a madman].

Edgar. Away, the foul fiend follows me! Through the sharp hawthorn blow
     the [cold] winds. Humh, go to thy bed and warm thee.

Lear. Didst thou give all to thy daughters? And art thou come to this?

Edgar. Who gives any thing to poor Tom? whom the foul fiend hath led
     through fire and through flame, through [ford] and whirlpool, o'er bog and
     quagmire; that hath laid knives under his pillow, and halters in his pew,
     set ratsbane by his porridge, made him proud of heart, to ride on a bay
     trotting-horse over four-inch'd bridges, to course his own shadow for a

traitor. Bless thy five wits! Tom's a-cold—O do de do de, do de. Bless thee from whirlwinds, star-blasting and taking! Do poor Tom some charity, whom the foul fiend vexes. There could I have him now—and there—and there again—and there.

Storm still.

Lear. Has his daughters brought him to this pass? Couldst thou save noth-
    ing? Wouldst thou give 'em all?

Fool. Nay, he reserv'd a blanket, else we had been all sham'd.

Lear. Now all the plagues that in the pendulous air
    Hang fated o'er men's faults light on thy daughters!

Kent. He hath no daughters, sir.

Lear. Death, traitor! nothing could have subdu'd nature
    To such a lowness but his unkind daughters.
    Is it the fashion, that discarded fathers
    Should have thus little mercy on their flesh?
    Judicious punishment! 'twas this flesh begot
    Those pelican daughters.

Edgar. Pillicock sat on Pillicock-Hill, alow! alow, loo, loo!

Fool. This cold night will turn us all to fools and madmen.

Edgar. Take heed o' th' foul fiend. Obey thy parents, keep thy word's justice, swear not, commit not with man's sworn spouse, set not thy sweet heart on proud array. Tom's a-cold.

Lear. What hast thou been?

Edgar. A servingman! proud in heart and mind; that curl'd my hair; wore gloves in my cap; serv'd the lust of my mistress' heart, and did the act of darkness with her; swore as many oaths as I spake words, and broke them in the sweet face of heaven: one that slept in the contriving of lust, and wak'd to do it. Wine lov'd I so [deeply], dice dearly; and in woman out-paramour'd the Turk. False of heart, light of ear, bloody of hand; hog in sloth, fox in stealth, wolf in greediness, dog in madness, lion in prey. Let not the creaking of shoes nor the rustling of silks betray thy poor heart to woman. Keep thy foot out of brothels, thy hand out of plackets, thy pen from lenders' books, and defy the foul fiend. Still through the hawthorn blows the cold wind: says suum, mun, nonny. Dolphin my boy, boy, sessa! let him trot by.

Storm still.

Lear. Thou wert better in a grave than to answer with thy uncover'd body this extremity of the skies. Is man no more than this? Consider him well. Thou ow'st the worm no silk, the beast no hide, the sheep no wool, the cat no perfume. Ha? here's three on 's are sophisticated. Thou art the thing itself: unaccommodated man is no more but such a poor, bare, fork'd animal as thou art. Off, off, you lendings! Come, unbutton here. *[Tearing off his clothes]*

QUESTIONS FOR THOUGHT AND DISCUSSION

1. In the first scene, what does Lear think he is doing in giving away his kingdom? What is he not giving away?
2. How do you react emotionally to Lear's infamous "love auction"? Is this "contract" giving or "charity" giving? What does it do to his daughters? How does it affect their relationship with him? In what ways can money turn children into "groupies" and all relationships into dependencies?
3. Do you find what Goneril and Regan say believable? Why do you think Lear believes them? What was Lear's deepest need that he sought to assuage in the "love auction"?
4. What do you think of Cordelia's response to her father? Why does she not play along? What does Cordelia mean when she says, "I love your Majesty/According to my bond, no more nor less"? Is she being harsh and proud or honest and loving?
5. Why does Lear respond so badly to Cordelia's forthrightness? What does he do? What does that mean for himself? What had been his expectations for retirement?
6. Which of Lear's daughters would you say demonstrates love in the first scene? Why? How can power and wealth distort love or create false love?
7. In the first scene, Lear based "love" on flattering words. In the second scene, how is he measuring the "love" of his daughters?
8. On the surface, Lear and his two daughters are struggling over the number of knights in his entourage. What do the knights signify for Lear? What solution do his daughters offer for his "need" of knights?

What would their solution mean for Lear? Digging deeper, what would you say is the real struggle over?

9. In the final scene here, what does the storm signify? What happens to Lear in the midst of the storm? What does he realize about himself? His daughters? What is the meaning of his tearing of his clothes?

10. What does the tragedy of Lear show us of the need to plumb our own motives in giving?

11. Do you know examples of generosity so dominated by the donor's need that the giving becomes self-defeating? What went wrong?

POINT TO PONDER:

Social Entrepreneurship Is One of the Deepest Investments of All

As modern giving and caring have developed and grown more self-conscious it has become plain that the best giving is a form of "venture capital for social change." It is motivated by the belief that "we can transform the world, one good cause at a time." One vital form is the new emphasis on the entrepreneurial element in giving and caring.

As we saw earlier, an overall trend in both business and philanthropy has been the distancing of the founder/creator of the fortune from its administration. Professional foundations and fundraising have removed the wealthy from the control of their wealth—in favor of experts, specialists, and professionals. This drift is now under attack politically, but it is potentially just as harmful in terms of declining vision and energy in an organization.

The last decade has witnessed the rise of an alternative model of philanthropy, one that carries none of the distancing tendencies of the general purpose foundation. The new model is philanthropy through "social entrepreneurship." That is, rather than wealthy people giving their money to existing institutions, wealthy people give themselves as well as their money by serving in as well as supporting *the organization in which they believe.*

Thus no distancing occurs between the creator of wealth and its administrators. More importantly, the creators of the wealth are able to bring to the organization the same business expertise that was vital in creating their wealth in the first place. Social entrepreneurship is therefore a gift of knowledge and money delivered along with the personal passion of an entrepreneur.

The term "social entrepreneurship" may be new, alongside other modern terms such as "social capital." But the idea is not new. William Wilberforce's cousin, Henry Thornton, for example, was far more than England's most prosperous late-eighteenth-century merchant who happened to support the abolition of slavery. He brought to the abolition movement the same entrepreneurial gifts that exemplified both early modern capitalism and the early abolition reform movements. In our modern terms, he was a social entrepreneur, a venture capitalist for social change.

Obviously, the idea of social entrepreneurship is not for everyone. Most wealthy people continue in the sphere in which they created their wealth. But this philanthropic model appeals particularly to those who realize—as we saw in the Introduction—that there is more to money than making money, just as there is more to giving than giving money. In the words of Bob Buford, chairman of Buford Television Inc., it appeals to those who desire to move "from success to significance." Realizing that life is more than "going for the gold," they invest their gold—and themselves—in a greater cause or calling.

❊ *Millard Fuller* ❊

Millard Fuller (born 1935) is the founder and president of Habitat for Humanity International. Established with his wife Linda in 1976, a decade after Fuller gave away his earned wealth, Habitat has grown into a worldwide housing ministry. As of 2000, Habitat volunteers, working with more than 80,000 families, have built decent, safe, and inexpensive homes for more than 400,000 people in about 2,000 cities and in 64 countries. Each family in the program not only invests "sweat equity"—their own labor to construct their house—but helps construct houses for other families as well. Construction costs are met from a revolving fund replenished by house payments that vary according to what new owners can afford.

Former President Jimmy Carter is a well-known board member, advocate, and participant. Jack Kemp, former Secretary of Housing and Urban Development, describes Habitat as one of the few "housing success stories." President Clinton called it "the most successful continuous community project in the history of the United States." Habitat for Humanity is a striking example of "social entrepreneurship" in action.

WHEN SUCCESS GOT IN THE WAY

"I was raised by a dad who was doing well in business, so he got me into business. I got caught up into making money and went off to college, where I formed a business with a fellow student. Over an eight-year period, the business grew and mushroomed and made incredible money.

"Then, in November 1965, my wife left me. My wife and children were very important to me, but I pretty much took them for granted—until I saw I was about to lose them. I pursued my wife to New York and convinced her we could start a new life. We agreed that I would leave the business and donate all of our money to charitable causes. We didn't sit around and ponder for weeks about the advantages of keeping the money and the advantages of giving it away; it was a decision that we made very quickly. . . .

"I am a Christian person, fired and motivated by the Christian faith, and I feel that it was divine guidance that caused me to take this step. I feel strongly that material abundance was getting in the way of my family relationships and my spiritual life, and that attachment to material things was what got me into trouble. Giving it all away was a dramatic, radical step, one which society might consider somewhat foolish, but I was raised in the Church and have done a lot of Bible study over the years. The teachings of Jesus are very clear. You cannot serve God and money—you have to choose."

—Millard Fuller, cited in *We Gave Away a Fortune*

The 1995 Builder of the Year ❧

Some builders build for profit. Others build because they like the kicks they get by creating something original. Millard Fuller is different. Millard Fuller builds for God.

Fuller, age 60, is president and co-founder of Habitat for Humanity International, a nonprofit ecumenical Christian housing ministry based in Americus, Georgia. His mission is simple: to eliminate substandard shelter, what he calls "poverty housing," not only in the United States, but everywhere from the face of the Earth.

Fuller has been instrumental in improving the lives of thousands of citizens around the world by building houses the poor can afford to own. In 1995, HFHI built its 40,000th house since Fuller and his wife founded the organization nineteen years ago.

Professional Builder editors have selected Millard Dean Fuller the 1995 Builder of the Year for his unique approach to building affordable houses. Fuller brings together the business community, local community groups, private owners, and the homeowners themselves (who otherwise would never achieve the American Dream) with the sole purpose of building simple, low-cost houses. Fuller is the first not-for-profit builder to be named Builder of the Year since *Professional Builder* began the award program in 1966.

In 1996, Fuller estimates Habitat will have built twelve thousand houses—four thousand in the United States and eight thousand elsewhere in the world. Habitat ranks fifth on *Professional Builder's* 1995 list of the nation's largest builders, based on housing starts. Habitat's homes are sold to families and individuals with interest-free 20-year mortgages. A second mortgage on the land is paid down as the families live in the house. That is, 1/20th is paid after the first year, 2/20th the second and so on. A Habitat survey of affiliates in 1993 found a 0.8% foreclosure rate. Next year, Habitat's twentieth, will see the first houses being paid in full.

ORIGINS OF HABITAT FOR HUMANITY

Fuller, who grew up in Alabama, graduated from the law school of the University of Alabama in 1960. A self-made millionaire by age 29, Fuller found his personal life in shambles. His wife wanted to leave him, and he developed nagging physical problems that were ruining his health. After consulting with their minister, Fuller and his wife decided to give away his fortune and start anew. (His salary was $43,000 in 1993.) He then worked on a number of projects, including fund raising for a college. In 1973, Fuller, his wife, and four children moved to Zaire to build houses for the Disciples of Christ Church.

In Zaire, Fuller faced challenges on a scale greater than any U.S. builder faces. As Fuller wrote in his first book, *Bokotola*, he had to overcome scarce labor, material shortages, theft, dwindling funds, and superstitious employees. Three years later, Fuller had developed a 100-house development. Homeowners' monthly payments went into a revolving fund to finance the construction of more houses.

In 1976, Fuller returned from Zaire with, he says, "a vision of forming a worldwide organization" to eliminate poverty housing. Nearly twenty years later, he is still at it. He says he wants to "make it morally, politically, and socially unacceptable" for humans to live in sub-standard housing.

He says he wants to "make it morally, politically, and socially unacceptable" for humans to live in sub-standard housing.

Fuller set up shop in rural Americus, Georgia, to replicate the plan he had used successfully in Zaire. But it wasn't until former President Jimmy Carter moved back to nearby Plains after he left office and signed on that HFHI began to take off. Carter raised the profile of Habitat for Humanity by donning overalls and building houses himself.

THE JIMMY CARTER WORK PROJECT

Carter, the nation's most socially conscious president of the post-war era, turned out to be the perfect front man. It is hard to imagine Nixon, Ford,

Reagan, or Bush swinging hammers side by side with the poor. Carter lends his name and time to a high-profile, week-long building program every year. This year, the Jimmy Carter Work Project built twenty-one houses in Los Angeles; next year it moves to Hungary. Habitat's first fund-raising letter (HFHI has a direct-mail list of 1.4 million names) comes from Carter who explains what Habitat is all about. If people respond to that letter, then all subsequent correspondence comes from Fuller.

Both political parties find something to like in HFHI's mission, be it the self-help aspect, the housing of the poor, or that HFHI builds without federal funds. Fuller sees Habitat as a facilitator in bringing together diverse groups.

"We live in circles and Habitat breaks those circles," Fuller says over a lunch of baked fish and cornbread in an old Victorian-era hotel on Americus's main street. "Habitat brings Gingrich and Clinton together, (Jack) Kemp and Carter, Catholics and Lutherans. That's the theology of the hammer." Both President Clinton and House Speaker Newt Gingrich have cozied up to Fuller for their own political reasons.

HABITAT: THE PERSONAL TOUCH

HFHI doesn't lobby for federal funds, but Congress is considering a $25 million grant to HFHI. Fuller would use the funds for land acquisition and infrastructure improvements. In general, though, Fuller avoids government involvement. "We're the personal touch. Government is cold," he says.

Habitat is located in a renovated warehouse in downtown Americus. It has a paid staff of 160 and 150 volunteers. Staff is young, and the dress is casual. Fuller himself wears a blue Habitat for Humanity workshirt. Each morning kicks off with a devotional service, attended by staff, volunteers, and any of the international partners who happen to be in town.

Habitat's day-to-day operations are headed by Senior Vice President David Williams. Associates describe Fuller's role in the organization as cheerleader, fund raiser, and public face. Fuller accepts those descriptions of himself and adds that his job is to keep the staff and the affiliates focused on building "simple, decent, affordable houses."

Building the houses falls to the more than twelve hundred independent Habitat for Humanity affiliates in the United States and the more than three dozen in other countries. The affiliates secure land and materials, arrange financing, select the families, and organize construction. Having the local affiliates choose the homeowners is Habitat's strength and a drawback, Fuller says. Because the affiliates have a personal relationship with the homeowners the tendency is to want to give them a bigger house with more amenities. But that only draws resources away from other houses that could be built. "This should not become 'lottery housing for humanity,'" he says.

Affiliates create their own house plans but the national organization provides design criteria governing size and amenities. The largest house (with four bedrooms) should not exceed 1150 square feet. A two-bedroom house should be no larger than 900 square feet. The basic house should have one bathroom, a covered entry, and no garage or carport. Families can budget for extra items such as picture windows, fencing, or an additional half-bath. The average three-bedroom Habitat house costs the U.S. homeowner $34,300; in developing nations it costs $600 to $3,000 a house.

Those are Spartan plans, but a walk through Habitat's international model home village near headquarters shows the relative grandeur of U.S. houses. American garages are more commodious than what gets built in Kenya, India, Zaire, Indonesia, and Guatemala. Yet the simple structures built in developing countries represent a vast improvement over the shacks families move out of.

Because volunteer labor builds the houses, building materials must be "volunteer friendly," says Sybil Carter, associate director of corporate programs. Product donations must also be low-cost because materials are figured into the value of the house. Thus, Habitat won't use gold faucets and bidets even if they are free. Building material companies that have participated with HFHI include Andersen, CertainTeed, Dow, Georgia-Pacific, Kwikset, Larson, Milwaukee Electric Tool, National Gypsum, Owens-Corning, Square, and Sterling Plumbing.

Centex Corp., the nation's largest builder, is one of many for-profit builders working with non-profit Habitat for Humanity. By the year 2000, Centex expects to have built two hundred Habitat homes.

Atlanta builder John Wieland, this magazine's 1993 Builder of the Year, has served on Habitat's board of directors. He builds houses every year for Habitat and strongly encourages his employees to participate. "There is a feeling in this company that everyone has made a fine living by housing the privileged, so it's time to help the less privileged," says Maureen Mercer who runs the John Wieland Family Foundation.

Builder Perry Bigelow, who builds low-income housing in Chicago, says that Fuller's activities make Bigelow's job easier. "Fuller's work calls attention to the need and that things can be done," Bigelow says.

Habitat's annual budget was $49.9 million in 1994, up 29.6 percent from

Because the affiliates have a personal relationship with the homeowners the tendency is to want to give them a bigger house with more amenities. But that only draws resources away from other houses that could be built.

"There is a feeling in this company that everyone has made a fine living by housing the privileged, so it's time to help the less privileged," says Maureen Mercer who runs the John Wieland Family Foundation.

$38.6 million in 1993. Most of its operating funds come from contributions. Nearing its twentieth year, Habitat finds itself the hot charity of the 1990s because it satisfies all the right needs of donors and volunteers. HFHI is not a giveaway program. Owners pay for their houses with a down-payment, monthly payments, and sweat equity. Volunteers who build with HFHI achieve emotional rewards, which they do not get from simply writing a check. They can point to a tangible result at the end of a day.

Business partners achieve something, too. Instead of the usual team building exercises of shooting the rapids or an Outward Bound adventure, some companies send employees to Habitat events instead.

Next year, Habitat will build its 50,000th house and possibly the 60,000th, Fuller says. Fuller calculates that in June 2000, the 136,000th house will be completed and the 200,000th in the year 2003. By then, Habitat will have housed more than one million people, based on Fuller's estimate that six people on average live in a Habitat house.

33 HOUSES EVERY DAY

The Blitz Builds are Habitat's high-profile events. Politicians, celebrities, and corporate executives turn out to build houses and to do good (and some arguably participate to score public relations points with their constituencies). What the public often fails to understand, Fuller says, is that Habitat builds all the time throughout the year. To build 12,000 houses in one year, as Habitat will do in 1995, means that it must build 33 houses every day of the year.

Fuller admits to being surprised at the success of Habitat for Humanity. His original dream was to eliminate poverty housing in the rural south and in developing countries. Today there are affiliates worldwide. The fact that some nations (such as the Netherlands and Sweden) have eliminated substandard housing, but not the United States, is a point of irritation with Fuller. "The measure of a great society is how it treats the least," he says. Thirty-eight million people in this country live in poverty, Fuller says. His work has no end.

"The measure of a great society is how it treats the least."
—Millard Fuller

James D. Carper, "Millard Fuller of Habitat for Humanity Is the 1995 Builder of the Year," *Professional Builder,* December 1995. © 1995 by Cahners Publishing Company.

SUCCESS TO SIGNIFICANCE

"My goals and motivations have changed. Instead of business, I am just pursuing the common good. As Dr. Martin Luther King said, we all should work toward the establishment of the beloved community. Jesus taught us to pray, 'Thy kingdom come, thy will be done on earth as it is in heaven.' If you work for the coming of the beloved community, you have to be as concerned about your neighbors as you are about yourself. In order to generate income and services and housing and food and clothing for your neighbors, you must have as much fire in your belly as if you were doing it for yourself.

"Unfortunately, many of the brightest minds are devoting all of their energies to making themselves richer. . . .

"People with privilege ought to become familiar with movements that are doing significant things. Maybe they should invest their funds to get themselves elected to be a different kind of politician. But they have to be very careful to guard their motives and not get caught up on an ego trip. Jimmy Carter is a person who remained pretty committed to his ideals, both as President and since he left office. He has worked with us at Habitat for Humanity, and he is committed to human rights and sharing with the poor. I think he is a great example today of someone who is quite affluent—in terms of material wealth, position, power, influence, and prestige—who is using those resources for the larger good. We can all be part of helping to usher in the beloved community, a New Earth where righteousness prevails."

—Millard Fuller, cited in *We Gave Away a Fortune*

QUESTIONS FOR THOUGHT AND DISCUSSION

1. How were the circumstances in Fuller's life and conversion similar to St. Francis's? Why did Fuller give away his money?
2. In what specific ways is Fuller's Habitat for Humanity an example of "social entrepreneurship"? Who has come together in this work? What is the significance for the homeowners? The communities? What are the challenges HFHI faces?
3. Where does social entrepreneurship find its roots? What type of giving is this?
4. How is social entrepreneurship decisively different from voluntary associations and foundations? How is it an answer to some of the problems endemic in the other two?
5. What about social entrepreneurship appeals to you? What are the pluses and minuses of this type of giving?
6. In what organizations or spheres of concern might your expertise be fruitfully employed?

POINT TO PONDER: _____

Giving Should Be a Commitment and a Life Goal

It is frequently pointed out in statistics about giving that, in the Western world, people with less money give proportionately more of their money than people with greater wealth. Why is this? One common answer is that poor people have a greater fellow-feeling for other poor people. From the Greek view of pity to the modern "NIMBY" factor, by contrast, wealthy people have had a series of social alibis to help them escape this sense of solidarity with those in need.

Another less obvious answer is that many poorer people tithe regularly—they follow the Jewish and Christian practice of putting aside a tenth of their income to be given to God and the poor. The potential consequences of such tithing are staggering: at any one moment 10 percent of the income of Jewish and Christian communities is circulating with the express purpose of meeting human needs as they arise. But in another sense tithing is simply the most common form of planned giving.

Today "planned giving" has become a technical term for bequests, life-income gifts, life insurance, pooled income funds, and so forth. Cynics dismissed much nineteenth-century philanthropy as "riot insurance." Similarly, they describe current planned giving as "giving when you cannot afford not to give"—to evade the taxman, the spendthrift heir, or whomever. Such cynicism overlooks the many true advantages that spring from planned giving. But limiting planned giving to such forms of bequest misses the simpler, more important place of planning in all our giving.

The previous readings should have helped us to reflect on our own settled convictions about money and giving. One obvious consequence of such convictions is that giving—however we are motivated and whichever avenue of expression we choose—is not a matter of impulse or spur-of-the-moment responses. It is a way of life that issues from a commitment and a plan. Only such planned giving creates the opportunity to address and remedy human needs constructively. Only when giving is a commitment and part of our life goals in this way does it reward the giver as much as those to whom it is given.

Andrew Carnegie

Andrew Carnegie was introduced earlier in part 3. In 1868 he realized he had been successful beyond his wildest dreams. He had $400,000 in assets, had made $56,110 that year, and was still only thirty-three years old. But he was not satisfied. Many of the most successful men he admired had only one ambition and one talent—money and the ability to make it. Not only were they big men in small worlds, they knew almost nothing of literature and culture, of Shakespeare and Robert Burns, which his father and uncle, poor though they were, knew so well.

So early on in Carnegie's rise to success he was restless. New Year's Eve was always a time of sober reflection for Scottish Calvinists and, atheist though he was, Carnegie the Scot picked up a pen and took a hard, unpitying look at himself and his situation. The result was a moral balance sheet to accompany his statement of business holdings. Intended only for himself, and not acted upon until years later when his stupendous wealth seemed to make a mockery of his youthful memo, this note has been quoted more than any other piece of Carnegie's writing.

STOCK TAKER

"This remarkable document of self-analysis and adjuration is surely unique in American entrepreneurial history, for neither Rockefeller, nor Ford, nor Morgan could have written this note, nor would they have understood the man who did."

—Joseph Frazier Wall, *Andrew Carnegie*

PERSONAL MEMORANDUM

December 1868
St. Nicholas Hotel
New York

Thirty three and an income of $50,000 per annum.

By this time two years I can so arrange all my business as to secure at least 50,000 per annum. Beyond this never earn—make no effort to increase fortune, but spend the surplus each year for benovelent [sic] purposes. Cast aside business forever except for others.

Settle in Oxford & get a thorough education making the acquaintance of literary men—this will take three years active work—pay especial attention to speaking in public.

Settle then in London & purchase a controlling interest in some newspaper or live review & give the general management of it attention, taking a part in public matters especially those connected with education & improvement of the poorer classes.

Man must have an idol—The amassing of wealth is one of the worst species of idolitary [sic]. No idol more debasing than the worship of money. Whatever I engage in I must push inordinately therefor should I be careful to choose the life which will be the most elevating in its character. To continue much longer overwhelmed by business cares and with most of my thoughts wholly upon the way to make more money in the shortest time, must degrade me beyond hope of permanent recovery.

To continue much longer overwhelmed by business cares and with most of my thoughts wholly upon the way to make more money in the shortest time, must degrade me beyond hope of permanent recovery.

I will resign business at Thirty five, but during the ensuing two years, I wish to spend the afternoons in securing instruction, and in reading systematically.

Joseph Frazier Wall, *Andrew Carnegie* (Pittsburgh: University of Pittsburgh Press, 1989), pp. 224–225. © 1970 by Oxford University Press; © 1989 by University of Pittsburgh Press.

QUESTIONS FOR THOUGHT AND DISCUSSION

1. Read the paragraph, "Settle in Oxford. . . . " What type of needs in his life is Carnegie addressing? Why?
2. What different type of needs is he addressing in the next paragraph? Have you considered such issues in your own life?
3. How does Carnegie, an avowed atheist, describe the power of money? What is the significance of this very radical assessment?
4. What does he mean when he says, "Whatever I engage in I must push inordinately therefor should I be careful to choose the life which will be the most elevating in its character"? What does this say of his own self-awareness?
5. He says, "to continue much longer . . . must degrade me beyond hope of permanent recovery." Recovery from what?
6. How was this personal memorandum played out in Carnegie's life? What do you think happened between this self-examining young man and the legendary multimillionaire?

7. Personal mission statements are in fashion today. What are the pluses and minuses in using them? What part, if any, do they play in your life?
8. Have you made a commitment similar to Carnegie's? What place do you give to planning in your giving?

For Further Reading

For those who desire to read further on money and giving, the following is a short list of books that are both helpful and accessible.

Peter L. Berger, *The Capitalist Revolution* (New York: Basic Books, 1986).

Robert H. Bremmer, *American Philanthropy* (Chicago: University of Chicago Press, 1988).

Jacques Ellul, *Money and Power* (Downers Grove, Ill.: InterVarsity Press, 1984).

Lewis Hyde, *The Gift* (New York: Vintage Books, 1979).

Jacob Needleman, *Money and the Meaning of Life* (New York: Doubleday, 1991).

Michael Novak, *Business as a Calling* (New York: Free Press, 1996).

Marvin Olasky, *The Tragedy of American Compassion* (Washington, D.C.: Regnery Publishing, 1992).

Robert L. Payton, *Philanthropy* (New York: American Council on Education, 1988).

READER'S GUIDE:

Using This Book in a Discussion Group

THE FOLLOWING SMALL-GROUP GUIDE OFFERS A FORMAT FOR LEADING EIGHT NINETY-minute discussions of *Doing Well and Doing Good.* Ideally, participants will read about forty pages of the book before each group meeting. However, it's possible for people to participate even if they have not had time to read the material beforehand.

The goals of this discussion group are to help participants:

- Understand money's *meaning* (as distinct from its obvious *usefulness* as a medium of exchange)
- Come to their own conclusions about who ultimately owns property and why money is a problem in so many lives
- Compare and contrast traditional views on money and giving: those of ancient Greeks and Romans versus those of Jews and Christians
- Decide for themselves whether and why giving will be a part of their lives
- Explore the history of philanthropy, with emphasis on competing schools of thought in the nineteenth century
- Evaluate contemporary challenges to effective philanthropy and consider possible solutions
- Move toward a personal philosophy and plan regarding their own money and giving

It should be emphasized that this group has no fund-raising agenda. As will become clear through the book, guilt is a poor motivator for sustained giving. If your group is connected to or sponsored by an organization that receives donations, please avoid including a "pitch" during any of these group sessions.

The eight group sessions break down as follows. The part numbers refer to the major sections of the book. The titles in " " refer to the various Points to Ponder, along with the readings that fall under them. In [ ] you will find selections from the book that may be omitted if your time is limited. In addition to the main readings marked here, you will sometimes discuss the short quotations scattered throughout the book.

1. Introduction; Part 1: "Money and Property—Whose Is It?"
2. Part 1, continued: "Money—Why Is There a Problem?"
3. Part 2: "Why Give?" [omit Consumer Giving, the Schmidt reading, and the Malinowski reading]
4. Part 2, continued: "Why Care for the Poor and Needy?"
5. Part 3: "Social Conditions"; "Competing Schools of Philanthropy"— Social Calvinism
6. Part 3, continued: "Competing Schools of Philanthropy"—Social Universalism, Social Darwinism, The Rise of the Foundation
7. Part 4: Contemporary Challenges to Voluntarism and Philanthropy [omit "The 'ODing' of Compassion"]
8. Part 5: Four Concluding Reflections

If you have time for an extra session at the end, you may want to take time to discuss what each of you plans to do during the next six months with what you've discussed.

The Leader's Role

You don't need any special background in order to lead this discussion group effectively. The readings in this book include background information about the writers and their ideas. This discussion guide offers help in small-group leadership. The format of the group will be discussion, not lecture, so you will not be expected to teach or answer questions. Any background you have (in history, philosophy, political science, and so on) will enrich the group, but your knowledge will not be the group's focus.

Your role is:

- To begin and end the meeting on time
- To introduce each reading
- To ask people to read aloud key portions of each reading
- To keep the group moving from reading to reading at a reasonable pace

- To select the questions that are most important for the group to discuss
- To ask questions
- To listen closely to answers and ask follow-up questions as appropriate
- To express your opinions at appropriate moments
- To set a tone of respect and free exchange of ideas
- To make sure that everyone who wants to speak gets adequate air time
- To help the group keep track of the big picture that the readings are sketching

Beginning and ending on time is a way of respecting participants. Latecomers won't mind if you start without them, and doing so rewards those who come on time. Likewise, even if you're in the middle of a great discussion, people will thank you if you cut it off when the time is up. Those who need to leave can leave, and if your host permits, others can stay and continue the conversation informally.

Each reading is preceded by a brief introduction about the author and the context. As you come to each reading, begin by summarizing this introduction in a few sentences. Then, ask someone to read aloud a portion of the reading that relates to the first question you want to ask. (This guide will suggest portions to be read aloud.) Reading aloud and asking questions will set the rhythm of the discussion. Reading aloud refreshes everyone's memory and involves people who may not have read the material ahead of time. (However, be aware that some people are uncomfortable reading aloud. You may want to ask people ahead of time how they feel about doing so.)

After twenty minutes or so, summarize the discussion about that reading and introduce the next one.

Most groups function better with two facilitators than with one. It's helpful to take turns guiding discussions on the different readings, or to let one person guide the discussion while the other keeps track of the time.

The Group's Emphasis

Some small groups emphasize the sharing of personal experiences and feelings. Many don't challenge people to think deeply. This series addresses whole people, the understanding as well as the feeling parts of them. Your task is to help the group think, understand, and draw conclusions together. However, the conversation will not be banter about airy notions. The questions are designed to be practical. The issues raised are relevant to the nitty-gritty lives of each person in your group. Ideally, people will leave each meeting with new thoughts about what they do all day: conduct business, raise children, vote for lawmakers, relate to neighbors, spend money. And you may be surprised at how emotional these thoughtful discussions become as people's hearts are pierced with new perspectives on their lives.

The questions typically progress along the following lines:

- What's being said?
- Is it true?
- So what?

That is, you'll begin by identifying exactly what the writer of the given selection is trying to say. Then you'll have a chance to react to it. Some people like to jump to expressing their opinions before taking the time to understand clearly what the author is saying. If this happens, it will be your job to slow participants down and ask them to look first at the text. An essential group skill is listening—listening both to the other members of the group and to the author of the selection being discussed. To speak one's own opinion without listening to others long enough to understand them is to shortchange oneself and the whole group.

Each session is designed to take about ninety minutes. During that time you will discuss as many as eight readings from *Doing Well and Doing Good*. Many of these readings are quite short. You might cover three big ideas in a session, spending just thirty minutes on each idea. Therefore, you won't have time to discuss all the questions listed in the book. It's not necessary to have an exhaustive discussion about any reading. Instead, you'll draw out the main points of each one so that group members can follow the inner logic that flows through the progression of readings. Do not get bogged down in one reading because you might lose the thread of the big picture. Another benefit of keeping up the momentum is that, in any given session, everyone is likely to find at least one of the readings especially meaningful to him or her personally. It is always better to cut off a good discussion than to drag it out until it dies.

This reader's guide will point out the questions for each reading that will be most helpful for group discussion. It will also trace the big picture from reading to reading so that you will have no trouble seeing where you're going. This guidance is meant to simplify your job. Nevertheless, you are still the group leader, so if you think your group will benefit most from questions other than those suggested here, follow your intuition. Instead of the pointed questions that follow each reading, you may prefer to use open-ended questions, such as, "What is your perspective, feeling, or reaction to this reading?"

The reader's guide contains no suggestions for worship, such as prayer or the singing of hymns. This format makes the group open to everyone, regardless of faith convictions.

Guiding the Discussion

Most groups depend heavily on the leader in the beginning. The leader asks a question, and someone answers. The leader asks another question, and someone answers. People direct their responses to the leader. However, an effective leader nudges participants toward talking to each other. The leader plays referee and timekeeper so that the group stays on track.

One tool for nudging people to talk to each other is the follow-up question. For instance, one type of follow-up question invites others' input: "What do others of you think about Terry's view?" Other kinds of follow-up questions include:

- Rephrasing the question
- Probing gently for more information ("Can you say more about that?")
- Asking for clarification ("So are you saying that . . .?")
- Summarizing a portion of the discussion

You will probably want to summarize (or ask someone else to do so) at the end of your discussion of each reading. This will help people keep track of where each reading fits into the big picture.

Maintain eye contact with all participants, particularly those on your immediate left and right, so that everyone feels included in the discussion. It's a good idea to arrange the room in a circle before the meeting so that people will be able to see each other's faces.

Avoid answering your own questions. Allow silence, especially when people are looking at the readings to refresh their memories. If people seem not to understand your question, it's best to rephrase it, rather than answering it.

Also, avoid commenting on each participant's response. Instead, ask a follow-up question to draw out others' comments.

Encourage participants to ask questions about one another's comments. Your ultimate goal is to foster a lively discussion among participants about the point under discussion. However, if you sense that the conversation is drifting off the main point of the reading, summarize the comments that have been made and move on to a new question that builds toward the focus of the reading.

Dealing with Talkative and Quiet People

In any small group, some people are naturally more talkative than others. While it's desirable for everyone to participate aloud, it's not essential for this group. One of the ground rules (page 294) is that everyone is welcome to speak, but no one is obliged to speak. There are several reasons why a person might be quiet during the meeting, and you'll want to assess which reasons apply to each of your quiet people. Reasons for quietness include the following:

- A person may be overwhelmed by the material and not be following the discussion. This person needs you to listen to his or her concerns outside the group meeting.
- A person may be processing the discussion internally. Some people prefer to digest ideas and feelings inside and speak only when they have thought through what they want to say. By contrast, other people think out loud. They often don't know what they think until it comes out of their mouths. It's possible that both the talkative and the quiet people are getting what they need in your group. Don't assume that silence equals nonparticipation.
- A person may strongly disagree with what is being said but may be uncomfortable with overt conflict. There are ways of handling covert conflict that strengthen the group. See "Disagreement and Conflict" on the next page.
- A person may want to speak but may feel intimidated in a group. It's usually best to draw such people out in conversation outside the formal discussion, but not to call attention to them during the meeting.

This is not an exhaustive list of reasons for quietness. The important thing is to gauge each person individually and ask yourself, "What might this person need?"

With people whom you think talk too much, knowing why they're talking is less important than assessing their effect on the group. Are the quieter people getting something out of what the talker is saying? Or are they wishing they were somewhere else? If you think someone's talking is excessive, there are several subtle ways to discourage it. You can sit next to the person rather than facing him or her. You can avoid making eye contact or nodding, because these are signals that the speaker should continue. In extreme cases, you can take the person aside after the meeting and enlist his or her help in drawing out the quieter group members.

Above all, take care that you are not the group member who talks too much. Keep the group focused on the readings, not on you. Resist the temptation to fill silence with your observations. Silence can be productive if people are thinking.

Disagreement and Conflict

In a discussion group of this kind, disagreement is good. *Tough-minded discussion* occurs when one person's ideas, conclusions, or opinions are incompatible with another's, and the two seek a deeper understanding of truth or wisdom together. Views are aired openly, and everyone has a chance to evaluate the merits of each position. Someone might even change his or her mind.

Debate occurs when people's ideas, conclusions, or opinions are incompatible; each person argues for his or her position; and a winner is declared. Debate is not necessarily bad in a group either. People may feel strongly that they are right and someone else is wrong. A strenuous defense of one's position is fair play.

Some ground rules can make tough-minded discussion and debate constructive:

- Genuine disagreement is an achievement because it enables people to learn. We assume that a disagreement is valuable until proven otherwise.
- Deepening our understanding of truth or wisdom is more important in this group than winning an argument.
- Respect is important in this group. The merits of a position may be debated, but persons may not be attacked.
- If people feel attacked, they will say so respectfully, and the group will assess the situation together.

Many people fear all forms of conflict, including controversy and debate. If you have group members who are uncomfortable with conflict in the group, you may want to have a discussion about constructive conflict. Explain that while quarreling is unproductive, disagreement is not. Emphasize that *concurrence-seeking* is less productive than open controversy. Concurrence-seeking happens when group members inhibit discussion in order to avoid disagreement. Concurrence-seeking can lead to *groupthink,* in which everyone feels obliged to think alike and people cease to think for themselves. Religious versions of political correctness are not uncommon.

A certain amount of concurrence-seeking is natural in a group of people who don't know each other well. However, the more you can draw covert conflict out into the open, the less likely people are to withdraw from the group because of unvoiced dissatisfaction. If you sense people simmering but not speaking, the best course may be to give a short speech about the value of healthy disagreement and to state some ground rules for tough-minded discussion.

The Big Picture

Because you'll cover a lot of ground in each group session, you'll find it helpful to keep in mind the book's "big picture." The readings have been arranged as a journey leading logically from point to point. Each reading contains many more interesting ideas than you have time to discuss, so you can avoid time-consuming side trips if you keep the "roadmap" in mind. See the section entitled "Roadmap to the Readings" in the introduction (pages 31-32). You may want to refer the group to this roadmap at the beginning of each session. This reader's guide will help you orient each session within the roadmap.

The main question this book addresses is: Why and how should we give to and care for others, especially those outside our own groups? Our society is preoccupied with making money and largely ignorant of the long debate in Western culture over matters like what "ownership" means, how money affects us, and what are the best ways of using the money we make. This book goes back to the roots of Western culture—Greece, Rome, and the Jewish and Christian faiths—to answer these questions. It then brings the discussion forward to the rise of modern philanthropy in the nineteenth century, its evolution in the twentieth century, and the situation we face today.

Each of the five parts of the book is introduced with an essay that states the theme of that part. Each part is then subdivided by an essay called "Point to Ponder." Under each "Point to Ponder" are the readings—selections from ancient and modern writings on the subject.

SESSION 1

Unless yours is an ongoing group, people will usually treat the first meeting as an opportunity to decide whether they want to participate. They will decide what they think about one another, the material, and the discussion format. Therefore, you'll want to do a few extra things in the first meeting that will help people feel comfortable with each other, have a sense of where the group is going, and become excited enough about the group to return.

Perhaps the best way to break the ice in a new group is to share a meal. Plan a simple enough meal that the focus will be on conversation. Schedule the meal so that people don't feel rushed as they eat, yet you still have ninety minutes for a full discussion session. You'll want the full ninety minutes in order to give people a realistic taste of what the group will be like. If sharing a full meal is impractical, consider planning a two-hour session in which the first half-hour is devoted to light refreshments and informal chatting.

Overview and Introductions   (20 minutes)

When the food is set aside and the group gathers formally, welcome everyone. Then take ten minutes to give people an overview of what to expect. Explain:

- *What the* Trinity Forum Study Series *is:* It makes the forum curricula available to study groups. It helps thoughtful people examine the foundational issues through which faith acts upon the public good of modern society. It is Christian in commitment but open to all who are interested in its vision. Issues are discussed in the context of faith and the sweep of Western civilization.
- *The theme of this particular study:* What does money mean? And in light of this meaning, why and how should we give to and care for others, especially those outside our own groups?
- *The goals of this study:* See page 285.
- *The big picture of this study:* You may want to walk the group through the "Roadmap to the Readings" on pages 31-32.
- *The format of the group:* Your discussions will take about ninety minutes. In each session, you will cover about thirty pages from the book. Ideally, everyone will have read the material ahead of time, but it is

possible to participate without having done so. As the leader, you'll select questions that you think are most helpful for the group to discuss. Your goal is an open give-and-take, and you will not be lecturing. Differing opinions are welcome.

Ground Rules:

Here is a list of suggested ground rules for your group. You may want to add to this list the ones about disagreement on page 291:

- *Leadership:* The leader is not an expert or an authority, merely a facilitator and fellow-seeker. All in the group are teachers, all are students.
- *Confidentiality:* All discussion is free, frank, and off the record. Nothing will be repeated outside the group without permission.
- *Voluntary participation:* Everyone is free to speak; no one is required to speak. The only exception will be in the final session, when everyone will be asked to share two or three things he or she has found helpful or striking.
- *Nondenominational, nonpartisan spirit:* Many people have strong beliefs and allegiances, both denominational and political. However, the desire here is to go deeper, so it will be important to transcend political advocacy and denominational differences. The book comes from the perspective of what C. S. Lewis called "mere Christianity" and reflects no particular denomination. Participants are welcome to express their own views and even to disagree with the readings.
- *Punctuality:* In order to get to all of the readings, the leader will keep the discussion moving. The formal meeting will begin and end on time.
- *Logistics:* Tell people anything they need to know about the location and schedule of the meetings. Explain that the group will finish promptly at the official ending time. That is the "soft" ending. However, if the host permits, you can also set a "hard" ending time thirty, sixty, or more minutes later. In that case, people are free to stay after the soft ending and talk informally until the hard ending time. (Setting a hard ending is a courtesy to the host if you are meeting in a home.)

Next, ask participants to go around and introduce themselves briefly. You'll go first to model the length and type of response you're looking for. That is, if your answer is one sentence, the others will usually give one sentence. If you take one minute, or three minutes, others will follow suit. The same is true for the content of your answer: if you say something brief and substantive, others will tend to do the same. Therefore, it will be a good idea to think ahead of time about how you can introduce yourself in a minute or less. In this way, you won't shortchange time for discussing the book. By way of introduction, ask each person to state briefly:

- His or her name
- What formal training he or she has had (if any) *in how to make money*
- What formal training he or she has had (if any) *in how best to use money once one has it*

In most groups, most people will have had some training in how to make money but little or none in how to use it wisely. If this is the case in your group, you might make an observation about that when participants are finished introducing themselves. The point of this group is to help participants become as wise in the use of money as they are in the making of it.

Introduction: Doing Well and Doing Good   (10 minutes)

The introduction lists four reasons why money, giving, and caring are worth studying:

- The recent explosion of wealth puts increased responsibilities on those who are earning or inheriting it. Success in making money does not automatically translate into success in enjoying it or giving it.
- Institutional philanthropy is at a crossroad, facing tough questions. For example, can institutions take up the slack as government programs are rolled back? Is their proper mission to relieve suffering (such as hunger and homelessness) or to enhance the quality of life (for example through libraries and the arts)?
- Dismantling government bureaucracies and returning care to local communities will succeed only if local communities have strong "social capital"—shared vision, shared trust, strong voluntary associations, and so on.

■ Western capitalism was built on a foundation of values from Greece, Rome, and Jerusalem. Now, having largely rejected those values, Western countries are exporting a form of capitalism stripped of values regarding spending, giving, and caring. There is great doubt throughout the world as to whether value-free capitalism is desirable.

Invite participants to share one reason why they are interested in studying money, giving, and caring. They may choose one of the reasons stated in the introduction or one of their own.

Money and Property—Whose Is It?

Money's obvious *purpose* is to provide a medium of exchange. But what does money *mean*? That is, what does it signify about us and our world? Is it really just a medium of exchange, morally neutral, or does it exert a power in our lives that is both moral and spiritual?

As the introduction to part 1 states, "The story of the rise of philanthropy in Western Civilization is a response to two leading questions about money: First, whose is it? And second, what is the problem?" For the rest of this session you'll address the first of these questions. In session 2 you'll look at the second.

To answer the question of who owns things, you'll look at three strands of thinking from the ancient world: a Greek view espoused by Plato, the Roman view expressed by Cicero, and a view held by the ancient Jews and Christians. Plato speaks for common ownership: the group owns everything; individuals own nothing privately but share everything. Cicero argues for absolute individual ownership: an individual property owner has the right to use, enjoy, and even abuse his property. The Hebrew Scriptures and an early Christian teacher claim that God owns everything and assigns individuals and groups to manage God's property. These three views of ownership have radically different implications for how we use property.

When you discuss these readings, you'll concentrate on understanding each of the three perspectives and deciding which you most agree with. In future sessions you'll look for the influence of these perspectives on classical, nineteenth-century, and current views of giving.

Plato   (20 minutes)

You have about an hour to cover Plato, Cicero, the Hebrew Scriptures, and Chrysostom. Thus, it won't be possible to have a long discussion about Plato's plan. Briefly summarize who Plato was and what *The Republic* is about. Ask someone to read aloud the first three paragraphs of the excerpt. Draw out the facts of the story with questions 1 through 4.

Read aloud the paragraphs that begin, "As law-giver. . ." and "We must. . . ." Discuss questions 6, 8, and 10.

Save time for question 12. Is there a role for giving if all property belongs to the community?

Cicero   (20 minutes)

Introduce Cicero briefly. The reading is short; ask someone to read the whole of it aloud. Discuss questions 1, 4, 5, 6, and 7.

Plato's view of property is widely scorned in our day because it is associated with communism. Cicero's is widely embraced because it fits so well with capitalism. Some people believe these are the only two options. Postpone a comparison of the pros and cons of each view until you have looked at the third one represented by the Hebrew Scriptures and St. John Chrysostom.

The Scriptures and St. John Chrysostom   (20 minutes)

Read aloud the three introductory paragraphs under "Ownership Is God's; Stewardship Is Ours." Then have three different people read the passages from Leviticus, Deuteronomy, and Psalms. Discuss question 1.

Read aloud the first three paragraphs of Chrysostom's homily. Discuss questions 4 and 5. Read the last sentence and discuss question 6.

Save a few minutes for question 7. It's important to understand the three views before you evaluate them, but this question will wrap up your discussion. Don't worry if you run out of time with people still eager to talk about their opinions—they can do this informally later, and their eagerness will motivate them to return for session 2.

The three views of ownership you've looked at in this session still echo through our modern debates about taxing, spending, giving, and caring. Encourage group members to listen for these echoes in the news media this week and to come back next time to share what they've heard. Also, ask everyone to read the rest of part 1 for your next meeting.

SESSION 2

In this session you'll continue to investigate the meaning of money from the perspectives of Greece, Rome, and the Jewish and Christian faiths. You'll explore two questions: What are the problems with money? And, why do these problems exist? While ancient people disagreed as to the roots of why money is a problem, they were united in believing that it is.

You have at least four major ideas to digest in this session: insatiability, commodification, excess, and idolatry. They fit together as a unit, so ideally you will get to all of them in one group meeting. Session 3 will be less demanding, so if necessary you can save idolatry for your next meeting.

The two problems with money that people throughout the ages have observed are insatiability and commodification. *Insatiability* expresses the idea that the pursuit of money and possessions all-too-frequently grows into a never-satisfied thirst. The more one has, the more one seems to want and the harder one clings to what one has. *Commodification* occurs when money assumes such a dominant place in human thinking that everything (and everyone) is seen as a commodity to be bought and sold. As you examine the readings on insatiability and commodification, help participants see and understand these two problems at work. Money is so prized in our society that it can be hard for us to see the problem with greed or with putting price tags on everything. The readings in this session are meant to overcome these blind spots.

Insatiability   (25 minutes)

The most important thing for your group to get out of the readings on insatiability and avarice is an understanding of what each of these problems is. It will also be helpful for participants to identify ways in which they have observed or experienced these problems.

To define insatiability or avarice, read aloud the second paragraph of the introduction to insatiability ("Avarice is often confused . . .").

The Greek writer Plutarch compares avarice to hunger and thirst. He shows how the craving for possessions is like and unlike those physical needs. Read aloud the last two paragraphs of the Plutarch reading and discuss question 3. Then discuss question 2 from your own experience. Has anyone in the group found that more things seem like "needs" now than they did when he or she had less money? Does any participant find that he or she "needs" things that less affluent people don't seem to need?

Plutarch also observes that some people go into survival-threatening debt to buy things they don't need for survival. Why is this ironic? Can participants give examples from their own or others' lives?

Next, read aloud the passage from Ecclesiastes, as well as Jesus' story from the Gospel of Luke. Discuss question 5.

Look quickly at the Tolstoy story. From its introduction, summarize what has already happened in the story, then read aloud the seven short paragraphs beginning with, "'I will go on for another three miles. . . .'" Read also the last four paragraphs. If you have time, discuss question 6. Be sure to save at least five minutes for questions 8 and 9. It will be tempting to spend more time on these fascinating issues, but if you want to finish part 1 in this session, you will need to move on and let people wrestle with these questions further on their own.

(Note: For those who enjoyed this excerpt from Tolstoy's story, the story is available in its entirety in *Steering Through Chaos* in this series, as well as in its own booklet form directly from The Trinity Forum.)

Commodification   (20 minutes)

Read aloud the third paragraph of the introduction to commodification ("The negative connotations . . . ").

Read aloud the third paragraph of the article, "A Mom's Plea to a Ballplayer." Then read from "When we arrived at the toy shop . . ." through "'But Mom, he didn't even look at me.'" Discuss question 2. Read from, "My husband and I slumped . . ." through "'But Mom, that's what Gregg Jefferies wants: *money.*'" Discuss questions 3 and 4.

In the box, "What Does an Economist Economize On?" read aloud the last quotation (the second from Barry Schwartz). Discuss questions 6 and 7.

Excess   (15 minutes)

You have just looked at two problems with money that people have been observing for centuries. Next you'll look at two explanations for such problems. Athens, Rome, and Jerusalem generally agreed on the seriousness of the problems, but they disagreed about the root causes. Greeks and Romans tended to see excess alone as the culprit: too much of a good thing becomes harmful. They thought if one sought moderate wealth, one would not fall into the cycle of insatiability nor start putting price tags on everything. Read aloud the last paragraph under the introduction to excess ("This view is helpful . . . ").

The Greek philosopher Aristotle argued that every virtue is the mean or middle ground between two vices, two extremes. The proverb, "Moderation in all things," began with Aristotle. Read aloud the second and third paragraphs of the Aristotle reading. Discuss questions 2 through 6. Many people may never have thought about the question posed in question 6, so if you are greeted with silence, let the question hang in the air and move on. Encourage participants to think about it further on their own or to come back to your next meeting with their thoughts.

Idolatry of Mammon   (20 minutes)

Jews and Christians did not dispute that excess is one cause of money's problems. However, the prophets and Jesus probed for another, deeper cause. Jesus used the Aramaic word "Mammon" (Aramaic was the common language of Palestinian Jews in his day) to convey the idea that money is an active agent with spiritual power. It is almost as though Mammon were a living spiritual being who solicits worship in a rivalry with God. Jesus did not speak of Sex, Pride, or Other People's Approval as though they were rival gods, so his treatment of Mammon in this way is provocative. Your goal in examining the readings in this session will be to assess whether you think money really does have the kind of spiritual draw depicted here. Do you agree with Jesus, or do you lean toward the Greco-Roman view of excess?

Read aloud Mark 10:17-25 and discuss questions 1 and 2. Because most participants won't know the Ten Commandments by heart, you might have a Bible available with a bookmark at Exodus 20:1-17. Or, you can just tell the group that Jesus omitted the commandments about having no gods ahead of God, making no statues or other idols for worship, treating the name of God with utmost respect, resting from work on the Sabbath, and not coveting anything that belongs to one's neighbor. What is significant about the commandments Jesus chose to omit?

Next, summarize the introduction to François Mauriac and *Viper's Tangle*. The excerpt is not long, so you can read the whole of it aloud. Discuss questions 3 through 6.

These readings focus on ways in which money enslaves the rich. While excess is undoubtedly a factor in this enslavement, it's worth noting that money can enslave the poor just as readily by making them dependent upon others for their support.

To close this session, read aloud the last paragraph in the introduction to the idolatry of Mammon (page 80: "Curiously, both these explanations . . ."). That paragraph forms a bridge from what you have been discussing in this session to what you will cover in session 3. Invite participants to notice their own experience with the problems of money during the coming week. Also, ask them to collect any fund-raising appeals they receive through the mail and bring them to your next meeting. Finally, ask participants to read the first half of part 2: "Why Give?" including Consumer Giving, Contract Giving, and Charity Giving.

SESSION 3

Begin your meeting by orienting the group, using the roadmap on page 31-32. You have looked at various views on who owns property and why money carries inherent problems for people. For the next two sessions you will cover part 2, which addresses the meaning of giving and caring. As in part 1, you will focus on the classical perspectives of Greece, Rome, and Jerusalem. You will be asking *why* questions. In this session you will examine the question, "Why give?" Advice on *how* to give and *to whom* to give bombards many of us. However, it is important to explore motives before delving into methods because motives have a way of determining both methods and outcomes. *Why* needs to precede *how.*

The problems of part 1 have suggested two motives for giving: to get rid of excess wealth that can debilitate us and to break money's power to enslave us. In this session you will consider two other motives that have been the main threads running through Western views on giving: *contract* giving and *charity* giving. (In the interest of time, you may leave the modern practice of *consumer* giving for people to read on their own.)

Before you get into the readings, invite anyone who has brought a fund-raising appeal to lay it before the group. Those who have not brought anything can think back to other appeals they have received, perhaps in television ads or by telephone. Ask, "In the fund-raising appeals you have received, what reasons for giving and caring have been stated or implied? To what motives do you think these pitches appeal?" Do they appeal to your guilt? Your pride—your desire to look good? Your fear of what may happen if you don't give? Your sense of belonging to the group who will benefit from your gift? Do they promise you'll get something if you give? Do they appeal to your love for others who can offer you nothing in return? Limit this conversation to five or ten minutes—it's intended simply to get the group thinking. As you move into your discussion of contract giving and charity giving, you may want to reflect back on the appeals you've discussed.

Contract giving was standard in the great civilizations of Egypt, Greece, Rome, and China, among others. Contract giving is giving in order to get. Giving to a person of lower status in order to win that person's allegiance and giving to a person of greater status in order to win his patronage are two examples of contract giving. Giving to political campaigns is typically giving-to-get.

Charity giving is uniquely Jewish and Christian. As with contract giving, there is reciprocity involved. But instead of giving-to-get, one gives-because-given-to.

(Consumer giving was unknown before the modern era. The ancients would have been astounded at how commercial ingenuity has turned celebrations of religion and family—Christmas, Easter, Mother's Day—into consumer festivals of commodity exchange.)

In this session you'll explore the differences among these reasons for giving and their implications for philanthropy. As you'll see in later sessions, why we give affects what and how we give. You'll also see how our giving affects both us and the recipients.

Contract Giving   (30 minutes)

Begin by reading aloud the seventh paragraph of "Why Give?" on page 90. It begins, "There are numerous benefits of contract giving. . . ."

To save time, you can skip the reading by Malinowski and focus on Plutarch's description of Pericles, the famous leader of Athens during that city's golden age. The citizens of Athens were complaining that too much of their tax money was being spent to build the Parthenon, but Pericles handled them shrewdly. Ask someone to read aloud the first two paragraphs of the Pericles reading. While they listen, the other participants can underline the reasons why, according to Plutarch, Pericles undertook this huge project. Then discuss question 4. Read aloud the fifth paragraph ("When the orators . . . ") and discuss question 5. Read aloud the last paragraph and discuss question 6.

Look at a few of the more recent instances of contract giving mentioned in the boxes. Read aloud the Henry Ford quotation from the box entitled "For the Sake of Honor," and the Scott McCartney quotation from the box entitled "Getting Giving Going." Discuss questions 7 and 8.

Charity Giving: Jewish *Tzedakah*   (30 minutes)

Have different people read the passages from Deuteronomy and Isaiah. From the reading by Maimonides, read all but the first paragraph. (To make this more interesting, you might have different voices read each of the eight degrees.) Discuss all four questions.

Charity Giving: Christian *Caritas*   (30 minutes)

The introduction to this section states three main reasons for giving from a Christian perspective. Summarize those for the group.

Have different people read aloud the passages from Matthew, Luke, and 1 John. Read the first paragraph of the passage from 2 Corinthians. Discuss questions 1 through 3.

Just as Maimonides taught that there was more to *tzedakah* than the giving of money, so Dostoyevsky's *The Brothers Karamazov* makes the same point about *caritas* or love. Set the stage for this conversation between Father Zossima and the rich woman: the woman has just asked Father Zossima how she can know for sure whether God exists. Ask someone to read Father Zossima's words and another to read the woman's. Have them read the first four paragraphs, beginning with the woman. Discuss question 4.

Have your "woman" read the fifth paragraph: "'Yes. But could I endure . . .?'" Discuss question 5. Have "Father Zossima" read the last paragraph. Discuss question 6.

Finally, compare contract and charity giving. What are the merits and drawbacks of each? To close, ask participants to read the rest of part 2 for your next meeting.

SESSION 4

In this fourth session you'll ask, "Why care for the poor and needy?" The same ideas that divide contract giving (well represented by the Greeks and Romans) from charity giving (represented by the Jews and Christians) also affect answers here. The give-to-get approach in Greece and Rome never produced private charity or concern for the neediest members of society. In this session, you'll contrast the Greco-Roman civic-mindedness and "concern for humankind" with the Judeo-Christian idea of personal compassion for human beings. You'll also consider whether compassion has a place today in our governmental and/or private dealings with the poor.

Greeks and Romans:
Concern for Humankind   (40 minutes)

In this excerpt from *The Republic*, Plato refers to Asclepius, the god of healing. Have someone read the entire excerpt aloud. Discuss question 1. What would Plato say in our modern debate about assisted suicide? About the rationing of healthcare? (Don't get into a debate about the merits of Plato's view, nor of assisted suicide or rationing. Your goal at this point is simply to understand Plato; you'll evaluate him later.)

Read aloud the first two sentences of the selection from Aristotle, and discuss the first part of question 2: What are the separate components of Aristotle's definition of pity? Note that he thinks pity is a feeling, is caused by the sight of something negative, is directed only toward one who we believe doesn't deserve the evil or painful experience, and is felt only toward situations we can imagine ourselves suffering.

Read aloud the rest of the Aristotle selection. Discuss the rest of question 2 and questions 3 and 4. If you have time, read the Bertrand Russell comment in the box, "The Careless Society," and discuss question 5.

Jews and Christians:
Compassion for All Human Beings   (40 minutes)

After reading Plato and Aristotle, it's easy to see why so many people in the Greco-Roman world were astonished and drawn when they encountered first Judaism and later Christianity. Jews and Christians had an entirely different outlook on human lives. Read the selections from Leviticus, Deuteronomy, and Matthew. Discuss questions 1 through 3.

The passage from Luke is the famous story of the Good Samaritan. In order to hear it as Jesus' first audience would have heard it, one needs to understand the place of priests, Levites, and Samaritans in that society. Priests and Levites were religious professionals, highly honored as men who kept the Law of God with great purity. Samaritans were considered ethnically and morally inferior. Ask participants to think of a group who would have the appropriate shock value for them: the good illegal immigrant? The good fundamentalist? The good Arab? Read the story and discuss question 4.

For the story about Francis of Assisi, be sure everyone understands what it would have been like to be with a leper. Leprosy is an infectious disease that causes nerves to go numb and extremities (fingers, toes, noses, and so on) to ulcerate and rot. Thus, lepers look and smell terrible, and many are contagious. Read aloud the fourth and fifth paragraphs of the selection, beginning with, "On his walks in this place. . . . " Read the eighth and ninth paragraphs, beginning with, "Francis started. . . . " Read the last paragraph. Discuss question 5. Get as far as you can with questions 6 through 8.

In session 5 you'll leave the classical and medieval worlds behind and leap to the nineteenth century. The different answers to the questions, "Why give?" and "Why care for the poor and needy?" lead to very different conceptions of philanthropy and society. Ask participants to read the first half of part 3 through Social Calvinism.

SESSION 5

Part 3 explores the rise of modern philanthropy in the nineteenth century. First you'll trace its origins in the voluntary associations of the early nineteenth century. Next you'll examine three competing schools of thought about philanthropy: Social Calvinism, Social Universalism, and Social Darwinism. Finally, you'll observe the rise of the philanthropic foundation toward the end of the century. Throughout, you'll see how the classical ideas of parts 1 and 2 recur in the various strategies and schools of thought. This session will cover the voluntary associations and Social Calvinism. Session 6 will finish with Social Universalism, Social Darwinism, and the foundation.

Rise of the Voluntary Associations   (50 minutes)

The Point to Ponder, "Social Conditions," sets the stage for the readings in part 3. Read aloud its first sentence: "If modern capitalism made modern philanthropy possible, modern poverty made it necessary." Summarize the rest of that section. Ask participants to remember anything they have ever read of Dickens. Read aloud the Wasserman or Olasky quotations in the box, "Dickensian." It's important for people to grasp that the new urban poverty of the Industrial Revolution was a different order of magnitude from the rural poverty of small populations with close family and religious ties. Pollution, crime, and appalling working conditions were worse than most of us can imagine. This human catastrophe led to new ideas about giving and caring: the possibility that private charity could not do everything and the desire to eliminate the causes of social ills, not just the symptoms.

The introductory section, "The Rise of the Voluntary Associations," makes several points worth underscoring. First, voluntary associations began to flower in the United States only in the 1820s and 1830s. Note from the fifth paragraph that a religious renewal was the catalyst. Note also the three roots of the movement: the disintegration of family- and farm-based life, the British abolition movement, and the disestablishment of the last state churches. Finally, read aloud the four fundamental ideas about voluntary associations beginning with the paragraph, "Whatever the causes . . ."

With this background, you may turn to Alexis de Tocqueville. Summarize the introduction to de Tocqueville. Note that he did his research from 1831 to 1832 when the voluntary association movement had just begun to spread its wings. In *Democracy in America* read aloud the first paragraph and a sentence or two of the third paragraph ("The English often perform great things singly . . ."). Discuss question 1. Read aloud the sixth paragraph ("Among democratic nations . . .") and discuss question 2. Read the Drucker quotation in the box, "Voluntarism in an Open Society" and discuss question 3. Spend a few minutes on question 4, but remember that you have several other readings to cover.

The Bacon reading shows how a nineteenth-century preacher applied what you saw in part 1 about the Christian view of property ownership. Bacon takes the biblical notion of stewardship, combines it with the Protestant emphasis on the individual rather than the church, and points to the new, democratic idea of the voluntary association. In the association, individual choice and democratic cooperation hold hands. Read aloud the second and third paragraphs, and discuss questions 2 and 3. Read the fifth paragraph and discuss question 4. Read the last paragraph and discuss question 6. Finally, spend some time on question 7—what has happened in the past two centuries that has dampened many people's enthusiasm for changing the world?

Competing Schools of Philanthropy: Social Calvinism   (30 minutes)

For the rest of this session, you will look at the first of three nineteenth-century schools of thought on how best to attack poverty. These philosophies were hotly debated among people who observed or participated in philan-thropic associations. Nor are they just ancient history: these same philosophies continue to underlie our modern debates about welfare, entitlements, and privately funded efforts to combat poverty.

From page 150 this section, read aloud the brief definitions of the three schools of philanthropy: Social Calvinism, Social Universalism, and Social Darwinism. Although you will have time only for Social Calvinism in this ses-sion, it will be helpful to have all three in mind. Also, read the central question that all three schools were trying to answer: How can a good society protect those who cannot protect themselves without being so generous that it sub-verts personal responsibility?

In the introduction to Social Calvinism, you may want to call attention to the bulleted list of this school's distinctive features. The main aims of your discussion will be to identify what Social Calvinism is so you can evaluate its merits and drawbacks.

You'll begin with an excerpt from Gurteen's *A Handbook of Charity Organization,* published in 1882. Reverend Gurteen wrote fifty years after de Tocqueville, when squalor from the Industrial Revolution was at its worst and when voluntary associations had had a few decades to learn by trial and error. Before you discuss Gurteen's ideas, it might be a good idea to acknowledge that elements of his tone will irritate many modern readers. "Kind words of encouragement and advice" from the rich to the poor may have a condescending ring, and many people today bristle at a distinction between the deserving and undeserving poor. Your task here will be to note both the strengths and the weaknesses of his views.

Gurteen begins by quoting from the 1868 report on the Edinburgh Poor-law. Read aloud his quotation from the Poor-law. Discuss question 1.

Gurteen's first principle is "Coordinate." He speaks of "the people, the citizens, taking the matter in hand, and seeking to co-operate with the Church, the State and the Municipality. . . ." He wants to "show what can be done in this matter of checking the curse of indiscriminate alms-giving by the diffusion of sound, practical views and the adoption of wise, discriminating action." What do you think are the strengths of coordinating a city's efforts to address poverty?

Read the paragraphs that begin, "The necessity of good works . . ." and "Coming to the attack . . ." Discuss question 3. Read aloud the paragraphs that begin, "The fundamental law of its operation . . ." and "But let us bring . . ." Discuss question 4.

Gurteen distinguishes "paupers" from "the poor." He compares "floating pauperism" (that is, homeless people in particular) from "the *resident* poor" (such as a working man who has slipped "to the very verge of poverty by no fault of his own"). And he contrasts "confirmed" paupers with "involuntary" poor people. Ask the group to look at the paragraphs that begin, "But let us advance a step . . ." and "It must be borne in mind . . ." to discuss question 5. What are the strengths and weaknesses of this distinction?

Question 6 relates to the paragraphs that begin, "The answer which the Society gives . . ." and "The Charity Organization Society, adopting this germ-thought . . ." Gurteen proposes to have rich people doing house-to-house visitation of poor people and becoming kind friends to them. What are his arguments in favor of this plan? What are its potential advantages and drawbacks?

Marvin Olasky writes more than a century after Gurteen, in 1996. Note from his biographical introduction that he is not just theorizing; he practices what he preaches. Ask participants to look at his seven basic principles and discuss question 7. If you have time, discuss question 8. Don't be afraid to cut off a vigorous discussion—you'll have more time when you get to the other schools of philanthropy in session 6. Ask the group to read the rest of part 3 for your next meeting.

SESSION 6

In session 5 you saw the roots of charitable voluntary associations in the 1830s and their development fifty years later among the Social Calvinists. In this session you will look at two other schools of philanthropy that flourished in the nineteenth century: Social Universalism and Social Darwinism. You'll also explore the rise of another kind of charitable institution—the foundation—by which a new generation of wealthy individuals sought to run philanthropy less like a democratic association and more like a business. You'll have the opportunity to assess the relative merits of the three schools of philanthropy, and you'll assess the strengths and weaknesses of the foundation.

Social Universalism   (40 minutes)

Those in your group who were bothered by the Social Calvinists' work-tests and distinctions between the deserving and undeserving poor will probably like Social Universalism better. It blames the problems of society on the system rather than sin, and it advocates both government involvement and universal entitlement. It lies behind the New Deal and the Great Society. Both a century ago and today, debates about poverty often pitted Social Calvinism and Social Universalism against each other as either-or alternatives. In your discussion, it might be more helpful to draw out the strengths and weaknesses of each school and consider how the best features of each might be married. If the problems of society are too great for private institutions to handle alone (as the Social Universalists argue), and if government programs create dependency and other problems (as Social Calvinists point out), what might a third alternative look like?

You'll begin with the Greeley editorial from 1847. Read aloud his first three paragraphs. Harking back to part 1, would you say he believes in common ownership of property, absolute individual ownership, or God's ownership and our stewardship? How does his view on ownership compare to Gurteen's Social Calvinist outlook? Note that he and Gurteen both begin with the Christian idea of God's Creation, but Gurteen takes stewardship in an individual direction (each individual property-owner is responsible to manage what God has entrusted to him for the good of all), while Greeley takes it in a communal direction (God entrusted the earth to humanity as a group, and the group is responsible to manage earth's resources for the good of the group). In both cases we have God entrusting and humans managing for the good of all, but there turns out to be a vast difference between individuals managing property for the good of all and large communities (effectively, the state) doing so. Your discussion will eventually draw out the strengths and weaknesses of each interpretation of the Christian tradition.

From Greeley's fourth paragraph, read aloud the sentence, "The absolute, indefeasible Right . . ." Discuss question 2. From the last paragraph, read the first two sentences: ". . . [Human desires are] good in themselves . . ." Discuss question 3. Read the rest of that paragraph and discuss question 4.

Bellamy's novel was published in 1888, at about the same time as Gurteen's book. To answer the various parts of question 5, read some excerpts from Bellamy's parable: From the first paragraph, read aloud the sentence, "Naturally such places were in great demand . . ." From the second paragraph, read the last couple of sentences. From the third paragraph, read the first sentence. Read all of the fourth paragraph ("I am well aware . . .") and the first sentence of the fifth paragraph.

For question 6, read the first two paragraphs of "The Golden Future of the Corporate State." Remember that Bellamy wrote at a time when socialism was a new idea, fashionable among the elite of many countries, and before it had been put to the test in any country. The Russian Revolution was still thirty years away. Big business was booming in the United States and brutally quelling strikes and protests by early labor unions. No government regulations protected workers' safety, child laborers, food safety, truth in advertising, or unfair competition. The idea of "the people" rather than the tycoons owning the mines and factories seemed like a vast improvement over the miserable working conditions in which most people suffered.

If you have time, read the box, "A War to End All Poverty?" and discuss question 7. However, you'll want at least ten minutes for the *Time* article.

The *Time* article was written in 1971 when the expansion of welfare in the 1960s was still new. At that time, the nation had not yet seen a whole generation grow up on AFDC without any working adults in the household. Gangs in the inner city were fewer, less organized, and generally armed with nothing more lethal than knives. The drug trade had yet to explode. Yet already two counties in California were showing the first signs of danger ahead. From the first paragraph, read aloud the last several sentences: "In the four years since NWRO had been in operation . . ." From the second paragraph, read the quotation from Mrs. Tillmon. Read the third paragraph and the last.

Spend at least a few minutes on question 9. This section has given participants a brief history of the ideas behind welfare. Where did the Social Universalists go wrong? And which of their views continue to be important parts of today's debate?

Social Darwinism (20 minutes)

Social Darwinism—the idea that the unfit should simply be left to die—did not last long as an overt school of thought. However, it lives on today in some people's hard-heartedness toward the poor. Indeed, one could combine the views of Plato and Aristotle from part 2 with a dash of Darwinism to justify leaving the poor, the disabled, and the mentally ill to their families or their fates. If your group scoffed at the high-toned ideas of the Social Universalists, remember that Bellamy (the Universalist) and Newcomb (the Darwinist) were writing at the same time. Social Universalism was in part a response to the *de facto* Social Darwinism of factory and mine owners in the late nineteenth century. As we address the failures of the welfare system, we need to ask ourselves whether another era of *de facto* Social Darwinism is really what we want.

For question 1, read the second half of Newcomb's first paragraph, beginning with, "Why are there no beggars . . .?" For question 2, read the first two sentences of the third paragraph. How does Newcomb's view of human nature compare with that of the Social Universalists? The Social Calvinists? (Greeley addresses the Social Universalist view of human nature directly in the early paragraphs of his reading. Neither of the Social Calvinist readings addresses this question directly, but their view can be inferred: They show more respect for humans than Newcomb's phrase "poor, miserable, and worthless" reflects, but they seem more clear-eyed about the human capacity for deception and folly than the Social Universalists appear to have been. The Social Calvinists believed firmly in human sin, but not human worthlessness.)

Look next at the paragraph that begins, "The way we deal with the poor and miserable . . ." Read aloud the second half of that paragraph beginning with, "We cannot evade the conclusion . . ." From the next paragraph ("Now, although at first sight . . ."), read a couple of sentences beginning with, "Love of mankind at large . . ." Discuss question 3.

Take a few minutes for questions 4 and 5. Note especially Social Darwinism's roots in the Greek views of Plato and Aristotle.

The Rise of the Foundation   (20 minutes)

The unimaginable new wealth of the late nineteenth century moved some of the great industrialists to search for a way to administer their wealth. They invented the philanthropic foundation based on the model of the business corporation by which they had made their money. Draw your group's attention to these roots in the business model and also to the foundation's philosophic roots in Greece and Rome rather than Jerusalem. While the voluntary associations drew their inspiration from the Jewish and Christian ideas of righteousness and love, and sought to relieve suffering and address the causes of poverty, the foundations were built to enhance the community through civic projects. Carnegie and Rockefeller had more in common with Pericles in his contract giving than with Maimonides and Francis of Assisi in their charity giving. Carnegie Hall and the Rockefeller Center hark back to the Parthenon. And today there remains a tension between those who believe giving should support efforts to relieve poverty and those who believe it should enhance public life through the arts, libraries, and the like.

Summarize the introduction to Andrew Carnegie. He published *The Gospel of Wealth* at about the same time as Gurteen, Greeley, and Newcomb—his sympathies lay with the Social Darwinists. Read aloud the first paragraph of Carnegie's words and discuss question 1. If you know anything about the conditions of the Industrial Revolution and the labor unrest that plagued that era, such information would paint the context of Carnegie's thoughts. Harmony between rich and poor was very much at a low ebb.

Read aloud the third and fourth paragraphs, and discuss question 2. Carnegie believed that as the head of U.S. Steel he was "forced" by "competition" with his rival steelmakers "into the strictest economies." It might be worthwhile to pause and discuss whether that was true. Could he have provided better wages and working conditions for his workers and taken less profit for himself? Was he "forced" to amass a huge fortune in that way? In part 4 of this book you will read about Henry Ford's very different choices in running his automobile business. You probably don't want to digress into a long discussion about shareholder and CEO profits versus workers' conditions, but you can raise the question and point out that Carnegie and Ford faced the same decisions a hundred years ago that corporate executives face today, especially in Third World factories.

Carnegie goes on to state three ways in which people can dispose of surplus wealth. They can leave it to their children—the paragraph that begins,

"There are but three modes . . ." outlines the problems Carnegie sees with this strategy. The paragraph that begins, "As to the second mode . . ." outlines the problems he sees with leaving wealth to the community at one's death. Have the group scan those paragraphs for answers to question 3. Read aloud the paragraph that begins, "There remains, then . . ." for Carnegie's description of the best way to use surplus wealth.

For question 4, you might look at the fifth paragraph, which begins, "Having accepted these . . ." Look also at the much later paragraph that begins, "The best uses . . ." Where are the echoes of Social Darwinism here? How would the Social Calvinists agree and disagree?

For question 5, read the paragraph that begins "The rich man is thus almost restricted . . ." You might point the group back to the biblical quotations in parts 1 and 2, especially Luke 12:15-21, Luke 14:12-14, and Luke 10:25-37. See also the passages on Jewish *tzedakah* and compassion for human beings. Carnegie says nothing about the Jewish notion of justice (which is reflected in wages), the insatiability of the rich man who hoards, the dangers of pride, compassion for the neighbor in need, the value of personal contact in giving, or the wisdom of secrecy in giving. On the other hand, he does see himself as a steward entrusted with resources that should be used for the public good, not just for his own good. Read the last paragraph (page 197), which begins, "The gospel of wealth but echoes Christ's words." Note the echo of stewardship, but also the craving for gratitude that you heard in the woman who talked with Father Zossima in *The Brothers Karamazov.*

For question 6, look at the box entitled "The Critics." See especially the Niebuhr and Dillard quotations, as well as Tucker's warning against the effects of patronage. Later, you'll see that instead of squeezing money from workers and then giving them libraries as gifts, Henry Ford preferred to let them have dignity of earning good wages.

Save a few minutes at the end of your discussion to assess the strengths and weaknesses of Social Calvinism, Social Universalism, and Social Darwinism (including Carnegie's idea of the foundation).

Your next meeting will cover part 4. It contains five contemporary challenges that are currently facing voluntary associations, foundations, and other forms of philanthropy. Because of the length of the readings and the seriousness of each challenge, you need discuss only four of them in your group. Ask participants to read the Orwin, McKnight, Reich, and Wooster selections. They may omit the final selection by Payton. As they read, ask them to think about personal experiences with each challenge.

SESSION 7

Much has happened since Carnegie wrote *The Gospel of Wealth* more than a century ago. The philanthropic foundation has become a fixture on the American landscape, and now the worlds of giving, caring, and volunteering face another period of transition that is testing their character and health. Part 4 examines five of the major challenges confronting philanthropy today: the way global communications shorten people's attention spans toward the needy; how professionalization undermines personal giving; the isolation of the rich from the rest of society; the indifference of some foundation trustees to their founders' wishes; and the compassion overload people experience when bombarded with images of suffering. This session will cover the first four of those challenges. Your goals will be to consider how you would like to deal with these challenges in your personal giving strategy, as well as how you think we as a society should deal with them.

Any one of the four readings in this session could occupy your entire meeting, so you will need a mind-set of exposing yourself to the four ideas but not exhausting them. You have probably already begun to find that your group discussion spawns informal discussions between meetings.

By way of overview, begin by reading the summaries of the first four challenges in the introduction to part 4.

The "CNNing" of Perceptions   (20 minutes)

The first challenge is the way in which television images of global suffering can desensitize us to suffering nearby and sustained suffering anywhere. Television has been much lauded for making us more aware of need; Orwin wants us to notice the downside of this awareness.

Orwin begins by duly noting the upside of television. For question 1, see the third paragraph, which begins, "Naturally this development . . ." Ask participants to think back through the past year or so to recall floods, famines, political oppression, or some other form of suffering that made the news. How did that coverage affect the way governments and private persons responded to the tragedy?

In the first paragraph under "The Need for Images," Orwin observes, "Compassion depends on the imagination." Read aloud that sentence and the sentence that follows. It echoes Aristotle's assertion that pity depends on our ability to imagine a similar evil befalling us or a friend, that the suffering has to feel close to us in some way. However, like those in the Judeo-Christian tradition, Orwin thinks it is possible to imagine ourselves close to—identified with—people who live far away or in economic or political situations very different from ours. In biblical language, it is possible to view even a stranger as a "neighbor" who deserves our love and compassion. All we need is concrete images by which to imagine ourselves in the other's shoes.

However, Orwin goes on, "while television doubtless renders distant sufferings more vivid, it does not thereby necessarily render them more real." To answer question 2, direct the group to the paragraphs that begin, "Of course, as we may as well admit . . ." and "Let's assume, however . . ." Read all or part of that aloud. Note that television distorts our perception of human need by giving us just enough to entertain us and enabling us to tune it out when we've had too much. It also blurs the "real" suffering in the news with fictional suffering in scripted shows—we get just as emotional about characters in shows as we do about real people.

Orwin discusses the paradox of question 4 in the paragraph that begins, "Can television . . .?" How does television both bring distant things closer and make them feel distant at the same time? How have you experienced this? Also, read aloud the paragraph that begins, "Nearby sufferings foster compassion . . ." and look at the one that follows for question 5. Finally, read the first couple of sentences of the last paragraph and discuss question 6. The most important part of this last question is the word "sustained." Do participants find that when they respond to a televised tragedy, they sustain that response for the whole extent of the need (which might go on for years in most cases), or do they find their attention snagged soon thereafter by the next big tragedy? Do they commit themselves to giving significant help in a few situations as longs as help is needed, or do they burn out by spreading themselves too thin? Most agencies like the Red Cross, Doctors Without Borders, Compassion International, and others report that governments and private donors often fail to stick around to deal with deep-rooted problems that could see lasting change if they had sustained attention.

The "PhDing" of Expertise   (20 minutes)

When the idea of the corporation was fresh, Carnegie and Rockefeller revolutionized philanthropy by setting up foundations that ran like corporations. While professionalism has brought many benefits, some critics have begun to warn that in service industries (including social work, counseling, medical centers, universities, correctional systems, and nursing homes), professionals and experts can actually *disable* rather than *enable* those whom they serve. John McKnight's 1995 article illustrates this problem.

Read aloud the fourth paragraph, which begins, "In 1837, a blacksmith . . ." and the seventh, which begins, "Initially, the soil was generous . . ." These summarize the effects of the John Deere plow. Then read the paragraphs that begin, "The new technology . . .," "As one can imagine . . .," "It is in these ways . . .," and "Finally, one day the aged father . . ." Discuss questions 1 and 2.

For question 4, McKnight lists four elements we should weigh when assessing the benefits or harms of a service technology: monetary cost (does the cost of a service like Medicaid consume too much of our total available funds for fighting poverty?), "specific counterproductivity" (does a given juvenile detention system actually increase rates of juvenile crime?), loss of knowledge (does our reliance on a professional pediatrician make us forget how to care for children?), and the tearing of the social fabric (does seeing ourselves as a nation of lone clients cut us off from communities even more than our mobile society already does?). Point out these four elements in the text. Ask participants to think of examples of each of these problems in a service with which they are familiar—healthcare, mental health care, education, child rearing, social work, and so on. (Question 6 will fit in here.)

Also, invite any participant to make the counter argument: if there were no grief counselor or professional social worker in your county, what would happen? Does a mobile, post-industrial society simply require professionals to provide services that families, churches, and communities once provided? Is the social fabric irretrievably tattered by other factors? Or, are there ways that professionals and citizens can work together to take advantage of what professionals can offer while limiting the monetary cost, rebuilding the store of knowledge among laypeople, equipping laypeople to do what they have done for centuries, and pushing against the notion that laypeople are incapable of being anything other than "clients"?

If you have any service professionals in your group, this could become a lively debate. Unless you have time for an extra session, you'll need to cut it off and move on.

The "NIMBYing" of Concerns   (20 minutes)

To combat the 'CNN' factor, we need to focus more on our neighbors, whom we can actually serve personally and over time, and avoid being distracted by myriad distant needs. The 'NIMBY' factor, however, warns us not to define our "neighbors" too narrowly. Affluent people in particular are all too willing to devote their time and money to services for their "neighbors"—the kind of people who can afford to live next door and enjoy similar interests. They often don't see the people who wait tables in their favorite restaurants or the people in the low-income subdivision a mile away as their "neighbors." Robert Reich urges the affluent among us to have the moral courage to cross the social lines and care for the poor and needy.

Read aloud some or all of the first five paragraphs and discuss questions 1 and 2. Also, read the paragraph in the middle of the article that begins, "But close examination reveals . . ." For question 3, read aloud the earlier paragraph that begins, "The secession is taking several forms." You can probably get through these factual questions fairly quickly and save time to discuss questions 4 and 5. For question 4, recall the contrast between Pericles building the Parthenon and the Jewish and Christian teachings about the poor.

The Reverse "*Cy Presing*" of Foundations   (20 minutes)

The fourth challenge you will discuss in this session is the trend among foundation trustees to disburse funds in ways their founders would abhor. To what degree should foundations be bound by donor intent? Martin Morse Wooster addresses this question by tracing the ironic history of the Ford Foundation.

For questions 1 and 2, read the paragraph that begins, "Ford often gave money . . .," the quotation of Ford that follows it, and the paragraph that begins, "For those who had experienced . . ." For the last part of question 2, look at the paragraph that begins, "On January 15, 1936 . . ." For question 3, have the group summarize the section under the subhead, "The Fund for the Republic." For question 4, read the paragraph that begins, "In the late 1960s . . ." Discuss question 5 with your remaining time.

Your final session will be devoted to part 5, in which four readings give you an opportunity to draw conclusions from what you've been discussing. Ask the group to read all of part 5 for next time.

SESSION 8

In this final session you'll reflect on the four concluding ideas of part 5. The purpose of these readings is more inspirational than analytical. Each reading makes one main point that will leap out to most readers, so it's not necessary to hash through every question. This is your chance to draw conclusions from what you've learned and envision your own life goals for money, giving, and caring. It's important that the group not conclude with a "hard sell" to contribute to any particular cause. As stated in the beginning, guilt and social pressure are ineffective motivators for sustained caring.

Generosity Is More than Giving Money   (15 minutes)

For questions 1 and 2, read aloud the paragraphs that begin, "I am well hardened . . ." and "There was a time . . ." on page 253. For question 5, ask participants to scan the paragraphs that begin, "But Benjamin wasn't the tenth . . .," "God knows . . ." and "And that's only the half of it . . ." Read aloud the final paragraph and discuss question 6. Discuss question 8 if you have time.

Always Be Aware of the Role of Need   (15 minutes)

Because it is poetry, some participants may struggle to understand this excerpt from Shakespeare's *King Lear.* You may want to highlight the main points in the introduction to this reading. First, there is a difference between needs and desires: "Just as we often desire what we do not need, so we often need what we do not consciously desire." Second, some needs such as food and protection are basic to survival. Other needs—dignity, respect, love, community, and freedom—are deeper but no less real. Freedom may be legislated, while love cannot be. The point of *King Lear* is that Lear gives because he thinks giving will fulfill his half-acknowledged needs for respect and love. At great cost, he learns that contract giving does not buy love.

Ask several people to read the parts of Lear, Goneril, Regan, and Cordelia. Set up the scene: Lear is "retiring" from his job as king and leaving his kingdom to his three daughters. He proposes to give the best part of the kingdom to the daughter who loves him best, and he asks them to declare their love. Ask

Lear to begin reading his lines from "(Since now we will divest us both of rule . . .)." Have the players read down through Cordelia's line, "So young, my lord, and true." Discuss questions 1 through 4.

Note that at the beginning, Lear says what he thinks he's giving: "Interest of territory, cares of state"—the work of running the kingdom. He doesn't think he's giving away his status, right of respect, power of influence over his daughters, freedom, or dignity. Like a company founder giving his corporation to his children, he thinks he's giving away the work, but not the headship of the family. He thinks he's trading land for love. As the story unfolds, however, this contract gift proves tragic because love cannot be bought. Regan and Goneril have no love to sell, and the love Cordelia would give freely cannot be purchased. Lear ends up with neither what he thought he needed, nor what he truly needed—with neither what he had at first, nor what he thought he was buying.

Questions 7 and 8 deal with the second scene of this excerpt. For Lear, the knights in his entourage represent his status, dignity, freedom, and respect. His daughters claim he doesn't "need" knights, but neither they nor he will talk about his real need—not for the knights, but for what they represent. This family quarrel appears to be about knights but is really about status in the family, about power.

The final scene occurs in a hut where Lear, his royal fool, and Kent (his friend and subject), take refuge from the storm on the heath. They have fled the unkindness of Lear's daughters. Edgar is one of Kent's sons, but neither father nor son recognizes the other immediately. Edmund, Kent's other son, has tricked Kent into believing Edgar a traitor. Edgar has therefore fled to the heath and, like Lear, is suffering some mental illness because of the shock. Kent and his family parallel and enrich our understanding of Lear's family. Lear and Kent are two much-deceived fathers who have failed to discern their true-hearted children from their false-hearted ones. Edgar is huddling in this hut naked except for a blanket. In the last speech of Lear's excerpted for this reading, Lear learns of man's true nakedness from observing Edgar. With this realization, he tears off his clothes.

You may not have time to work through the whole excerpt from the play with your group. Instead, you may want to skip to question 11.

Social Entrepreneurship Is One of the Deepest Investments of All   (15 minutes)

The first and third paragraphs of the introduction to this reading explain what social entrepreneurship is. You may want to read them aloud or summarize them. Millard Fuller, the founder of Habitat for Humanity, is a model of the social entrepreneur. The most important element of this reading is the way Fuller illustrates the entrepreneurial model of giving: serving in as well as providing funding for the cause; focusing on addressing one need over a sustained length of time, rather than spreading oneself thin from one charity to the next; and giving out of love rather than from a contract motive.

Read the first five paragraphs of this reading, and discuss question 2. For the challenges HFHI faces, you may want to look further down at the paragraphs that begin, "Building the houses . . . " and "Affiliates create their own house plans . . . "

Do your best to reach back in your memories to answer question 4. For example, recall that in the voluntary associations such as Gurteen's, the rich were giving to the poor and so there was a certain patronizing tone. Was this poor person really "deserving"? Gurteen wanted to build relationships between the rich giver and the poor recipient, but this was for the poor person's "improvement," so again, the patronizing tone grates on our modern ears. HFHI puts the giver and receiver on an equal footing: the giver is doing manual labor alongside the receiver; receivers help to build their own houses and continue to pay for them, so their dignity is upheld throughout. They are not treated as "clients," and there are no handouts.

Unlike most foundations, which can fund a broad spectrum of projects, HFHI focuses on addressing one narrow slice of the world's needs and doing it well over years and years. In this way, it resembles a focused new corporation that seeks to make and sell one product or service effectively.

Try to save time to address questions 5 and 6.

Giving Should Be a Commitment and a Life Goal   (15 minutes)

Read aloud the last paragraph of the introduction to this final reading on page 280. Here we have a more-than-a-century-old memo by the 33-year-old Carnegie, who might be building a high-tech company if he were alive today. He predicts that in two years he will have enough money to lay aside business and devote himself to things he believes are more deeply important. Read the paragraphs, "Settle in Oxford . . . " and "Settle then in London . . . " What did the 33-year-old believe were the most valuable things he could do with his life?

Read the paragraph, "Man must have an idol . . . " Carnegie knew himself to have a driven personality. He was the type to "push inordinately" at whatever he decided to pursue, so he knew he needed to choose his goal wisely. Good intentions and good mission statements, however, are not enough. Carnegie did not follow this written plan, but instead continued to pursue business ruthlessly. He couldn't shake off the idolatry of money. As you saw in Annie Dillard's critique of Carnegie at the end of part 3, "his steel-workers worked twelve-hour shifts on floors so hot they had to nail wooden platforms under their shoes." When, as an old man, Carnegie eventually sold his steel company to begin his philanthropic efforts, Pittsburgh had the highest death rate in the country. What life-lesson do you draw from Carnegie's example?

Closing Thoughts   (30 minutes)

To close your session, let each person respond to this question: "What key thoughts, ideas, and comments struck you personally during our study? What stands out to you?" Think carefully ahead of time whom you will ask to answer this question first, because that person's answer will set the tone for the other responses. Choose someone who you think is reflective and has been taking the readings to heart.

Thank everyone for participating. Some light refreshments and informal time to talk would be a fitting way to end the meeting.

AUTHORS

Os Guinness is a Senior Fellow at The Trinity Forum in McLean, Virginia. Born in China and educated in England, he earned his D.Phil. from Oxford University. He is the author or editor of numerous books, including *The Call, The American Hour, Invitation to the Classics,* and *Time for Truth.*

Karen Lee-Thorp (author of the reader's guide) is the senior editor of Bible studies and small-group resources at NavPress and the author of more than fifty study guides. Karen has spent almost two decades exploring how people grow spiritually. A graduate of Yale University, she speaks at women's groups and writes from her home in Brea, California.

For a catalog of The Trinity Forum's publications, including others in this series, please write: The Trinity Forum, 7902 Westpark Drive, Suite A, McLean, VA 22102. The catalog is also online at The Trinity Forum's website, www.ttf.org.